P.S. JACK PAAR

P.S. Jack Paar

BY JACK PAAR

1983
DOUBLEDAY & COMPANY, INC.
GARDEN CITY, NEW YORK

Grateful acknowledgment is made to the following for permission to reprint their copyrighted material:

"I Give You Jack Paar" by Sidney Carroll. Reprinted from *Esquire* (March 1946). Copyright 1946 by Esquire Publishing, Inc. Reprinted by permission of Esquire Publishing, Inc.

Excerpt from *The Odds Against Me* by John Scarne. Copyright © 1966 by John Scarne Games, Inc. Reprinted by permission of Simon & Schuster, a division of Gulf + Western Corporation.

"Just One of Those Things" by Cole Porter. Copyright © 1935 (Renewed) Warner Bros., Inc. All Rights Reserved. Used by permission.

The estate of Alexander King.

Library of Congress Cataloging in Publication Data

Paar, Jack.
    P.S. Jack Paar.

    1. Paar, Jack.   2. Television personalities—United
States—Biography.   3. Comedians—United States—
Biography.   I. Title.   II. Title: PS Jack Paar.
PN1992.4.P3A35   1983   791.45'092'4   [B]
ISBN 0-385-18743-2
Library of Congress Catalog Card Number 82-45938

To Miriam and Randy,
to Amani, the best lion I ever knew,
and to Lisa Drew, who encouraged me to
type like I talk and let me
leave the room whenever I raised
my hand.

Contents

P.S. JACK PAAR

1

Least But
Not Last

POSTSCRIPT: When I finally decided to stop appearing on television some eight years ago, I said, "Everything I wanted to say I have said twice," but now here I am again with some new thoughts, experiences, and observations. Also there are many leftovers, things I didn't wish to say or write about in my last three books.

Up to this moment I have had a very interesting and exciting life; I have known some of the most famous and celebrated people of the past twenty-five years: from Fidel Castro to Dr. Albert Schweitzer, Richard Nixon, all of the Kennedys, Marilyn Monroe, Noël Coward, and just about everybody who was in show business or politics in the United States or England from 1950 onward. Some I knew very well, and many were strangers in the night who had appeared on my television show.

Many amusing things happened to me which are funny now but which at the time I tried to cover up or forget. For instance, who else do you know who was sued by David Begelman? (He lost, of course.)

Who else do you know that was booed for ten minutes and

now wants to write about it? It happened this way: When I was on the "Tonight" program, I was considered very controversial; and while the show was a phenomenon in its day, there was a dichotomy of opinions about my personality. The expression "What is Jack Paar really like?" became a cliché of the sixties. I found that being considered eccentric, unpredictable, and flintily honest gave me a cover for my private life. Since many people didn't believe that anyone really would behave that way, they looked for many other mysterious causes which allowed me to go about my life just as I appeared on television. However, there were many who became so confused that they came to really dislike me for whatever reasons they could conjure.

Well, for some reason I found myself in Chicago appearing before a big audience in Soldier Field. The event was a stock-car race, and I was to appear as the guest star. There was a long oval track for the car races, and it was somebody's idea (a bad one, it turned out) that I should make an entrance in a little electric car by myself going around the track at no more than six or seven miles an hour. I was to make a complete circle in front of thousands of people in the stadium.

The stadium was dark with a spotlight on me in this clown car, and I heard a little booing which grew louder and louder. There was no way for me to turn the damn car around or speed it up. I just smiled and waved and died!

Nothing had prepared me for this, and the last five minutes were a disaster, but looking ahead I figured another five minutes and it would all be over! It went on for ten minutes and then, I had to believe, it became an audible way of pulling my leg. People who really love me, I kept saying to myself, are getting their kicks booing. Well, I learned a lesson: never appear or compete with a crowd who came to see a Chevrolet smash into a Buick.

The reason I open with a story like this is that I don't want you to think this is to be a book about how wonderful Jack Paar is or was—actually I was a real pain in the ass to many people. But I really think, or wish to think, that I was interesting and one of a kind. Since I already have the money, it doesn't matter now. Besides there were some of you who thought I was peachy.

My only defense is that always, but always, I gave you my best shot! Sometimes I was frightened, but I never backed away from a fight with the press when they were untruthful or when I told the United States Congress to go to hell! I said on two occasions, "Call me before a committee or leave me alone."

Many of you good people might consider that anyone who drove around Westchester County in a Rolls-Royce with a lion in the back seat was unusual, weird, eccentric, or—God forbid— *nouveau riche!* Not at all. It will be perfectly logical when I explain it.

First, the Rolls: Long after I was a grown man, my mother sent me, as she did throughout my early life, five dollars on my birthday. It had something to do with my youth, I suppose, but I really looked forward to the five dollars in the envelope every May first. When I was a kid, it meant money that I could spend on anything I wished, but even when I was in my late thirties and making a million dollars a year, I still got a kick out of the five dollars from Mom.

One May first, with the five dollars in my pocket, I went to a small luncheon with my staff to celebrate my birthday. I had a bottle of wine. When my friends had gone back to our office, which I hardly ever went to, I had to kill time until that night's show. Feeling rather melancholy because the party was over, I drove down Park Avenue past Inskip Motors and saw this beautiful sable-colored Rolls with orange leather upholstery in the window. I had never even thought of buying a Rolls. It just wouldn't go with my peasant image of myself. But I found myself asking to see the manager and saying that I would like to buy that car. He explained that it was a special one made for the recent auto show.

I reached into my pocket and took out my mother's five dollars and said, "You see, it's my birthday!"

The manager wished me a happy birthday, took the five dollars, and said there was still the small matter of about eighteen thousand dollars. He asked if I had a check for the balance. I never have checks, and I don't know how to write them. I suggested that he call this number and tell my wife, Miriam, that I had just bought a Rolls-Royce with the money from my mother, and would she send a check for the rest. I said, "Miriam might faint, but when she gets up off the floor, I am sure she will not wish to spoil my birthday. Since I am in good health, there will be many more birthday five dollars to follow that she can apply to this purchase."

The story became a legend among the Rolls sales staff. I kept the car for nine years, and it was worth more when I sold it than when I paid for it. So you see, it wasn't weird or eccentric—it was good business. I drove a Rolls for nine years for nothing.

Now about the *lion* in the back seat. . . . Well, that's a very sad story. My wife Miriam, our daughter Randy, and I had been to Africa several times and had many good friends in Kenya. Two of our closest friends there, Jock and Betty Leslie-Melville, live in Nairobi. They sent me a wire saying that the Kenyan government had changed a policy and after a certain date no one could keep lion (they always use the singular) in a *boma* (a caged or fenced-in area) privately. All lion held on ranches or farms had to be released or shot.

Three lion used in the making of the motion picture *Born Free* would have to be shot in two weeks. They wanted to know if I could find a place for them in some zoo in the United States.

I thought it would be easy and wired them to tell the government that I would be responsible and to give me time to check the zoos here, but by all means, not to shoot them, because my word was good! I figured that any zoo would want the lion that were seen in that wonderful picture *Born Free* and that I could easily obtain the airfare from one or two airlines with whom I was friendly.

Now the disappointments: First, no zoo wanted them because lion breed well in captivity, and domestic lion are better suited for captivity than African animals that have been living in a large, open area. Second, upon checking with the movie studio that made *Born Free* I learned that they were not the lion used in the picture at all but were the cubs of the animals. And third: since they were nearly fully grown weighing more than three hundred pounds apiece, no airline could give up that much space simply for publicity. So I was really in a jam, but I had given my word and they were being shipped via Athens and London to JFK in New York. I finally found a home for them in West Palm Beach since they had a Safari Park there.

When I checked the airfare for crating three beautiful lion, thinking it would be a few hundred dollars, I was told that it would cost nine thousand, and I had to put the money up in a few days. I knew there was no way one could deduct on his income tax "airfare for three lion," but I could not and would not back out. I sent the money and told my friends in Kenya to ship them.

The next night at two o'clock in the morning our phone rang. Sleepily I answered to hear; "Jack, brace yourself. I have terrible news. They just shot Bobby."

I said, "They promised they wouldn't. I kept my word and sent the money. Damn! Those bastards!"

You see, I was under the impression that one of the lion was named Bobby—

A broken voice repeated, "No, Jack, they have just shot Bobby Kennedy in California! This is Carmen [an associate of mine]. I am in California, and the news just broke here. I just wanted you to know."

Randy and Miriam heard my sigh, and it was one of the worst moments of my life. It was one of the few times I have ever seen my wife or daughter cry—they simply are not the type to show emotion—but Bobby Kennedy and Miriam and I were close personal friends. And my daughter worked for the senator in Washington during the summers.

Well, the next day I was in a daze because I had lost a good friend, the father of eleven children. I was asked by Lem Billings, one of Bobby's closest friends, to come into the city and help in any way I could. NBC sent a car to get me, as I was in no shape to drive. They wanted me to speak of my friendship with Robert Kennedy for several hours on the network since all commercials and regular programs had been canceled. I knew I was pretty incoherent, but who can be sure when Jack Paar is being incoherent?

The next morning I went to have breakfast with young Robert, Jr. We never spoke of his father but kept talking about the shipment of lion en route, which I would take him to see. Later in the day young Bobby and I went to St. Patrick's Cathedral and were part of the honor guard that stood by the casket of his father.

Then after lunch we, or rather I, continued the nonstop conversation about Africa and lion. He asked if it was possible that I could get a lion cub for the zoo up at his school in Millbrook, New York. I promised that I would try. It was arranged that I would get one from the Safari Park in Florida, but for some reason they sent two, so Miriam and I had to take the other poor little fellow. We named him Amani, after the Swahili word for peace. We had no safe place to keep a growing cub, so I drained the swimming pool and kept both of them there until I could get one up to Millbrook and then built a place for Amani in our second garage. I gave Randy my little Mercedes sports car to make room, and she took it up to school at Harvard (Radcliffe) in Boston.

Now a small lion away from its mother has to be fed by bottle with a concoction of "bitch's milk" and vitamins. This had to be mixed twice a day in a Cuisinart, and it made a mess in the kitchen because it hardened quickly into a plasterlike substance. Also, because it was unnatural to feed the cub that way, we had to burp him over our shoulders several times a day. Needless to say, Amani received a love unknown to any wild creature.

Our home was fenced in, and the little lion followed me everywhere. He had to sleep in his quarters in the garage, but the rest of the day he never left my side. I adored him.

After a few months, when he was the size of a small German shepherd, Randy took him up to her dormitory at college. She had to continue to feed him by bottle, and many of the students helped. When some of the faculty discovered nursing bottles in the kitchen, it was assumed that one of the students had had a baby and was trying to hide it. When they found out it was only a lion, they were even more surprised. Amani was the only lion ever kicked out of Harvard!

I was so fond of the lion that I took him everywhere, and naturally he was always in my Rolls-Royce as we would go driving around Westchester County. So isn't that a logical explanation of why I was seen with a lion in my car? There was nothing weird or bizarre about it at all. The next time you see a man with a lion in a Rolls-Royce, don't jump to conclusions. It could be a perfectly normal set of circumstances. It could even be St. Francis of Assisi, who has just come into some birthday money.

I spent the next seven months raising Amani and enjoyed the experience so much that for a period of six months I never went into New York City. I spent nearly all my time filming the lion at home. I had cameras and lights set up to go on electronically whenever there was any action, and during that time I made a really wonderful television documentary entitled "Jack Paar and His Lion." It was a big success and has been repeated several times. But of course the TV critics called it "just a home movie." Fair enough, but they might have noted that it was the first of many "Paar home movies" that made the top ten in the weekly Nielsen ratings. No one, but no one, had ever pulled that trick off before or since!

The reason I put together the lion show, besides my sheer love of animals, was that it would be a way to recoup the nine thousand dollars I had tied up in getting the big cats over here. If I could do a program and sell it, then the transportation costs could go into that budget.

One funny thing happened after I had done the program: An auditor from the Internal Revenue Service came to our home to examine the books for the television program. You won't believe this, but he wanted to know the life-span of a lion (in the wild, it is about fourteen years) and wanted to write the nine thousand dollars off over fourteen years. Imagine, the IRS wanted to amortize three lion! I began to laugh, and then, in fairness to the IRS man, he began to laugh too and the charges were dropped. Can you imagine the legal hassle that would have ensued if the IRS had to set a precedent or find something in the legal code about "amortizing lion."

P.S.: Now I must tell you the sad truth. When Amani was about seven months old, his paws were larger than my hands. He was so powerful that I couldn't actually hold him, so I knew I would have to take him back to the Safari Park in Florida. It was around Christmas time, and he could easily knock over the big tree in the living room. It broke my heart, but I knew that he had to be returned. I intended to spend much time in Florida, and we could continue our relationship after he had been placed running free with others of his own kind. Miriam and I got an animal man to take Amani to the airport in a Carey Cadillac, to see that he was comfortably caged, and to accompany him to West Palm Beach. I admit I cried when the little fellow in the back of the Cadillac looked back at me as it sped away. The only consolation was that we were going to Florida right after New Year's and I would be with him again. I looked forward to that so much.

I telephoned Florida daily to see how he was adjusting and was always assured that he was fine. Then, just after the first of the year, I got a call from the veterinarian at the Safari Park the day before I was leaving to go to Florida. Not wanting to spoil our Christmas holidays, he now had to tell me that Amani was dead. He had died a week after his arrival.

The reason given was that he had been raised in the sterile environment of our home and had not developed immunities against the diseases that were natural to the wildlife environment he had returned to.

God, it was a blow! But worse than that, when I went to Florida a few days later and talked to the young lady who had taken care of Amani, she said, "You know, and I shouldn't tell you this, but I really think he died of a broken heart."

My life has been a bouquet of anecdotes: funny or sad, but usually both at the same time.

All my life I have been a verbal person, and conversation on a professional or theatrical level has always been easy and enjoyable for me. However, I find the discipline of writing a book hair-raising (but I can use it, especially in the front). If I could just tell my stories door to door, it would be easier. I suffer from total recall except for recent memory. It has been said that I could remind elephants. (They say an elephant never forgets, but even if he can remember, what can he do for you?) Last-hour memory is the problem. Each day I go through the same routine: Where are my car keys, where did I park the car, which car was I driving, and what the hell am I doing in Westport? I thought this was Greenwich!

Late middle age has it's problems, but so far nothing has happened to me as crazy as what happened to my friend, the author

Vance Packard, who lives near us. He rushed off to La Guardia Airport to catch a plane for a lecture in Michigan. He parked the car on the third floor of the parking lot and then rushed to the plane. He found out two days later upon returning that he had failed to turn the motor off; he was now out of gasoline, and the battery was dead. Now that's a problem!

I have another close friend (no names please), who confessed that he often forgets whether or not he has taken a shower. And now if he feels the towel and it's *wet*, he knows he *has*. Dear God, is it going to be like that for me?

I remember everything that ever happened in my life if it happened before breakfast. It's from the orange juice to the present that it's touch and go. For instance, I have no idea why I am sitting here at the typewriter, unless it's to write my Uncle Harry—but I think he's been dead for twelve years.

Oh well . . . I guess I'll write a book. Now where is the typewriter?

2

Heeeerre's Jack

For many years, I did a program on television that opened with that line. The same as Johnny does. I am sure by now that Steve Allen believes he invented "Heeeerre's Jack" and "Heeeerre's Johnny" along with his discovery of penicillin. I am fond of Steve Allen, but not as much as he is.

Chemically or biologically speaking, I am allergic to bullshit. Why Steve, a versatile and talented man, continues this charade of "Mr. Show Business" I cannot understand. For instance, when he is introduced on talk shows or in advance publicity these phrases constantly precede him: "Known as the Noël Coward of America." "There probably hasn't been a more durable, able, and admirable personality in the history of the medium." "Steve Allen has written more than four thousand songs." "The author of twenty-five best-selling books."

Well, recently Bob Metz of the New York *Times* wrote a book on the history of "The Tonight Show" and discovered that Allen has a prepared advanced-press release on his introductions. This explains the hyperbole.

The last time I saw him on television, and remembering the press kit, I really roared with laughter. His, in more ways than one, introduction went something like this: "One of the most talented men in show business. He is working on fifty different projects at the present time. In the past twenty years, there is not

an hour of the day or night, somewhere in the world, where Steve
Allen cannot be seen or heard. Welcome, this giant, Steve Allen."
Applause. Applause.

I am even applauding. Then he tops his own introduction,
which he had written, by bowing and saying quietly, "Much that
is being said about me is highly exaggerated. Actually," he continues, "I think of myself as a *singer.*"

That old rascal has it both ways. He is not only the most talented man in the world, now he is the most humble! Another
modest ploy of his is when he says, "I am supposed to be a half-
assed authority on comedy." (He's a quarter right.)

I think he suffers from a disorder that one, to coin a phrase,
could call *manic-excessive.* He makes many of us feel like we were
only in the chorus of *Annie.*

If I sat here for an hour, I could not compete with him at inventing glowing phrases about my own career. I can only think of
funny put-downs or hostile quotes of my pilgrimage through show
business:

"Jack Paar's mind is one part genius and two parts chocolate
fudge."

"A bull in his own China Shop."

"Little Lord Fauntleroy with a switchblade knife."

"The world's tallest elf."

"The Paar show is one hour and forty-five minutes of inter-
ruptions, with time out to remove the wounded."

"A Methodist minister after four martinis."

My only real public claim to fame is that I am a direct descen-
dant of Adam and Eve. But if pressed, and I am, I can quote a
few lines from *Time* magazine after a visit I made to the Soviet
Union, including, "Paar's comments and observations on the
human level in Russia were the best reporting recently on the Soviet Union."

There is no question that Steve Allen is a talented man, but I
fear for his safety. I must write his peachy wife, Jayne, of my concern. You see, if Steve insists on being "Mr. Show Business" and
trying to do everything, there is a danger. When next the circus
comes to Los Angeles, I am afraid that Steve is going to try and
get up on that high wire and do a few back flips. The chances are

he may fall and break his glasses! Only a real friend would intervene as I have.

Dick Cavett, one of my early students, who was graduated from my staff to a unique place in television, has recently taken up tap dancing, card tricks, and gymnastics. I liked him better when he first brought his considerable intellect and charm to television. I must point out that Pablo Casals was the world's greatest virtuoso of the cello, but had he gone on to the banjo, he would not be revered as he is today.

Dick was working for *Time* magazine, as a researcher for sixty-five dollars a week, when he joined our staff as a "booker" and later as a writer. He was the most starstruck young man I had ever met. And now that diminutive Dudley Moore has become such a big hit, I hope that Cavett will be given a chance in pictures. Dick is a handsome young man but short. I recall when first he worked with me, I used to take him down to Fifth Avenue and hold him up to see the parades. I even bought him a balloon.

Merv Griffin frequently replaced me on the "Tonight" program and is a quick study. I would have to give him an "A" in economics, because he knows more about the money end of television than anyone. (He will never need food stamps.) He will probably outlast Johnny Carson and all the rest because of his "laid-back" approach. He is a decent and likeable man.

Actually, I can still recall several nights when I would look into the wings of the NBC theater and see three young men as onlookers watching with great interest as if there was some secret to doing that kind of show. If there is a secret, I never knew what it was. The three young men were Dick Cavett, Merv Griffin, and David Frost. I liked all of them very much and am happy that they have found work.

However, some nights seeing those three eager faces in the wings, I felt a little like the actress played by Bette Davis in *All About Eve*. It definitely crossed my mind once when I walked into my dressing room and found Dick Cavett standing on a chair, looking into the mirror, and with his right arm raised in the Paar salute, saying over and over, "I kid you not! I kid you not!"

I feel that Cavett is the most like me because he's more interested in conversation than asking questions. I think I was different from the others in that I was just as happy if no guests showed up, providing that I had recently returned from some interesting place in the world with stories and experiences. If I did anything well, that was it.

David Frost had a smaller success than the others, but the fact that he lasted two years is amazing considering his handicap of a different speech pattern—and his not really understanding the American psyche. He wins the award for asking the second dumbest question ever on TV. "What is your definition of love?" he asked night after night.

But the all-time Olympics award for the dumbest question on TV has to go to Barbara Walters. I shall never get over the shock of hearing her ask three times in one night, "If in another life, you come back as a tree, what tree would you like to be?" My three dogs, who are interested in trees, crawled under the bed. And I wanted to be a cactus.

Returning to David for the moment, it should be said that his long interview with Richard Nixon was outstanding. I know of no American broadcaster who could have pulled that off with such a mixture of interest, understanding, courteous probing, and finally a real zinging finish. I think in this case being British detached him from the rest of us, as if he were from another planet, which helped the historic interview. Mike Wallace or Dan Rather, and many others, would have clobbered Nixon in five minutes, which might have been easy to do; but they probably would have lost in the long run, since many people don't like seeing anyone embarrassed for five hours. I feel that getting a portrait of a man is more illuminating and helpful than interrogation in the manner of those who act like Torquemada in the Spanish Inquisition.

As far as I can recall, the only time I embarrassed anyone on the air was an angry moment with William F. Buckley, Jr., a man I had always respected and admired. But on the air one night, he became a smart-ass, I felt, and made some unwarranted personal remarks about my earlier interview with Fidel Castro. I was usually ready for such tactics simply by being interested enough in my guests to read some of their thoughts and writings beforehand. I had had no intention of using any of this background material, but after his comments, I began to shift the attack onto his own magazine's staff. "Why," I asked, "were so many writers employed by *National Review* former Communists?" (There *were* several.) "Did you have to be a Communist and repent to be a good American?"

Buckley's eyes rolled back into his head like a cash register's numbers. My point was that I wouldn't necessarily think that being a former Communist was sound intellectually. Sin is forgiveable, but ignorance is forever.

Buckley became angry and lost his cool, unusual for him. I then asked him, "At what point should we begin to treat African nations with some understanding and helpfulness?"

He replied, I am sure not realizing what he was about to say, "When they stop eating each other!"

The audience groaned. He got up and stomped out of the studio. I felt sorry about that—really I did! I have since tried to be friendly and helpful. When he once mistakenly wrote about "the tigers in Africa" and later about "Swahili being spoken in South Africa," I pointed out in a note that there are no "tigers in Africa"; they are only in India and other parts of Asia. And that Swahili is spoken only in a portion of East Africa. I got back only a mimeographed postcard.

I was later surprised to hear Dick Cavett one night use a French term (*déjà vu*) and pronounce it *deja* VEE, when it is *deja* VOO. My goodness! What are they teaching at Yale? Too much boola-boola and not enough schoola-schoola.

I have enormous respect for Johnny Carson—not just because of his talent—for only he and I know what it's like to do what is the most difficult show in television ever! Don't knock it, if you've never tried it. It looks easy—and if there is a trick, that's it! Johnny replaced me many times going way back to my "Morning Show" on CBS. I doubt if anyone will ever come anywhere near Johnny's success.

After five years on "Tonight," when it was a longer version and live for two years, I really had had enough! There was no problem of money; I never asked for more. It was just beginning to affect my personal happiness. NBC had many thoughts about my replacement, and some they tried. I had always thought that Carson was the best. He still is.

I can take no credit in recommending Johnny. I wanted to get away so badly that I would have accepted, if I was asked, to be replaced by Vincent Lopez or Yogi Berra. It's just that Johnny was my choice, and being stubborn I like to be right!

The most bizarre interview I can remember watching on TV was with the singer, Andy Williams, a really very nice and charming gentleman, and a host who shall be nameless. The interview went roughly like this:

HOST: You know, Andy, I really miss those wonderful Christmas shows that you used to put on during the holiday season—you had on the program you parents, your brothers, your wife, and children. They were wonderful.

ANDY: Well, I miss doing them, but no network seems to want to put them on anymore.

HOST: I think it's unfair of the networks to stop a fine, family holiday program just because you and your wife have separated. After all there are many separated couples now, and they should be represented at Christmas time.

ANDY: Well, after my wife and I separated, we still did one more Christmas program together, but that was the last one. I would like to be on with my wife or without her—it's the Christmas season that's important.

HOST: Just because a couple are separating and getting a divorce shouldn't stop a fine family program.

As Tiny Tim would say, "What a crock!" (It was not mentioned that Andy's wife had recently been accused of shooting and killing a man, allegedly her lover, at a ski resort. Not even Noël Coward could have handled that noel situation.)

Of the newest personalities, David Letterman will unquestionably be a big star. He has an original style and winning manner that is lasting. He will go the distance.

The most pleasing memory I have of my contribution to the genre is that without exception the staff—the writers, directors, producers, and associates I was fortunate to have working with me—are now important members of all the other shows I have mentioned. This is not to say that I taught or trained fifteen or twenty people because there was nothing to teach. You either have it or you don't. I hope that they can all honestly speak well of me. I would like that.

I never realized when I began talking to people on television that it would become such an industry and that the format we used would be the most copied. I guess that history will record that my only contribution was the davenport. Well, to steal a line from Charles de Gaulle: "*Après moi le déluge*"; and Charlie stole it from Mme de Pompadour, who said it in the eighteenth century.

I am sure that the first "talk show" was in a cave, around a fire, and the host carried a club. The reason he had the club was to keep Zsa Zsa from interrupting.

3

Some of My Best Friends Are Me

This is being written in a loft of our home, Long Barn, in the woods of what is called the Lost District of Connecticut. Our house, which we built, is five miles from the nearest village. As I look out the window, I can see acres of snow, evergreens, and every now and then, five or six large deer cross our land. When the house was being built, I was reading the diaries of Harold Nicolson and his wife Vita Sackville-West. He was the brilliant British writer and diplomat of the World War II years. They called their home Long Barn. It was in the country, some thirty-five miles from London. Our home, while we were in construction, fit the description of theirs, and since we didn't want our name on the rural mailbox, we chose that.

We are very happy here fifty miles from the Big Apple. I have always had ambivalent feelings about New York City and think the distance is just right. I was not certain that I would want to live *fifty-five* miles from New York but have always been a country-type person and think of myself as a farmer or rancher. However, that is a pretension as I have only a station wagon and one head of German shepherd.

We have a tennis court with television cameras for taping, a swimming hole that looks quite natural but actually was built and heated, a large garden, and more friends than I deserve. I told Miriam the other day that we had too many friends and should have an audition to cut some of them out.

My wife and I met while I was in infantry training at Indiantown Gap, Pennsylvania. The camp was near the beautiful little village of Hershey, and although my wife is a Hershey, contrary to rumor, she is not an heiress of the chocolate family. There were no heirs to that fortune; it all went to a Boys' Town–type orphanage. The rumor that my wife inherited a great deal of money, resulting in my independence and not caring about a career, is not true. What we have is what I earned by hard work, a lot of luck, and remembering everything that happened everywhere.

We have been married for more than thirty-five years. Marrying Miriam and enlisting in the Army were the two smartest moves I ever made. A few years ago on our wedding anniversary, I was playing in a tennis tournament in Monte Carlo. Merv Griffin found out about the anniversary and arranged a surprise party after the sporting event in our honor, and Prince Rainier and Princess Grace attended. We've come a long way, baby.

There are people who think that I am a loner (true), an *iconoclast* (I don't know—I'll have to look the word up), and a square (I am practically a cube). For instance, I don't believe that I have ever seen marijuana and wouldn't even think of sniffing baking soda. In a theatrical way, I have said that I could be *fascinating*. That was just being campy. What I am is—*interesting*. When I was on television, it has been said that I was so interesting, you could forget you were not being entertained.

One of my staff has been quoted as saying that my personality was not only split, but was shredded. My darling assistant, Mitzi Moulds, when she left to get married said, "It was great working for a *team* like you."

I am very aware that I appear complicated and seem to have

two personalities. One: On TV I was very unconscious of discussing the more intimate details of my life and did it quite naturally. Two: I cannot speak to strangers on the street and will run from anyone I know slightly who might engage me in conversation. I avoid crowds and have never, but never, attended a cocktail party. I have seldom been lonely.

Johnny Carson has said much the same thing. His reasoning was that on television *he was in charge,* and that makes for a great difference. Without exception according to published reports, Steve Allen, Dick Cavett, Carson, and I are known as distant, aloof loners. I think it comes with the territory we cover.

People see you in a grocery store and know you from watching you for years on the tube, but you do not know them! They cannot understand this: TV only goes one way.

Besides, conversation with strangers is difficult when it begins with, "Jack Paar! I want to talk with you as we have so much in common." What we have in common, it turns out, is that we both drive station wagons. Such a tête-à-tête is awkward and goes downhill quickly.

That was why I not only wore dark glasses but began to wear a simple veil. Most people thought I had taken religious orders, and many believed I was trying to get the hornets out of the garage.

I think of all the pleasures of life: good food, a bottle of cold Chardonnay, sex, reading. *Reading* holds up the best in one's later years. Last night I read my friend Andy Rooney's book. I finally figured out how easy his writing seems. It's quite simple. All it takes is talent and complete honesty. I enjoy Andy more when I read him than seeing him on "Sixty Minutes." He appears on television as very dour and grim with those bushy eyebrows. Andy is the only one I know whose eyebrows become bangs.

Recently I have had several uneasy moments reading in bed. I have been skimming through a book about Benita Hume. Let me tell you about her. She was married to Ronald Colman and later George Sanders. I never knew her but would see her every week in the Brown Derby in Hollywood. She was terribly attractive, chic, and witty, with a marvelous British accent. I really had quite a crush on her from afar. Well, my dears, the book consists mainly of letters she wrote to her friends. And in one letter written in 1959 to a friend in England, my mad passion writes, "The rage here in America on late-night television is a Jack Paar. People think he's witty. I don't care for him at all."

Later that night I picked up another book on my night stand. It was *The Duke of Deception* by Geoffrey Wolff. It's a true story of a father-and-son relationship. The author speaks of his father coming home late one night quite drunk and going upstairs to his room. The family hears a gunshot, and all rush up to his bedroom expecting the worst, only to find that he had shot a hole into the television set spreading glass all over the floor. The father says, "I am glad I finally shot that son of a bitch. I have killed Jack Paar!!"

A few nights later, skimming through Jackie Cooper's cowritten autobiography, I was quite surprised to read that he didn't like me and that no one else he knew did either. Now "Skippy" and I shared a tent in World War II for many months on the island of New Caledonia in the South Pacific. He was in the Navy, and I was in the Army, but we both were assigned for a short time to working on the "Mosquito Network," an Armed Forces Radio Service. I always thought that for a spoiled kid movie actor, he was good company. I know of not one single moment with him that was unpleasant. I have seen him many times since, in New York, Palm Springs, and Hollywood, and it was always very amiable and nostalgic. When our mutual friends asked him why he wrote the remark, he claimed that he didn't but that his ghostwriter did. It would seem to me that if these actors can't write their books, they should at least be able to *read* their books.

His comment about me was minor when one read the vicious, gratuitous attack on Alan Alda for many pages. Now if there is anyone in the Hollywood community who is unanimously respected and liked, it's Alan.

"Skippy" is of the Shelley Winters, Britt Ekland school of fornicate-and-tell literature. His biggest moment in his career is when he confesses (though no one asked him) that as a teenager he had a sexual liaison with Joan Crawford. No wonder Wallace Beery slapped him. Joan Crawford should have hit him with a coat hanger.

Some people might think that once one is famous and a celebrity that he is known forever. Happily, I found that there is a life after television, but fame fades quickly. For more than two years, week after week, my name led the Sindlinger Report—a poll taken for the media that sampled public opinion as to who was the most discussed person in the nation. I was later replaced by Elizabeth Taylor, Richard Burton, and then Jacqueline Kennedy. I had been on the cover of *Time, Newsweek, Look,* and *Life* twice, and five or six times on *TV Guide.* I was caricatured by artist Al Hirschfeld many times in various publications. By hard work and clean living, I had earned the hatred of columnists like Walter Winchell, Dorothy Kilgallen, Westbrook Pegler, and many more who have gone on to the great rest room in the sky. All this I accomplished without a personal press agent, but that's blood over the dam.

I have found that one can go from "fame" to "what's-his-name" rather suddenly. Several times a week someone, after much staring, will say, "Didn't you used to be somebody?" or "Weren't you a celebrity or something?" When I answer that I used to be Mary Tyler Moore, it usually concludes the conversation.

I have never missed being on television. I find that many people cannot believe a person could give up all that fame and money. For me it was easy. The wonderful thing about a democracy is that a man doesn't have to be on television if he doesn't want to.

A few weeks ago, I gave my credit card to a lady clerk in a hardware store. She noticed the name, went into a small swoon, and told me how much she missed me. I was her favorite. She wanted to know when I was coming back on television.

"Never," I said.

Her reply really was a surprise as she said, "Oh, dear—to think that I'll never hear you *sing* again."

Later I walked into an electronics store and found the owner mumbling into the microphone of a tape recorder. He stumbled, reading his message and then began again while I waited. I realized that he was trying to record an announcement for his telephone answering service. I could see he was never going to make it and offered him help. The announcement, which he had written in crayon block letters, said, "The number you have reached is not answering at this time because of the press of business. All the salesmen are busy serving customers on the floor. Please leave your name and number, and we'll get back to you as soon as possible."

This amused me as it was a broken-down little store with no other salesmen, telephone, and not much of a sales floor. Well, I read for him in my best announcer's voice, and the owner was very impressed. He just said, "You ought to be in show business."

He never recognized me nor cared. Now when I told this story at dinner parties, people said they didn't believe it, and I would ask everybody to come to the phone. I would dial the number, and sure enough there I was, and still may be, my voice reading away. So, if anyone in America misses me, I have this number you can call.

About eight years ago, when Johnny Carson was still coming from New York, I was driving on the West Side Highway and was signaled to pull over by a police car. I obviously had been going too fast and offered no excuse. But I noticed the officer with great sadistic relish wanted a confrontation. He was, unusual in my experience, combative and wanted to argue. I wondered why. Then he said, "This gives me great pleasure. You are such a wise guy on the tube every night ripping into the police department. Now the tables are turned."

I was really puzzled by all this anger, since I had not been on TV in five years. Then I realized that he thought he was talking to Johnny Carson. I said, "Look, if I was speeding, I deserve the ticket. But why all this hostility unless you think that I am Johnny Carson?" "Mr. Smart Ass, I've watched you for years," the cop continued.

I then showed him my driver's license and for the first time flashed my New York Honorary Detective Badge. He became so embarrassed that he told me to drive on and to be more careful. I then felt sorry for the poor guy, but it was true that Johnny Carson and I did look very much alike until Johnny got older.

Sometimes being recognized can be a great embarrassment or a compliment. The drugstores in California are enormous. They sell tires, liquor, tennis rackets, asphalt, etc. The store in Palm Springs is easily the size of a basketball court. It was crowded on a Sunday afternoon, and I meekly sought the solace of some Preparation H. For some strange reason, it got around that Jack Paar was in the store, and a few people were following me around while I was looking for the anal department. I finally bought everything that might help and then grabbed a magazine to put over my various remedies. At the checkout counter, with several people watching me, the clerk picked up each item and rang it on the register. She picked up the last item and turned it over and over, looking quite distressed; then she pressed the button on the counter microphone and in a clear, loud Jane Pauley voice said, *"Pricing Information."*

A cavernous voice, with an echo yet, replied, *"Yes."*

Miss Large Lips, the Ethel Merman of Rexall, shaking the rafters of this enormous store, bellowed, "What is the price of HEMORRHOID SUPPOSITORIES?"

All eyes were on the checkout counter. I whispered, "Any price will do. Any round figure. I am not a comparison shopper. I don't want a bargain."

A voice from the bowels of the store insisted on padding his part on the public-address system and so replied, "A box of twelve or twenty-four?"

Dying, with an acute case of discomfort, I said, "Could I just take one? I'm not expecting an epidemic."

Another problem for any male celebrity is at theater intermission when there is a mad rush for the rest room. There is always a long line of men who have anticipated the punch line of the first act. Then, as you are standing awaiting your turn at the urinal, you realize that you are recognized, and the word spreads that "stars" pee. You count the line and see that you are eighth. But then, like looking for a place to park on a diagonal street, when you think, "There's one," you pull in and find the rear end of a short Volkswagen sneering at you. In this case, the *eight* turns out to be *ten* because there is little Leroy and Melvin, whom you didn't see standing in front of their father. This is bad enough at a Broadway theater, but if it's a Saturday afternoon at the circus, forget it. Sometimes, because of your fame and age, a younger man gives you the golf-courtesy of letting you "play through."

You accept because there is an older man behind you breathing down your neck.

Finally you reach the porcelain and find that—with all eyes on your performance—you cannot! What to do? They are all watching! You panic because now they might think you are some kind of weirdo or voyeur looking around. You press the handle of the urinal, you whistle, and you wish you could get the battery-jump starter from the trunk of your auto. You think encouraging thoughts, hoping that it's a mental block, but find that your sphincter muscle has never heard of you.

I had a sponsor on the "Tonight" program which made men's slacks, and I was given and wore many of them. Their unique feature was that they had a Velcro fastener on the fly. Now you know that when one tears open a Velcro fastener there is a loud, ripping noise. Everyone turns. You now are not only a peeping Theresa but a *masochist*. I tell you, it's very hard being a star in a men's room.

Many of my friends here in Connecticut are writers: Herman Raucher (author of novels like *The Summer of Forty-Two* as well as many screenplays and dramatic television programs); Evan Hunter (*The Blackboard Jungle*, as well as a popular detective series written under the pseudonym of Ed McBain); Gerald Green ("Holocaust" and *The Last Angry Man*); and a man who lives in the city, Sidney Carroll (the screenplay of the Academy Award–winning *The Hustler* and many Emmy-winning television scripts). When I see them socially, I go on and on about experiences, opinions, and stories. They have wanted me to write them down, but I have delayed until now.

However, I have cowritten three books, two of which were best sellers. While practically every word was mine, they were dedicated or taken from transcripts of "The Tonight Show" and from years of conversation with my late, dear friend, John Reddy of the *Reader's Digest*. To you now, I make no claims of skill in matters of style or syntax. I could include words like *morphology* just to prove I have a thesaurus. But what I am is a storyteller, an observer.

Much of the time when I speak, even when I am serious, I hear laughter (some of it mine). Always, the laughter of my wife

Miriam, who perhaps has given me a false sense of this small talent. I can get up in the middle of the night and say, "I am going to get a glass of water," and Mim says, "Now that's funny!"

It could be something idiosyncratic because of my stammer. Perhaps, it's the way I speak, in which case I am in trouble when writing. After all, Truman Capote is said to be very funny, but I have seldom heard him speak with any wit. He *sounds* funny. Close your eyes and listen to him, and you would think you were hearing Janet Gaynor. Really, I'm quite serious.

I was talking the other day to a friend, Lisa Drew, an executive editor at Doubleday, and she said, "Do you think you're a writer?"

I explained that I enjoy being alone more than performing. I love books and language. I am awake much of the night making notes. I have a small penlight fastened to a pencil so that I can write down a thought without waking my wife or the dogs, and the next morning I rush to the typewriter, having no idea what the notes mean. I begin each day by sharpening pencils and emptying ashtrays. I straighten out everything on the desk, and sometimes I even tidy up the bathroom. I drink too much coffee, and I have trouble spelling—also punctuation is an arcane mystery for me.

Lisa interrupted with, "Boy, are you a writer!"

About spelling—Jack Kennedy was a terrible speller, and yet he became a famous lover—here is what has been going on lately. I was on the third floor in my office in the loft, and Miriam was two floors lower sewing. We were connected by an electronic communications system.

JACK: Miriam, how do you spell *hootspah?*
MIRIAM: What?
JACK: *Hootspah!*
MIRIAM: Are they in the book?
JACK: Are *who* in the book?
MIRIAM: The *Spahs.*
JACK: Perhaps, under *Hoot.*
MIRIAM: We don't know them.

JACK: They are not a *them;* they are an *it* . . . it's a Yiddish word
  meaning George Jessel.
MIRIAM: You have a book by Isaac Bashevis Singer. Thumb
  through it till you come to it.

I called Herman Raucher. Wow! Is he a speller! The word is
chutzpah, and it means a person who is behind you in a revolving
door and yet comes out ahead of you.

The best thing about a storyteller who writes is that he cannot
be interrupted. We talkers hate that. If you want to say anything,
hold up your hand. Wait till the end of the next sentence, and
then, for God's sake, speak up!

Our close social and tennis chums, besides the aforementioned
writers, include Lou Weiss, head of the television division of the
William Morris Agency, and Mike Dann, the respected TV and
media consultant. Both Lou and Mike are funnier than most, if
not all, the comedians they ever hired. They're on a very fast
track, this group. Sometimes in the living room, we use the bak-
ery system: You have to get a number from the rack if you wish
to speak. And try not to inhale or you have to get a new number.

One night, Alan King began a very interesting, but involved
story and was being stopped by Eydie Gormé, the singer and darling. Eydie, as you know, has a great giggle and is pretty swift
with a *bon mot.* She was giving Alan trouble, so Alan stopped
and said, "Please, Eydie dear, listen, you're in the story."

Eydie's eyes opened and her mouth closed, and she listened for
three minutes, enthralled. Alan finished, and as you may have
guessed, she was not in the story, but boy did she *listen!*

Now in our crowd, if one says, "Please, you're in the story,"
you freeze!

So watch it!

I have always felt that people who deal in anecdotes should be
given a depletion allowance. The problem is to get started from a
sitting position. I feel like Telly Savalas (as Kojak) in the morning when he shaves—where does he begin?

It has been said that asking Jack Paar a question is like taking
your thumb out of the dike. Oscar Levant, a great wit and an old
adversary in living rooms, was annoyed when I held the floor too

long one evening. He couldn't wait any longer for his turn and stopped me by saying, "Jack, are you *reading?*"

I also have an unusual curiosity about most things and am genuinely interested in information and other people's views. However, when I am talking to someone and the subject hits on something that I have read, experienced, or thought, I cannot wait to contribute. Once, on television, I found myself explaining to Bishop Fulton J. Sheen that Jesus Christ spoke in the language of Aramaic, not in Hebrew or Greek. I had just come from a trip to the Holy Land, and in my enthusiasm I assumed I had the latest word.

The greatest and funniest put-down of my enthusiasm on the air, was by the smooth, articulate Alistair Cooke. We talked for a few minutes on the program, and then he mentioned a mutual friend, Malcolm Muggeridge, the brilliant British iconoclast. Well, my dears, I went on for six minutes with stories about Malcolm, and then time was up. I thanked Alistair for coming and said what a pleasure it was to have met him. He simply said, "I want to thank you—for your questions and your *answers.*"

I was always verbal. I can remember when I was in grade school in Detroit, from the fourth to the sixth grades. Teachers actually promised the students that if they behaved and were attentive for the hour-long class, the last five minutes before the bell rang she would let Jack Paar talk. I usually made up silly stories about giants and monsters. However, to this day I do not understand how I did it, because I have no talent for fiction and wouldn't think of trying it.

One of my favorite companions, Robert Morley, the British actor, said, "Show business and writing are quite simple. You tell the people what you are going to do, you do it, and then tell them that you've done it!"

So here I come. I warn you I digress a lot. One of the best television critics, Jack O'Brian, a constant booster of mine, has written, "That Jack Paar has never had an unspoken thought." There must have been one, but I can't think of it.

A love of reading stimulates the wish to write. It's something like being on television but without commercials. Many a night on TV, I couldn't wait to hear what I was going to say. And I am now anxious to hear about my life since I have had it on "hold" for many years. This is not to be an autobiography but a memoir; actually all I really wish for is that it be an *entertainment.*

This book should be unusual by today's standards in that it will have no overt sex scenes in it. My reasoning is that I don't know any more about it than you do. There will not be any confession about dope addiction. I am a cocaine virgin. There will be one vulgar word in the writing because that word played an important part in my life. So read on—

I was born in Canton, a small town in Ohio, and was later raised in Michigan. My first memory—really the earliest thought that I can recall—was of being told that I had a false sense of modesty. When I was two or three years old, I was constantly being corrected when I was being dressed or undressed. Getting out of a wet bathing suit, if there were relatives or neighbors present, I always turned my body *frontward.* I actually thought that it was the *behind* portion that was private and sacred. So even when I was two, my mother said I was different. I was not a two-year-old "flasher." I was just trying to do the right thing, but my problem was that I didn't know which was the important part of my body. Still to this day, I seem to get everything *ass-frontward.* I don't know my *navel* from a hole in the ground!

The next memory is of when I was about five years old. My Uncle Harry lived with us, and we children were crazy about him. My mother worried because he had a bad temper and had quite a string of profanity that he would use with great creativity when angered. I was in the bathroom, I remember, getting ready for school and heard this swearing going on in the driveway directly below. My uncle was trying to crank his car on a cold morning in Detroit. For those of you too young to remember, one sometimes had to start a car by placing a crank in the opening below the radiator and making a fast turn upward. It was dark, and I could see him cranking away with the car headlights on (in those days the battery ran only the lights, and the starter itself one had to do manually). After many attempts and after inventing many new words, he stopped. Very quietly and with great dignity, he withdrew the crank and said, "All right, you son of a bitch, I am now going to *blind you!*" With that, he took the crank and knocked out both headlights!

I attended school until the eighth grade. I developed tuberculosis when I was twelve and was confined to bed for a year. I still recall the doctor's office after a series of X rays were taken and was asked to wait outside. I had no idea what was wrong with me but was traumatized for life when I saw that my mother was helped out of the physician's office crying hysterically. That has left a mark on me to this day. There must have been a better way of breaking the news to a frightened youngster. No one said a word to me, but I rather got the idea that my days were numbered and I really wouldn't need that bicycle after all.

No one discussed the problem because they were all too busy playing their scene. So I began to pray by myself that if I could live and get the bicycle, when I grew up, I would become a missionary. I still have guilt feelings that I never kept my word.

As I write this book, I am discovering that I seem to have had a great many guilt feelings that were innocent. Maybe I'll discover what Jack Paar was *really* like. It would be nice after all these years to learn that I really was as nice a person as I always thought I was. If, however, I discover that I was not, then I will be perfectly honest—I'll just keep it between me and me.

After one year in bed with tuberculosis, I recovered and had to repeat my first year in high school. We had then moved to Jackson, Michigan—a great place to grow up, with lakes and fishing and woods everywhere. A few months later, after returning to school and being a year behind, I became the light-heavyweight wrestling champion of the Jackson, Michigan High School.

I still remember the school paper announcing the championship wrestling match—"Rough House Paar Versus The Black Panther, High School Band, Admission Five Cents"—although I was more of a showman than a great athlete. I used to attend the weekly professional matches and saw all the famous wrestlers. I had picked up all those grunts and stances unheard of in high school wrestling. Anyhow, I won by scaring the poor black kid to death. A few days later, going home with the letter on my sweater, I was surrounded by a small gang of black kids who wanted a rematch for the Black Panther. I said, "Why not?" and that was a mistake. I really got beaten badly. I learned a lesson that later I have used. Quit while you're ahead! I did on most shows I had on television.

Later I turned to high school journalism. I was the only kid who had read Walter Winchell or cared about show business. So I was given a column to write about school activities: basketball games, dances, exciting marble-shooting contests, etc. Well, I was removed from the column when I used as a lead item: "School Principal and Wife to Have a Baby." They really were, and I found out about it. This kind of reporting was simply not done.

Then one day a male teacher hit a boy whom I really think was retarded. I confronted the teacher and told him never, but never, to pick on that boy again, or he would have to deal with Rough House Paar. The authorities called my mother but never could reach her, as Mom would always assume a Southern black accent and say, "Mrs. Paw is not heah. What is the problem?"

My father was tougher with me and would listen to their complaints. As he put it, "Jack is an unruly student, and he is not turning in his homework. All he seems interested in is vaudeville, movies, radio, and leading a band."

My father then would have a talk with me and ask me to do better. "There is no question," he said, "that you are a bright and informed young man, but after all, you're only a teenager and have to get along within the system."

I explained that I would try, but that there was nothing the teachers knew that I wanted to know. I tried to point out that I felt different from the other students. My future was not to go to college but to be on radio. I said, "Pop, do you know that there isn't one teacher who ever heard of Fats Waller?"

My mother was always very supportive of my wish to be in show business because she once knew Clark Gable when they were both very young in Cadiz, Ohio. I was always referred to by Mother as her problem. I recall her once saying, "You are my cross to bury."

Perhaps, because I was seriously ill as a child I was spoiled by my parents. When I didn't want to go to school, I would tell my mother I wanted to stay home and read, and would ask her to write a note to the teacher. I did this so often that I remember my mother ran out of excuses. I liked the dramatic even then, and I recall actually dictating my own excuses to my dear mother. One note said, "My son, Jack Paar, could not attend school yesterday because of snow blindness."

Incidentally, I was a fashion setter in school. I loved clothes and looking smart and sharp. My shoes were always shined, my hair combed, and I wore a sharp tie. Now this is what you won't believe, and there is no reason to make it up. If I am going to create an eccentric persona, I can do better than this. I wore a sweater and *spats*. For you dummies, *spats* are a felt covering worn over one's shoes. I always wore them, but it was also the fashion among other teenage *bon vivants*. Here I was in a sweater and spats. I could outtalk anybody, including the teachers, but I couldn't spell. Who needed to spell, if you were going to set the world on fire talking with a stutter and hearing laughter?

I started then, and have continued, to read, three or four books a week—mostly nonfiction—and the best magazines I could get my hands on. So I am not formally educated, but I'm interested in practically everything. My parents have told a story about how curious I was. For Christmas one year they gave me a snare drum, and I took it apart to see how it worked. A boy like that can't be all bad.

I began skipping school and hanging around the local radio station. I ran errands and did anything to learn how to read well. You see, in those days an announcer only read copy. Informal ad-libbing was unknown and forbidden on most stations. All I would have to learn to do was say, "This is WIBM, in Radio Block, Jackson, Michigan. Eight o'clock, Bulova Watch Time." This was done at station breaks every half hour, and at midnight there was the legally required sign-off when you gave the station's call letters.

So at the age of sixteen, I quit school and became a radio announcer at WIBM in Jackson. You see, I never stuttered when I read, only when I talked spontaneously, which was practically all the time. The problem was to get an audition reading copy, so I had to get my tongue in the door. I read very well, had a good radio voice, and was given the job as the night announcer from 9 P.M. till midnight. I was surely the happiest young man in America.

En passant, as they say—or as I sometimes say when I am faking an education, *Entre nous*—there is an apocryphal story I tell about my experiences at NBC. In addition to me with my stammer, NBC had Tom Brokaw, who has difficulty with certain letters, and Barbara Walters, who cannot pronounce L's or W's. Well, a viewer called NBC and complained about Paar's stammer and also about Tom's and Barbara's problems. The viewer asked to speak to the president of NBC. There was a pause, and then a voice came on the phone saying, *"Haw-woah."*

Back to Jackson. So I went on announcing each night, including Sundays, for two years. Oh yes, besides announcing I also had to empty the waste baskets, which I did very well. The high school authorities tried very hard to get the station to fire me and send me back to school. I told them that I could not return as they were not teaching anything that I wanted to know. Fran Liebowitz recently wrote a marvelous line when she explained that in the real world there was no such thing as algebra.

True. I have made millions of dollars stammering on radio and television, and never once have I had to use algebra. I can multiply very well if you stick to fives or tens. I consider any number from two to four or six to nine as fractions. If I come across a problem in division, I call my wife or daughter. They are both college graduates, but they can't read a Bulova commercial worth a damn.

Well, after my great success just as a radio announcer from nine to midnight, our station bought its first news teletype machine. And since I have always been very mechanical, I was the only one on the staff who could change the yellow paper rollers on the machine. So at eighteen I became the news director. All I had to do was rip off the news and read it.

During the early part of the Italian War in Ethiopia, names and many phrases in the news were Italian. I learned to fake that by a kind of "baby talk." You would be surprised how close you can come if you use that method.

Examples:

Scusi	(Excuse)
Così così	(So-so)
Tutti frutti	(All fruit)
Patata	(Potato)
Zuppa	(Soup)

And *ciao*, which means "Hello," "Goodbye," "Have a nice day," "Aloha," and "Batteries not included."

The station at that time didn't have a local news reporter, and if you wanted to know what was going on in Jackson, Michigan, you had to open the window and look outside.

One embarrassing thing happened when I began to lift local items out of the Jackson *Citizen Patriot*, our only newspaper. They printed this item: "Meti Nelots, a visiting Russian diplomat, was in the city." I used the item but was clever in changing the words around a bit, and the next day the paper printed a banner headline that read: "METI NELOTS, spelled backwards was: 'STOLEN ITEM.'"

I was trapped. So back I went to my Italian baby talk and the war in Ethiopia. Nobody could check up on that. Who's going to argue with a guy who wears a sweater and spats, and who can speak Italian?

4

Swing and Sway

When I was eighteen years old, I left my starring position as radio announcer and news reader (at fifteen dollars a week) in Jackson, Michigan, and worked at many stations in the Middle West: at WIRE in Indianapolis, WKBN in Youngstown, Ohio, WCAE in Pittsburgh, and finally WGAR in Cleveland, Ohio. I stayed in Cleveland nearly four years, and it was the happiest time of my life up till then. WGAR was an important CBS station, which meant that I would be on the CBS network late at night announcing dance bands. If you ever heard on your radio, "Swing and sway with Sammy Kaye," chances are that was me with my hand cupped around my ear and wearing the latest thing in Bond clothing. I announced for many of the big bands of that era: Eddie Duchin, Jimmy Dorsey, "A rhythmic New Deal with Dick Stabile," "It's Tommy Tucker time"—it was all great fun. And I was making sixty dollars a week. This was during the Depression, and no teenager was making that kind of money except Mickey Rooney. Besides, it was an education. I learned to *count* by working with Lawrence Welk.

When I was twenty years old, I was perhaps the youngest announcer on the CBS network, certainly the youngest ever to be the commentator of the Cleveland Symphony conducted by Artur Rodzinski. I carefully learned to pronounce phonetically all the Italian names for the musical movements, and rattled them off like I knew what the hell I was saying.

WGAR in Cleveland at the time was owned by G. A. Richards, who also owned WJR in Detroit. He was a man best described as a "Citizen Kane"–type person. He was extremely reactionary politically and was one of the original backers of Father Charles Coughlin, a right-wing priest. Richards had formed a special radio network for Coughlin's hourly program, which was broadcast on Sunday afternoons. And since I was the youngest member of the staff, I was always the announcer on duty on Sundays. There were no telephone operators on Sundays, so I had to take the constant beating of enraged listeners who would call in. Someone had to answer the phones—ME! I did more ad-libbing off the air than on the air, always on Sundays.

One Sunday evening at eight o'clock on CBS there was a wonderful program called "The Mercury Theatre on the Air," featuring a new dramatic star, Orson Welles. I made the eight o'clock "break" and then rushed down to the drug store to get my big dinner of the week: a malted milk and a club sandwich. (I spent all my money on clothes. I was the best dressed but most poorly nourished young man in Cleveland. The rest of the week I had to live on cottage cheese.)

When I returned to the top of the Statler Hotel, where our studios were, I sat down to listen to this new program. I became, I admit, quite confused, having missed the beginning. There was something about men from Mars landing in New Jersey. What confused me is that they used some well-known news announcers' voices on the program. This had never been done before and is illegal to do today.

I had just finished taking a beating because of Father Coughlin, and now I had to answer questions from hundreds of listeners on the phone about what they should do in view of the men from Mars landing.

There was nothing in the *Announcers' Handbook* about what to do in case of an invasion from Mars, so since I was the only one in the studio, I had to make a decision. The telephone trunk lines were all alight, and I killed the network button on the control panel and spoke somewhat hysterically. "Please do not phone this station as this is a drama—I think . . . !"

Later I again broke into the network with, "Upon checking,

[not clear who with] I assure you this is a drama . . . I am almost certain! Be calm—have I ever lied to you before?"

Grace under pressure!

The phone calls increased with comments like, "You are only trying to calm us. You know there are people landing, and what are we to do?"

I called the manager of the station, John Patt, and told him we had a problem and that maybe we were being invaded. He was very angry and said that he too thought it was a drama and that I would never be an important radio announcer until I learned to control my emotions, but he would call New York and see if anyone was landing in New Jersey. Many people believed it. I will go further and say that MOST people believed it the way it had been presented. You see, it opened as a regular program of "The Mercury Theatre" and then was switched to this "special event." It was the greatest put-on in the history of broadcasting, and if anyone tried it today, it would mean the loss of billions of dollars as the entire network's stations would lose their licenses, and rightly so. However, it made a star of Orson Welles, who later became famous for his designer jeans.

The newspapers sent cameramen to the studio, and I was photographed as the man who calmed Cleveland. I became a "half-assed" hero overnight, and the management, who had wanted to fire me, realized that I had become the hottest property they had. The truth is I was a nervous wreck. There was no use in any of them passing judgment on the dramatic situation which had never happened before or since. I admit to you now that I really half-believed it; it's a good thing I was not working for a station in New Jersey, or thousands would have perished wading into the Atlantic.

To this day, when I hear on radio or television, "We interrupt this program to bring you a special news broadcast," I go into a quiet panic. It's not that I am cowardly; as a matter of fact, I am quite stupidly brave and courageous, but I would frankly never live in New Jersey.

A few years later, on Sunday of course, I came to the studio about two o'clock in the afternoon, all excited about the big event of the week, my malted milk and club sandwich. I went into the announcers' booth and heard some strange crackling from a shortwave news broadcast from CBS. It was not quite clear, but someone was being bombed at a place called Pearl Harbor. Now, all of you younger smart people know about Pearl Harbor now, but we at that time never had heard the name, and none of us knew where it was. It was never clear in the early hours of the broadcast who was bombing whom and where! It was December 7, 1941. No matter what you may think now, the war was unexpected and unbelievable. I wasn't sure what to do as the phones began to ring again. Since I had saved everybody from the invasion of New Jersey, they expected me to save them again. Well, enough is enough!

I called John Patt and told him we had a problem. He berated me again and said, "Do not push 'off' the network button. You stay out of it. If it's war, I don't want you involved."

Patt continued, "I will call New York and see if there is any trouble at this so-called Pearl Harbor. I will even check New Jersey. And you, Paar, are becoming a problem."

Now I was being blamed for World War II!

The next day war was declared, and my first thought was: Who has the best uniforms? I decided that the Canadian Air Force had the most unusual ones and made inquiries as to how one could join.

Before I was fired by the Cleveland management, that nut, G. A. Richards, had another crazy idea. It was at the height of "swing music"; Benny Goodman, Artie Shaw, or Woodie Herman were on the network each night, and "G.A." had decided that he would not permit any sacrilege of his favorite songs in a "swing" arrangement. So I had to sit by the control panel each Sunday, and if there was any modern version of "Annie Laurie," "My Old Kentucky Home," and others, I had to push the CBS network button off and apologize and fill in with a recording in the studio. This was also done at WJR in Detroit. So between Orson Welles, Father Coughlin, World War II, and G. A. Richards, I had more responsibility than a twenty-two-year-old could handle.

Although later on "The Tonight Show," I was convinced that Richards was silly with his censoring of swing music, many years later my aversion to rock music and its stars played a small part in my disenchantment with show business.

One of the reasons that I left television many years later was that I could not understand or appreciate the vogue for rock music. I found it embarrassing or, at best, amusing. In spite of this, I was the first to bring the Beatles to America. I had them filmed by the BBC for my program, and the only reason was that to me they were a new phenomenon like the Hula-Hoop or swallowing a goldfish. It turned out I was quite wrong, as they were lasting and wrote some beautiful melodies.

What I really dislike is the crazy, punk, screaming beat of what I considered a pagan culture. The beat goes back to the apes, but think of how many thousands of years it took for man to discover *melody*. Gershwin's *Rhapsody in Blue* cannot be played on a drum, and thank God there are no words to it.

I think it was Baudelaire, the French writer, who observed, "That which is too silly and stupid to be *spoken* can always be *sung*."

Many of the rock singers that I hear sound idiotic, which is an insult to the less fortunate. And the dope culture which goes with this trash turns me off and out. Never trust anyone under thirty!

At the time, I told my staff on "The Tonight Show" that I could not introduce these ridiculous performers in their under-wear! Can you imagine Perry Como, Frank Sinatra, or Andy Williams coming on stage wearing jockey shorts? Picture that for a moment!

I have a friend whose son was in architectural college for three years. The boy became restless, and his father sent him to France for a year to photograph the great buildings in Europe to renew his interest. Well, the kid came home and announced that he didn't want to be an architect, he wanted to be a rock musician. His dad went along with it and supported him while he took a course in *remedial* guitar. After a few months, the boy announced that he was ready to perform for his family.

He sang, "Ah loof yah bahbee, I need yah bahbee, gives it to me bahbee."

The father said, "You are practically a college graduate and went to the best prep school. You speak French and were raised by intelligent parents. What in hell is this 'Ah loof yah bahbee' crap? At least say, 'I love you baby'!"

The son began again, "I love you baby, I need you—" He broke off and said, "It won't work that way. You've got to sound *retarded!*"

But I have digressed. During my last days in Cleveland, despite the neurotic behavior of our management, it was a happy place to work and had become "my home," as I had left my family when I was sixteen years old and was on my own. The other announcers were older than I and were by my standards very sophisticated. They were like brothers. And it became for me a college education. I picked up manners and a love of literature, music, and drama from them. I learned to write well enough to sell several pieces to national magazines. Since I was the youngest member of the group, much was forgiven, as one does with a problem child. I was the outspoken one on the staff, and as a result I would talk myself out of Cleveland.

Each Christmas old G.A. would give a bonus to the employees, several hundred dollars that we all really began to count on, and the next holiday was approaching. I had already spent a good portion of mine buying a very fancy dog, a Sealyham. Then old G.A. called the staff together and—a little loaded, I thought—told us that this Christmas there would be no bonus because he, looking out for our welfare, had invested what would have been our money in a "new invention" for the railroads.

I mumbled, too loud obviously, "I hope it's not the *wheel*— they already have that!"

I was let go with a month's salary the next week. I was stunned! To this day, I awaken many a night with the recurring dream of being fired and separated from a group that had become my family. Each time I awaken from this dream, I have to remind myself that I survived and could at this moment buy WGAR if I wished. Later I did buy a television and radio station in Maine. I outbid my old manager John Patt, who later took a great interest in me after my career in the Army and my success in television. The truth is that I loved them all very much but never got over being fired. When last I saw my old employers, they felt that firing me was the greatest thing that could have happened, but my recurring, weekly dreams tell me differently.

In 1946, after returning from the war, I was honored by thousands of people in the Cleveland auditorium as the local boy who made good—but you know, I have never dreamed of that and only faintly remember the event. I think one is marked and obsessed by rejection; I have *never* had a dream of success!

Radio, the network radio of thirty-five years or so ago, still to me was the greatest entertainment form of all broadcasting. Fred Allen, who brought literature to radio comedy, Jack Benny, Fibber McGee and Molly, Duffy's Tavern brought "imagination and fantasy" to the medium far better than television does today. And none of those great stars were really as successful in the newer medium of television. Two men in a Chicago studio could act and write for years the story of two black taxi drivers and actually close the entire country down at seven o'clock each evening as Amos and Andy did. There was nothing racist about it other than the fact that they were white men portraying likeable blacks. Later, when black people played the parts on television, it became embarrassing for all.

Radio allowed each listener to form pictures in his mind, to use muscles in his brain—and that experience will never be known by the younger half of this country. To them radio is a cigar-box–sized little plastic thing in the kitchen that broadcasts news, the weather report, and music. In reality, radio was then half the size of your refrigerator, placed in the living room, and was quite wonderful.

I later had a friend, Hy Averback, who is now an important television and motion picture director who worked with me in radio. When he became the father of two sons and television was all the boys knew, he sat them down one evening and made them listen to one of the few radio dramas that was to be repeated. He sat the kids down on chairs and told them to listen; to picture for themselves the scenery, the faces of the characters in the story; to use their imagination. They simply could not listen and asked to leave the room because, they said, "We don't know where to put our eyes."

The one thing I missed the most about leaving Cleveland was the weekly broadcasts I would do backstage from the Palace Theatre, the vaudeville showplace of that city. We also broadcast from the legitimate theater, the Hanna. Over the years I had met and talked with the great stars of the stage. I knew many of the players who toured and even had early love affairs with some of the young ladies. One in particular, Doris Dudley, was playing opposite John Barrymore in *My Dear Children*. She played his daughter, and through Doris I got to know Barrymore as much as anyone could know him. Later Katharine Cornell and Jean-Pierre Aumont were starred in another show featuring Miss Dudley. I used to spend my weekends with a loan from everybody on the radio staff and visit the nearest city where Doris was playing.

Our romance was complicated by the fact that she was touring, and I was confined to my WGAR microphone, but I managed to woo her by means of the airwaves. Those were the days when I would be on CBS several nights a week announcing the big dance bands from the hotels and ballrooms in Cleveland. She would listen wherever she was, and I would introduce a number with such lines as "And now for a certain someone, somewhere, 'All the Things You Are'"; or "Now for that certain someone, somewhere, 'Who's Your Little Whoozis.'" This kilocycle idyll was abruptly terminated when CBS sent WGAR a teletype saying, "Tell Paar to stop making love on our network." Since one of my duties was also taking care of the teletype messages, the management never saw it.

Deprived of this channel of romantic communication, I pursued the young lady to Detroit by train. She had left the road company of *Margin for Error* a few weeks earlier, and when that company arrived in Detroit, she decided it would be great fun to play a practical joke on her former fellow troupers. Enlisting me in this skullduggery, she led me to a novelty shop where we stocked up on such trick items as exploding matches, glasses that dribble, and itching powder. Then we headed for the theater and went backstage well before curtain time. She was warmly welcomed by the stage hands, whom she knew, and had little difficulty surreptitiously substituting her trick glasses, exploding matches, and other instruments of torment for the real stage props.

Then, as the curtain rose, we took our places down front to enjoy the proceedings. The Clare Booth Luce play was about a Nazi consul in America and the Jewish policeman assigned to guard him. As the action unfolded, the Nazi consul, played by Kurt Katch, nonchalantly struck a match, only to have it explode with a loud BANG, startling him so that he almost fell into the orchestra pit. He had scarcely recovered from this when he raised a glass to toast *der Führer*. As he touched it to his lips, the wine dribbled down his chin, splattering the front of his suit. Each of these diabolically inspired mishaps was greeted with howls of laughter by my pretty companion.

As the actors proceeded warily through their lines on the booby-trapped stage, the Jewish policeman, played by Sheldon Leonard, now a prominent Hollywood director, began to twitch like a cooch dancer.

"I put itching powder in his puttees," my friend announced, gasping with laughter, as the harassed actors glared over the footlights at us.

"Come on, let's go back and see them," my young lady said as the final curtain rang down. "You'll love them."

Dubiously I followed her backstage. The cast understandably seemed less than overjoyed to see their nemesis, but her coltish spirits and hearty greeting quickly melted their irritation. "It was all in fun," she bubbled. "Here, have some gum as a peace offering."

Several of the cast took the gum, and we said goodbye. As we went out the stage entrance, I noticed that several of the actors were clutching their throats and otherwise looking apoplectic. "It's hot gum," my fair companion giggled. "Isn't that a riot!"

It may have been little things like that which eventually caused our romance to pall.

Being exposed to "backstage" at the Palace Theatre made me want very much to get into "real show business." At this time I met and became friendly with a great star of vaudeville, Frank Fay. Unlike the "baggy pants" comedians, he wore a dark suit, with a carnation on stage, and he had a most imperial manner. I wanted to learn to do this too because I never was, and never knew how to be, physically funny as were the great clowns of the theater. In vaudeville, Fay was known as a "talking gentleman"; he just stood quietly and said the most outrageous things. I used him as my model. I already had two dark suits, so all I needed was money for a carnation.

While working at the station, I devoted much of my spare time to trying to learn to be a comedian. I'd appear anywhere for a chance to get up and tell jokes.

I popped up at high school assemblies, Polish weddings, political rallies, grape festivals, bazaars, and benefits of every description. For anyone who wanted a few words said, I had a few thousand ready.

One night I was thrilled to get a call from a theater. This was to be an actual professional job for real pay. I arrived at the theater breathless and eagerly asked the manager, "Where are the other acts?"

"There aren't any other acts," he said sourly.

"But I can only do about a half hour of jokes," I protested.

"Nope, no jokes," the manager said. "If you tell jokes, the show runs longer and the projectionist gets overtime. I just want you to raffle off some turkeys."

Deflated, I was led backstage and presented to my supporting cast—a half dozen trussed-up turkeys thrashing about indignantly in protest against their plight.

"Where's my dressing room?" I inquired, by now prepared for anything.

"There isn't any," the manager said. "You just sneak on stage during the newsreel."

So that's how I made my theatrical debut, sneaking down the aisle in the darkness while the audience booed Hitler in the newsreel. It was pretty discouraging, following a warm-up by Hitler. But the end of this story is sadder than the beginning.

I'd come back each week and pass out turkey while the bank night cash-prize jackpot mounted in value. These were recession days, and the avarice of the audience mounted each week with the amount of the jackpot.

Finally one night came the drawing for the jackpot. In order to be sure that there were no suspicions, I invited members of the audience to come up and witness the drawing. After much urging, only one lady consented to come on stage. She eyed me suspiciously as I picked a child to draw the winning number. I spun the barrel mixing the thousands of stubs. The moppet then reached in, picked one, and handed it to me. With a flourish, I read the winning name. "My God, that's me!" the lady shrieked, nearly collapsing.

I saw several members of the audience coming over the footlights and didn't wait to see more. I escaped backstage and out a fire escape, while the angry crowd milled around the beleaguered manager.

I can remember just two big jokes from my early act. The first went like this: "A funny thing happened to me on the way to the theater," I would begin. "A sweet old lady walked up to me on the street and asked, 'Will I get an electric shock if I put my foot on that streetcar track?' 'No,' I replied, 'not unless you throw your other foot up over the trolley wire.'"

The other joke was about a farmer whose wife was giving birth on the farm without any electricity. The farmer asked a hired man to go get a flashlight and help him deliver the child. The first child was born, and as the hired man walked away, the wife again went into labor, and the farmer asked again for help with the flashlight. After the second baby was born, the hired man again went to put the flashlight away when a third child was born. When things quieted down, the hired man said, "Can I go now?"

The farmer said, "Yes, I think it's the *light* that's attracting them."

As I write this, I remember the indignity of going to my theater appearances by streetcar all dressed up with the dark suit and wearing the carnation. But what the hell, I was in real *show business!* I even bought a tube of suntan stage makeup, just like Frank Fay. I was on my way to bigger "gigs" and began to read *Variety*. I played better theaters and county fairs and made an extra hundred dollars every now and then. I was never very good with money and even had to buy my wonderful Sealyham dog, named Kipper, on time.

Once, while playing county fairs, I met some smaller vaudeville performers who made their living going from one date to another and staying in dinky motel rooms. Actors as a class, and particularly in vaudeville, were very cheap. I have known many who became big stars in radio and television but who never got over their frugal days. I can say almost without exception that stars who were making thousands of dollars a week or a million a year were still very tough with a buck—cheaper than any used-car salesman or person of smaller income.

Well, there was this one guy with whom I worked named Jimmy Edwards. He later became "Professor Backwards" and appeared on "The Ed Sullivan Show." He was a good performer, but he lived on Cracker Jack and wouldn't even rent his own room, choosing instead to move in with me and sleep on a chair rather than spend his money for a night's lodging.

He heard that I had a new apartment in Cleveland and said he was sending me a gift. When it arrived, it was a big twenty-inch outdoor clock with "Pepsi Cola" printed in large letters on its face. I wouldn't know where it could be hung except in William Randolph Hearst's little pad at San Simeon.

Well, Jimmy played mostly in the South and the Midwest. His agent, MCA, booked his act from their Chicago office. Jimmy was too cheap to actually pay for a phone call and ask for his next date, so it was arranged with the MCA secretary that he would use a code. He would telephone the office person-to-person and ask for himself. When the operator would report that "Mr. Edwards was not in," Jimmy would request the operator to ask the secretary where he could be reached. The dumb operator would repeat the message and the secretary would say, "Mr. Edwards can be reached at the Claypool Hotel in Indianapolis on June fourth." This meant that Jimmy had a date at the Claypool Hotel in Indianapolis, on June fourth.

Not content with that free information, Edwards would say, "Operator, would you ask the secretary what room he'll be in." This meant "How much does the date pay?"

The innocent operator would repeat the question and ask for the room number. The secretary would then reply, "Room 450," meaning that he would get four hundred fifty dollars. Now wanting to bargain, Jimmy would tell the operator to try and put Mr. Edwards into Room 500. The secretary at MCA would by now be quite fed up with this long bit and would say, "Tell the gentleman that Mr. Edwards is lucky he will not be in Room 375 as he was last year!"

After being fired from my radio job and running out of money, I took my dog, Kipper, home and gave him to my mother and father. I then made the smartest career move ever—I enlisted in the Army. I would have been drafted sooner or later, and the chic thing to do then was to enlist. Everything that happened to me since springs from that enlistment—World War II became bigtime show business. One day I was a bewildered private, concerned for the future, frightened by the discipline and danger, and the next day, I was a *star!*

5

Uncle Sam
Needs Me

As usual, I begin this chapter in the middle in order to get your attention. Later on, I can fill you in on the hows and whys after the shock of the next few moments.

I did not become a success in show business in the traditional way because I had never appeared at the Palace or Loew's State Theater. I *played* World War II! As show people say when they are talking about being a hit, the South Pacific was *my room*.

I was in charge of a small unit of Special Service Infantry Soldiers, who were picked to entertain in the forward areas. The 28th Special Service Unit consisted of men who had basic infantry training but had special skills in civilian life not only as entertainers, but as athletic coaches, newspaper writers who set up camp newspapers, even librarians to distribute paperback books in advance areas. We also had four soldiers who were concert musicians and who gave separate string quartet recitals in the hospital tents and mess halls. Can you picture a guy carrying an M-1 rifle and a cello? Well, that was the crazy 28th Special Service Unit.

The shows I wrote and starred in were put on by a twelve-piece band of former top musicians from famous orchestras; several singers, including a trio of guys from Charlie Spivak's band, and two very funny burlesque comedians who did sketches. Our shows were later described by war correspondents as possibly the best entertainment in the South Pacific. We later were given a Unit Citation and the Meritorious Service Award.

Now a "theater" in that area was in the open jungle with palm trees cut down to make seats and oil barrels with planks on top for a stage. Every division, brigade, or battalion had many "theaters" in their areas. There were also mobile hospitals, even remote antiaircraft units with twenty men far out on a point that would have a stage. Many times a week they would have movies, but the big event was our show. This was all before USO and the appearance of Hollywood stars.

Now would you believe that at one time a show could "play" every night for three months on Guadalcanal and never have a repeat audience? That's how many men there were in the Army and Marines on that one island. We could spend weeks going out on barges and board the navy war and supply ships and do our thing. When we finished the tour, we would rewrite, restage, and begin again. Also, during the day we would go into the tented hospitals and play for the wounded. The worst cases I can still remember were the pilots who were burned and had to be wrapped in ointment and covered with tissue paper since they could not stand the pressure of a sheet. I am still haunted by the odor of burned flesh. We served on guard duty like all the infantry soldiers, but I also had my own jeep and would go out to the units with magazines and paperbacks. I was really fortunate compared to the other poor bastards. I have always been lucky, not only when the chips were down but even when the chips were *up*.

Well, what I am trying to get to are some stories I have never told and could not tell on television. On the "Tonight" program there were several phrases which evolved that became a part of the language—"I kid you not" and, after a story had died, "You had to be there."

But there's another phrase attributed to me that I've never been able to use publicly. For the first six months in the South Pacific there were no women or Red Cross girls in these areas, so the language was bawdy. Once Eleanor Roosevelt flew in, and we

had to change the whole damn show, but the following is a story
I told each night:

"The King and Queen of England were awarding medals for
bravery to two British soldiers and one American soldier. The soldiers were at attention as the King passed down the line. Before
the first British soldier, he said, 'I present to you the Quam de
Quam, the highest honor of the British Empire. This is given to
you by your King, Keeper of the Faith, Ruler of All the Domin-
ions Beyond the Sea: New Zealand, Australia, Kenya, Uganda,
India, Bermuda, the Bahamas, Canada, Jamaica, Fiji.'

"Then the King moved to the next British soldier and made
the same long speech. When he got to the American, the Yank
said, 'All right, King, stop the bullshit!'

"Looking shocked the Queen said, 'What did he say, dear?'

"The King said, 'Something about stopping the bullshit.'

" 'Well,' said the Queen, 'fuck him, George. Don't give him the
medal.' "

You cannot believe the laughter in front of a thousand men.
Because I looked so innocent and had said nothing the least bit
risqué prior to that, it was a smash.

Later, when the First and Third marine divisions returned
from their invasions and the wounded were in the field hospitals
(they were actually at best Quonset huts), I would walk from
bed to bed and talk to the men.

One wounded marine called me over and said, "We didn't yell
'Geronimo!' in the invasion and all that movie crap; the battle cry
was, 'Fuck 'em, George!' " It was my greatest moment, and now
my wife doesn't want me to use the words, but there they are!

After the war, in Hollywood, when I was signed by RKO Pictures, I walked onto my first movie set to be given a screen test. I
had been signed to a three-year contract in New York unseen by
the Hollywood executives. I was signed on the strength of an
eight-page article in Esquire magazine, written by Sidney Carroll,
the war correspondent, who had seen me in the Pacific. As I
walked onto this dark movie set, having no experience as an actor
in this kind of glamorous world, I only had one thought—to get
the hell out of there—but then I heard my battle cry again. Will
Price, RKO's test director (then the husband of Maureen

O'Hara) and a man whom I had never previously met, turned out to have been a captain in the Third Division; so were some members of the crew. *"Fuck 'em, George!"* they yelled. I relaxed —these were my kind of people.

So maybe if the Japanese had not bombed Pearl Harbor, I would now be selling live bait in Fort Lauderdale.

Another time we were to do a special show before a mixed audience of soldiers, sailors, marines, and army and navy nurses. This had to be impeccable in the sense that there was to be no rough army talk or sketches. The top brass of all the services were to be there. It was in the best "theater" on the island with a crowd of two thousand, but it was still in the jungle, with the officers sitting on chairs in the front called "officers' country." The enlisted men were on the usual palm-tree logs that had been cut down on a hill, making it into a primitive amphitheater. There is never such a thing as a dressing room in these places. The acts would be waiting in the dark jungle among the trees.

The orchestra on the stage was tuning up, and I was pacing, waiting to go on with all the new material I had written. I first went behind a tree to take a pee only to "spritz" the palm tree and spray all over my pants. I always wore a pressed khaki uniform and dressed as well as I could under the conditions which prevailed. I really was in a panic. How could I walk out on stage with my pants all wet in front?

The officer who accompanied the show was Lieutenant William Rogers, a wealthy Philadelphia socialite and a great friend and protector of mine. He saw the problem and said, "Come back here." He took off *his* trousers and gave them to me. I took off mine, and as we were the same height and size, they fit. I heard my introduction and "play-on music" and went out and did my usual routine of officer put-down comments.

The irony was that here I was insulting the officers wearing their own pants! And my officer, Lieutenant Rogers, was hiding behind a tree in his shorts for an hour and a half. God only knows what would have happened if he had been seen by the MPs or a stray Jap.

When I enlisted, I was sent to Camp Custer in Michigan for assignment. I always prayed, "Dear God, anything but tanks."

Well, I was sent off to a staging area at Indiantown Gap, Pa., to a Special Service Unit that was on alert to go overseas at any moment. The one hundred twenty men had already had basic infantry training, and as the latest and last man, my training took place alone. Picture a drill field with only one soldier (me), marching around to the commands of a screaming sergeant. I have always hated bad manners and loud talk and was quite melancholy about the whole experience. But when that hell was over, I found out that the main purpose of our unit was to entertain troops overseas in the foreward areas. Now since I could write and talk and started what became a minor legend by commenting on how officers were different from the rest of us, I quickly caused attention. I was funnier than anyone else in the show and in a month had taken over the whole damn company. My army humor was different from the other army comics whose routines usually included wearing balloons in their shirts and mimicking "*Bei Mir Bist Du Schön*," a popular recording of the day.

So I was sent out doing my little talks around the area, but one night something important happened. Some officers of the Indiantown Gap reservation took me to Washington to do my routines in front of the top officers in the Pentagon. I was driven there by a Colonel Kitay. On the late midnight drive back to the Gap from Washington the colonel said, "Soldier, you were a big hit there tonight. There are some of us who would like to pull you out of that unit and station you in Washington for special assignments. But *say nothing*; it will have to be done quietly and quickly."

Well, since I had already met the girl I was to marry, who lived in Hershey, Pa., eighteen miles from the Gap, I was delighted. But old *big mouth* had to talk. I told my pals, "I probably will not be going with you chaps, but that's the way the K Ration crumbles."

A few days later, when everyone was packing and I was unpacking, the captain sent for me to report to the orderly room. He said, "I hear that you are not planning to join us overseas! What a pity when we have you trained practically as a commando. And now all that terror for the enemy we have instilled will be wasted. How sad." The joke was over. He turned bitter and really angry.

"I want you to tell me who gave you the impression that you can be removed from my command?"

I did not want to name the colonel as I had broken my word of keeping silent, but to a direct order I said, "Colonel Kitay did, sir."

The captain then said, and this is important, "No *kike* colonel is taking you from this unit."

I saluted and figured I had better start packing as it was bon voyage time. Returning to the barracks, my friends were waiting to hear what the hell was going on with me and the Army. I repeated exactly what I said and what our captain told me about the *kike* colonel. Now it just so happens that the three friends were older than I, and they all happened to be Jewish. They explained that they wanted to talk among themselves and asked if I would join them later. In a whispered meeting that night in back of the barracks, they told me that they had a plan. They wanted to go to Army Intelligence, G2, and bring charges against the captain as anti-Semitic. Wow! That was an important move and frightening, because if the charge didn't hold and we were alerted to be shipped out as a unit, the captain would have four soldiers who could be shafted for the next few years or whatever.

I stammered, "Look, if it's just my word, that isn't enough. What evidence of this anti-Semitism will *you* offer? I really cannot ruin an officer's career on one stupid, bigoted remark. And besides, guys, as I look among you and on your arms, I see sergeants' stripes. Each of you are Jewish and all are sergeants. There are others in the company who are both. That would negate prejudice charges. I am not even a PFC and am a Presbyterian. I will repeat what he said *only* if you have other evidence and join me, but to go to G2 alone is asking too much."

But now for the O. Henry finish to this tale. I did not go to Army Intelligence. I did go overseas. I never saw any other evidence of prejudice. But the other three sergeants, because the rules were changed at the last moment and because of their age, never had to go with us.

I am glad it turned out that way because our captain showed enormous courage and affection for his men in the years we spent in the South Pacific. He had strong political connections in Congress, and I recall him once saying to a superior, "Sir, I want my men moved to the front. We are sick of this rear area duty."

The area commander said, "Captain, you will move when you are ordered. Those men you have are lovers, not fighters. The invasion of Saipan does not need a string quartet!"

And I actually heard our captain reply, "As you say, sir. But I am writing Senator Byrd in the morning."

Holy Cow! I thought, our captain is more outspoken than I am!

One time I was taken off a stage for some remarks I had made and was put under guard by a navy commodore. Here's what happened: It was at a naval hospital in New Caledonia. We were putting on a show for several thousand men, many of them wounded and in wheelchairs or on stretchers. The time came to start, but we couldn't begin the show until the commodore arrived. The men were getting restless, and so was I. At last the commodore appeared, nearly an hour late, with a pretty USO girl on his arm. On stage, I said as they made their way to their seats, "You wouldn't think that one man and a broad would hold up two thousand men." The men howled, and I felt encouraged. So I continued, "The USO girls were supposed to do the Dance of the Virgins for you, but they went to the Officers' Club last night and broke their contract." The men loved it, but the commodore didn't. I was taken off the stage by the shore patrol and locked up. Our captain then went to the commodore and said, "Sir, you outrank me, but only in the Navy. This is a navy area, but that boy and I are army personnel. Release him to me. He's not well." And you know, we both walked out of that trap!

Here is another example of our captain's courage. If you remember the play or picture of *The Caine Mutiny*, you may recall that it is about a crazy navy captain of a ship who went berserk and was replaced under duress by his junior officers. There is such a rule in military code. This actually happened to our troopship. The ship was run by the Merchant Marine . . . but the ranking officer of the ship was an army major who would be in charge of all army troops aboard. This major turned out to be a drunk and stayed in his cabin most of our forty-four-day ordeal from Staten Island, through the Panama Canal, and into the Coral Sea.

We soon learned by his crazy commands from his cabin over the public address system that he was cracking up. One day when the ship was going into combat waters, he began screaming that we should all stay well away from the ship's rails. It came to a climax when we heard, "Now here this. I have told you sons of bitches before, and I repeat: You bastards had better obey. Keep away from the ship's rails."

The men were hungry and scared, and resented this. The public address system stayed on as we heard a scuffle. Next we heard our captain's southern voice, "I apologize for the manner in which you have been given orders. I assure you it will not happen again."

What later happened was that junior officers tried their drunken superior secretly and relieved him of his command. He was locked up and never heard from again. That takes guts.

A little footnote here: Many people, if asked, would identify the phrase "I kid you not" with me. Actually, it came from the picture *The Caine Mutiny* and was first said by Humphrey Bogart in the film. I used it because it amused me and sounded so baroque or Elizabethan. I was once on a TV award show honoring Jack Benny and Humphrey Bogart posthumously. They showed film clips of Bogart. When that scene from the movie came on and he said, "I kid you not," the audience roared, thinking that Mr. Bogart had stolen the line from me. He did not. It was written by the author Herman Wouk.

The ship we were on was not a regular naval vessel. It was rented, not from Hertz but from the United Fruit Company. It had been a former banana boat plying the Caribbean trade. We ate down in a hold that usually had five inches of water on the floor. Rather than go through that misery, we for the most part lived on candy bars for forty-four days. I believe that it was one of the longest continuous voyages by a troop ship without touching land, on record. We were not in a convoy but were bouncing along alone most of the time.

Morale was a serious problem. When we entered the Coral Sea, we had our first submarine alert. I cannot tell those of you who have not experienced the utter panic—quiet panic, mind you—when you hear on the horn, "Now here this. Battle stations for all naval personnel. Army troops go below."

Now what happens to a man who's really frightened is that he cannot make his lungs work. They will not go in and out on their own. Real fright means that you cannot breathe. We would all rather have stayed up on deck than to go three decks below on a broken-down banana boat. I have never been that scared again, not ever!

When an all-steel ship starts firing its guns, you are in an echo chamber below. You cannot tell if you are being hit or are firing.

I do not wish to prolong this story. When it was all over, we were told to come topside. Nothing was explained to us, but I was told, "Paar, put on a show." What show? I had exhausted every joke I ever knew and was a pretty melancholy soldier. But I can recall climbing up on a lifeboat where they had a microphone on the ship's system, and a thought came to me which turned out to be my best extemporaneous routine. I'll never top it!

About fifteen hundred men gathered around below the lifeboat, and I said, "I have been informed by the command that it was definitely a Japanese submarine off the port bow a few minutes ago. Unfortunately, the navy gun crew drove them off. I say 'unfortunate' because the Japs were trying to bring us food."

We arrived on Guadalcanal, and the work of building an area in the jungle began. We lived in tents with plywood floors, four men to a tent. We then began our job of entertaining the Army, Navy, and Marines.

My routines, which I had prepared myself since we had no writers, were comic, serious-appearing lectures with charts and a pointer, à la my hero Robert Benchley's famous "Treasurer's Report." I gave lectures on "How to Cheat at War" and "How to Avoid Venereal Disease Where There Wasn't Any." (You see, for the first six months there were no women on the island and no native people as they had all taken to the mountains.)

I began to express with humor the disgruntlement that we were all experiencing. I was able to say what the men were feeling but could not even write home about it because of censorship.

I was putting into words their own gripes and frustrations and loneliness. "Soon our day will come, men," I would tell them. "Someday we'll all go home and be free again. We'll join the American Legion and carry on its great and noble traditions—we'll goose old ladies and throw toilet paper out of hotel windows."

Often we played to war-weary, begrimed men, just back from killing Japs in the jungle, but they always responded with humor. I used to kid ourselves. "The only battle star I have," I would say, "is for being booed at Bougainville. But we, too, sometimes face danger. Just today I reported to our commanding officer, 'Sir, mission accomplished. Two of our banjos are missing.' "

I have kept some of my old jokes and am including a few as historic evidence of some of the dangers our fighting men had to face in the jungle warfare of World War II, although to *really* enjoy them, "you had to be there." Here they are . . .

I have announcements to make: The captain is censoring the mail again this week, so let's cut down on those big words . . .

The command is sorry about the foul-up on our Christmas packages from home. We'll get them as soon as they finish breaking them. However, there is an unclaimed package which just arrived for Sergeant York. I don't believe he's in this outfit or this war . . .

All of you men turn in your helmets—we're taking the rearview mirrors off the jeeps and putting them on your hats so you can see the lieutenants during combat . . .

Why is it that on every invasion this outfit makes, the officers in Headquarters Company are so far behind the Japanese lines that they may get bombed by the Nazis?

The only way the guys in Headquarters Company are going to get the Purple Heart is if they get caught between two desks coming together . . .

Next week when you go in, you are going to have your top-ranking officers with you on the beach. You'll hear their voices yelling "Geronimo," "Gung ho," and "This is a recorded announcement."

Besides, if we all went home now, there'd be no place for us to live. They can't start putting up new homes for us until they finish building the bowling alleys . . .

One guy I know got a discharge, got married, and lives in a Quonset hut. Last month I heard his first child was born round-shouldered . . .

I spent the next twenty months in the South Pacific islands. When I think back now, I wouldn't want to have missed the experience for anything. I made friends with the air corps pilots by entertaining and by driving around in my little jeep, giving out the latest magazines and paperbacks. The pilots would take me on training flights in the B-25 bombers, the first time I had ever been in the air. I hung around the then-famous Henderson Field and was always begging for a ride.

I finally ended up as a patient myself in one of the hospitals where I frequently entertained. Nothing heroic mind you, but I contracted a foot disease and my toes became webbed from the infection so that I could not wear shoes. I had to have my feet scraped surgically every few days and a purple lotion applied.

Well, one day, someone came to visit me just as I had been doing for other soldiers. It turned out to be Jack Benny, one of my heroes. He had heard of my performances and stopped to chat. He told me to look him up when I got back. I did and ended up being his summer replacement and went on to a career in radio.

However, since I couldn't walk very well, I was sent on rest leave to New Zealand, alone. And that was the first sign of civilization or civilian people that I had seen in fifteen months. I was given a one-week leave, but if you played your cards right, you could stretch it out to three weeks since there were only a few planes a week in or out of Auckland. The planes would be overbooked with other wounded or ill soldiers and officers, and you would wait for your turn. Three weeks! However, the strange part is that I was begging to be sent back to the Solomon Islands and my unit at the end of five days. What happened was that seeing a streetcar and being on an elevator in New Zealand made me more homesick for my real home and life than before. Besides, in the only other home I knew, a tent, I had friends, a way of life I was used to, and most important, mail call. My wife's letters were really everything, and I would only get them while I was with my unit.

Incidentally, we were never allowed to state where our outfit was, other than to mention a general area such as the "South Pacific." Any mention of an island or specific place would be cut out of our letters by the officers. I had a code with my wife. The problem was that I could never explain the "key" to the code. But I would say something like, "Give my regards to Wayne and Maurie and especially Richard Tregaskis." Miriam would have to figure out the meaning of this. She knew that I had friends in Cleveland, Wayne and Maurie, but who was Richard Tregaskis? She knew that I didn't know anyone by that name, and then she realized that a Richard Tregaskis had just written a book, *Guadalcanal Diary*. She always knew where I was. After all, I didn't go to the tenth grade for nothing.

When I returned from New Zealand, there was another piece of cake! I got assigned to the "Mosquito Network" of the American Armed Forces Radio Service. I lived in a great big Quonset hut with eight former radio guys from Hollywood. One among them, Sergeant Hy Averback, became and is still my best friend.

There was also Jackie Cooper of screw-and-tell fame, the Mickey Rooney of the minor leagues. It seems strange that Jackie and I lived together in a tent for many months, and he never once told me that story about Joan Crawford raping him. But then I never confessed my mad liaison with Edna May Oliver. (She only tried to pinch me.) What is interesting is that Hy and Jackie both became award-winning directors for their work on the television series "M*A*S*H." The way we lived then is very much the flavor of the present TV program. Our tents, our bizarre clothing, our lack of formal discipline, and the crazy Javanese servant—all were right out of "M*A*S*H," or vice versa. Because we controlled the music, news, and motion pictures on all the ships and islands, we could barter anything. We had two jeeps to ourselves, and we chipped in and had our own laundry done. A local native boy kept everything ship-shape and pressed our uniforms. We were the elite of the island. We had martini-and-chili parties every Sunday evening, plus the latest movies for a few select people. We had no prejudice and even occasionally allowed officers to join the martini-and-chili bashes. I swear to you that there were officers as high in rank as major trying to get in with us and be our friends.

Sergeant Hy Averback was a young actor from Hollywood radio shows. He was elegant with a great speaking voice, a grand manner, and the best-looking uniform on the islands. All the USO girls were trying to meet him. When I grew up, I thought, I wanted to be just like him. Well, we had all the movies and saw them first privately at night and in our own bar.

But there was one new movie which we didn't control that had come in on a navy ship and was playing at a large army area for one night. It was our only chance to see it. I said to Hy, "What the hell, we've got the jeep, let's go over and see the movie."

Hy replied in his Orson Welles–imitation voice, "You really mean, we would go and sit with those *soldiers?*"

It was a sad day for me when Hy was pulled out of the unit and was sent to the Japan invasion. He became famous in Japan as "Tokyo Mose," an armed-forces radio disc jockey.

He was a hell of a guy. And after this buildup, if this were a motion picture, surely Hy would get killed in the war. But think nothing of it. He returned, became a big success as a director, and has prostate trouble like the rest of us.

I really wanted to go with Hy into Japan because there he teamed up with the most polished, and one of the finest gentlemen I ever knew, the late, distinguished Hans Conried. What a time they must have had while I was stuck with the jeep, a Quonset hut to myself, a servant, and all those martinis. War is not only hell, it made me simply furious.

During a show one day at a field hospital on New Caledonia, a war correspondent named Sidney Carroll had chatted with me. Later we corresponded, and he said he was going to do a magazine story about me for *Esquire.* I heard no more about it, and my fellow GI's took great delight in ribbing me about the supposed article in *Esquire* which never appeared. When we arrived back at Camp Stoneman in California, I called my mother in Indianapolis.

"The movie studios have been calling," she said, "and the radio networks."

"The movie studios?" I echoed blankly. "What for?"

"They've read the *Esquire* story," she told me. "They want to sign you up."

I raced frantically out to find a copy of *Esquire*, but there was none in camp. To complicate matters, just then we were herded aboard a train for Camp Atterbury, Indiana, where we were scheduled to be discharged. There was no chance to get a copy of the precious *Esquire* to read what was causing the excitement. As we rode eastward, my mind was spinning like the wheels of our troop train.

Finally our train stopped in Cheyenne, Wyoming. We weren't allowed off the train, but I spotted an Indian dozing near the station. I beckoned him over, handed him a dollar, and said in my best Apache, "You gettum *Esquire* magazine." The Indian disappeared into the station, and when there was no further sign of him, I decided my dollar had likewise disappeared for good. The train started to pull out of the station, but just then the Indian bolted out of the station waving the copy of *Esquire*. The train was gaining momentum, but the faithful redskin put on a burst of speed and tossed the magazine through the train window to me.

Dazed, I sat back in my seat and began reading . . .

I GIVE YOU JACK PAAR
By Sidney Carroll

"I had been hearing stories about him for ten thousand miles. I know it started somewhere in the Solomons. It was at a USO show in the jungle, and I thought the comic was pretty funny and I made the mistake of laughing out loud. The kid sitting next to me, a marine private, seemed to resent my laughter. He turned and said, "You think this guy's funny? You should hear Jack Paar!" And then from the kid sitting next to him he turned to me and said, "Yeabo! That's my boy!" That was the first time I ever heard Paar's name. I was to hear it many times in the next few months. All through the Solomons, whenever I'd hear Marines discussing the shows they'd seen, I'd hear the inevitable names of Bob Hope and Jack Benny. But then somebody would bring up Paar's name, and that would be the clincher. Hope and Benny had left some fragrant memories behind them, all right, but this Paar was obviously the favorite of favorites.

"I did a lot of traveling before I caught up with him. His name kept popping up here and there, until I felt I was chasing rainbows. He was up and out of the Solomons before I could see him. He passed through Tulagi three weeks before I did. When I got to Fiji, they told me he had been there—and they looked at me with pity, and perhaps with contempt, because I had not seen him.

" 'You never heard Paar? My achin' back—he's got more noive than any bastid I ever seen!'

"He was panicking them all over the Pacific Ocean, and he was always just out of my reach. And then I caught up with him.

"It was in New Caledonia, and it was an accident. I was out at a field hospital called MOB 107 one day, and a Special Service captain named Carter told me there'd be a show for the wounded men that night and would I care to come? 'You'll like this one,' he told me. 'It's got a kid in it named Jack Paar, who'll kill you.'

"That night at MOB 107, it would have been beautiful beyond words except for the fact that when I looked around at the audience, I saw legs in splints, and many wheelchairs, and men with bandaged stumps on their shoulders. At least, I thought, this Paar boy picks himself some audience to make laugh. And while I was figuring his chances of creating general hilarity among these men, who'd been torn to pieces and who generally didn't give a damn about laughing at anything anymore, the sun went down and the light went up, and Paar came out and the show was on.

"To a lieutenant who kept talking out loud all during the show, Jack turned and said, 'Lieutenant, a man with your I.Q. should have a low voice, too.' Later he turned to the commanding officer. 'My dear sir,' he said, 'and you are none of the three.'

"The show went on and on, getting warmed up. It went all through the Solomons for twenty months. It touched at places which the geography books neglect but the sand ticks and the heat certainly do not, and Paar made the men laugh."

That story in *Esquire* went many pages and was the biggest thing that ever happened to me. To tell the truth, I was different! I was even good, but I wasn't that good. My "re-entry" was another piece of cake. I had offers from several movie studios and all the radio networks when I got home, although no one in the United States had ever seen me or heard me.

I never forget the kindness of a friend. Sidney and his wife, June Carroll, became our friends and protectors. Their children and our daughter, Randy, grew up together. Sidney went on to become one of the most sought-after writers in motion pictures and television. June Carroll became a singer and song-writer. Much of the music in all the "New Faces" shows are hers, such as the great "Love Is a Simple Thing." I have tried to help others as Sidney helped me. I'll always be grateful to him.

6

My Big Break
And How I Cured It

When I returned from the South Pacific with a discharge from
the Army, I returned to Hershey, Pennsylvania, to renew a relationship with my bride that for two years had been by letter only.
I had met Miriam one night, proposed marriage a few days later,
and was married two months before going overseas. So except for
the mail, we were almost strangers. For those of you who like
happy endings, we have been married for more than thirty-five
years.

Her family had a large dairy farm outside the Chocolate Dis-
neyland of Hershey. It was beautiful country, and I knew it very
well because I had marched over a good part of the county in infantry training. While her mother was a relative of the Hershey
family, her father, though well-to-do, was not in any way as-
sociated with the wealth of the Hersheys.

Her father took a great liking to me but was completely unaware of anything called "show business." He made one attempt
to keep us down on the farm by offering to buy a small movie
theater in a town nearby. It was a kind gesture, but upon return
to the United States I was getting offers from all the networks

and many of the motion picture studios. But first I had to go to
New York to appear on many important radio shows as the unknown army comedian who became famous overnight because of
all the publicity, especially the article in *Esquire* magazine.

I appeared on many radio programs, including "We the People," "Hall of Fame," and another show whose name escapes me,
with another unknown, Doris Day.

The big thrill of all time was appearing on the "Jack Benny
Show" from New York. Not only had Jack kept his word to me,
so long ago promised in that hospital on Guadalcanal, but the
main guest was Fred Allen—my hero! I had sent Fred, whom I
had never met, many letters during the war with material hoping
to impress him with my ability as a writer.

When I first met Mr. Allen, I stammered, "You are my God!"

Fred said, "There are five thousand churches in New York, and
you have to be an atheist!"

There were several offers from motion picture studios in Hollywood for a screen test, but a talent scout for RKO in New York,
Arthur Willie, made an offer for a firm contract that would guarantee me a salary for a year, sight unseen. Now I swear to you as
an amateur gentlemen that being a motion picture star was the
farthest thing from my mind. I wanted to be in radio. I wanted
to someday be like Fred Allen—to say funny things and have everybody fall down with laughter.

The more I resisted the motion picture offer, the more interested they became. I recall saying in a meeting with Mr. Willie
and a producer from Hollywood, Bob Sparks, that I never
thought of myself as an actor and said, "I wouldn't know how to
walk through that door."

Well, that did it! They both said, "What naturalness, what
honesty—we'll sign you now and send you to the Coast and then
make the screen test. You'll have a guarantee of a year's salary no
matter."

I didn't have an agent but inquired as to how I would get to
Hollywood. They said, "By Pullman train, first class!"

I knew one was supposed to bargain, so I asked, "And what
about Miriam?"

"We will have a compartment for the both of you. Is it a deal?"

I agreed and was more surprised than they were, because I did not, and never have, thought about being an actor. We took the money for the train fare, and with what Miriam had saved from my army pay, we bought a used Chevrolet convertible and headed for the Coast.

Now the important people in Hollywood had never even seen me. They had read the stories about my army career and had heard me on the radio shows from New York, but they had no idea what they were getting.

It had been said by guys in the Army that I looked like Alan Ladd, a big star at the time. Now some of this immodesty rubbed off on me because I began to think of myself as Alan Ladd. So I, upon arrival in Hollywood, bought a trench coat like the one Ladd wore, tried lowering my voice, and began to smoke cigarettes, which I had never done before. I coughed a lot, and the paper kept sticking to my lips.

The day I made my first appearance at the studio, I practiced with the trench coat, a cigarette dangling from my mouth, walking slowly, and with a lowered voice said, "Hi."

As I walked into the board room, with ten or more of the top RKO producers and directors waiting to meet this new discovery, I tightened the belt on my trench coat, lit my cigarette, coughed, and thought of Alan Ladd. Some men who are not used to smoking cigarettes do it rather effeminately. I kept thinking of Alan Ladd but looked, I am sure, like Ida Lupino.

I walked slowly into the room, faced the gentlemen, pulled the cigarette from my mouth taking off a small portion of lip, and said in a low, deep voice, "Hi."

I swear that one of the producers said with great enthusiasm, "KAY KYSER WITH WARMTH!"

This is no reflection on Kay Kyser, a Southern bandleader, but that was not the image I had in mind. Later, when I met Alan Ladd, I realized that I really didn't want to be him either. He was very short and had the strangest capped teeth I had ever seen. As I remember, his teeth were taller than he was. At that moment,

my first reaction was the right one for me. I didn't care about
being in pictures, and that indifference gave me a reputation as
an eccentric personality which helped my security if not my picture career. I kept saying, "I really don't care about pictures. I am
not an actor. I want to be a radio writer-humorist."

The more I said it, the more the studio kept thinking I was
unique, and they kept saving me for the special, big picture that
was coming up. In any event, my act of indifference kept me
under contract for three years at RKO, so I had an income beyond my dreams at the time. I was then able to spend all my
effort and enthusiasm in creating a radio program.

The best part of living in Hollywood was the reunion with my
two old army friends from the South Pacific, Hy Averback and
Hans Conried, who were then establishing themselves as radio actors on the Coast. With them were Jack Douglas, Hal Kantor,
and Larry Gelbart, who turned out to be three of the best writers
in radio and later in television. We wrote a script, and for a few
hundred dollars, we went to the Armed Forces Radio Service and
got them to record it in front of an entertainment-hungry GI audience. It was truly a smash and a different kind of radio program
than the big old vaudeville stars of that day who dominated radio
were doing. We didn't have a continuing theme, or running characters, or a story line. Each program became a series of short satirical pieces quite new to radio at that time. It was sold in a few
days and with Jack Benny's help was put on NBC at seven
o'clock Sunday nights as Jack's summer replacement, certainly the
biggest break for an unknown ever. We won many awards that
year and then went on to a winter program for the same sponsor
on ABC.

Although the program was critically acclaimed, we ran into
trouble with the advertising agency as they wanted it changed
to a scripted, situation comedy–type format, which I couldn't,
wouldn't, or didn't know how to do. The agency hired a so-called
expert on comedy shows to analyze my character, and he found I
didn't have any. I was a voice, an observer, a satirical commentator. I certainly was not either Amos or Andy, Fibber McGee or
Molly; nor did I have the great vaudeville and character personality of Jack Benny, Bob Hope, or Red Skelton. (Only last year I

was at the home of Bob Nye, our producer, who showed me some old memos from the sponsor to the agency that said, "Paar will never make it because he speaks too well and too softly.")

About that time, the agency hired a man, a very nice guy whose name was Ernie Walker. He had invented a machine that could analyze a comedy program. A running seismograph-type tape was run during the program that recorded the levels of laughter, and then the script was compared with the tape. Ernie would then point out that the laughs were as big as Bob Hope's or Benny's but that they didn't mean anything because they didn't come from a character trait: stinginess, drunkenness, egotism, cowardice, etc. It was Ernie's theory that the great comedians got laughter not from wit or humor, but from their "character." In any event, true or not, the agency bought the idea, and Walker, the comedy genius, drove us crazy.

One night he came to our home and took out what looked like a roll of wallpaper, attached one end to the floor with a thumbtack, and kicked the rest of the roll across the living room: twenty-five feet of this crazy chart which proved I would never make it.

Every joke was then analyzed. This went on for hours until I began to believe it and to figure I had better start looking for another line of work. It became so late that he asked to stay overnight, and we kept talking into the bedroom. I got out a pair of pajamas for him, and we kept talking of my lack of "character" as he undressed. When he finally got his trousers off, I was amazed to see that this new agency whiz, this guru of laughter, this one-thousand-dollar-a-week consultant was wearing the most ragged underwear I had ever seen! It was in shreds. I felt then, and still do, that one should never listen to or take seriously a man with torn underwear. I have followed this rule all of my life and so was able to retire at fifty. It became the eleventh commandment.

A few years later, my writer friend Jack Douglas wrote a book with the title *Never Trust a Naked Bus Driver*. This circuitous logic also applies to network and agency executives: Before you get involved, always check their underwear. My mother always was a great one for telling us that we should always be aware of our shorts. She would say, "Make sure that your underwear is in good condition in case you are run over by a truck; what would the people at the hospital think?"

I would always reason that the people at the hospital would consider that I had just been run over by a truck! However, as I grow older I have found that mother's observations are usually right.

You would expect in a book by me that I would have a few critical words to say about advertising and network executives. I do not. Nearly all were unfailingly kind to me, and I never once heard anything about the twelve-year-old mind of the audience. The only executive with whom I had some unpleasantness left the business and is now a forest ranger. I kid you not!

The problem usually was with some hanger-on, some noncreative person who had a theory and sold it to the advertiser. It's like the story of a young, virile tom cat who was jumping over a fence and got hung up on the top barbed wire and tore his male appendage. He fell to the ground and looked at his private parts and realized he would no longer be a great lover. His life as a Romeo was over. The poor tom cat said, "I was the greatest lover of the alley. I was the best; now look at me, I am ruined forever!"

And his cat companion said, "Don't worry, you can always become a consultant!"

And about agency people who were sometimes ashamed of all their commercials, I commiserated thus: It has been discovered that several hundred years before the birth of Christ, the harlots of the day in Greece used to have a marking on the heel of their sandals. As they walked about, it left an imprint in the sand, which when deciphered meant, "Follow me." This constituted advertising for the Second Oldest Profession in the World!

However, my first attempt at network comedy was canceled after a year and I went on a very successful radio quiz show called "The Sixty-four Dollar Question." This program was very popular but not at all what I wanted to do, and I left it. Hy Averback, my old army chum, and I did it together; it was an easy living.

Miriam, Hy, and I were usually together and had a wonderful time. We had bought a home, a very small one, but on Beverly Drive. The people who sold it to us were named Smith, and all I knew about them before the sale was that in this small little house, they had a gigantic St. Bernard dog. The dog, a "she" (I hate the word *bitch*), was so incongruous in such a very little house. Well, a few weeks after we moved in, there was a knocking at the door one afternoon. A couple wanted to know if they could speak with the Smiths. I explained that they no longer lived there, but that we did, and we didn't have the Smiths' new address.

The visitors were very perturbed and explained that they had brought their female St. Bernard for mating with the Smith dog, and their dog was in heat.

I looked out at their station wagon, and sure enough I saw this big female drooling and giving even me the eye. I said, "Forgive me, but I happen to know that the Smiths' dog was called Betty, that she was also a female, and that there must be some misunderstanding."

Now, only in Hollywood would you hear this reply. They said, "We don't care—they promised!"

When times were good, we had a wonderful housekeeper, a black lady called Merdes. She was a great addition to our family at the time our daughter was born, Miriam and I were three thousand miles from our relatives and knew nothing about taking care of a baby. Merdes was very important, and we would have been lost without her care and help. She taught Miriam and me about raising a small child. We were helpless without her. There was just one problem. When the race track opened, and there were several in the area, our dear Merdes would not show up for a few days. We would always get a phone call from the guy she lived with, Ronnie, who would say, "Mr. Pah, Merdes cannot come today because she had an operation on her ankle, but she be in on Wednesday."

This would happen every few weeks, and we knew it had something to do with the race track. Each time Ronnie called, it would be a different operation, but then she would appear in a few days with no sign of a medical problem. Then again in a few weeks, the morning phone call. Ronnie used up every part of her anatomy, so finally I just stopped asking him what the reason was.

Since I had stopped asking, he didn't offer any further excuses.

This went on for a few months. Then one day the phone rang
and Ronnie said, "Merdes be in on Thursday." He was not ready
with an excuse.

I asked, surprising him, "What is it this time, Ronnie?"

He said, after a pause, "Merdes had to go to New York . . .
on business!"

Now that's creative.

Besides my wife and daughter, my pride and joy was a new
MG sports car that I bought. Many years later I had an Aston-
Martin and a Rolls-Royce, but they never meant as much to me
as the MG. And the reason was that the other two exotic cars
came easy to me, but the MG I couldn't buy until I had saved
the money—it took months. I used to hang out at International
Motors on Sunset where all the sports-car people gather. There
you could meet Clark Gable, who had a Jaguar sports car, and
Gary Cooper, who also had one. On a Saturday morning I would
see them having their expensive cars tuned, and I was in line with
my MG. I taught Clark Gable how to wrap his steering wheel
with cord and then how to apply many coats of lacquer over the
roping as racing drivers did. I liked him very much but never
cared for Humphrey Bogart, who was a rude and surly boor. The
mechanics didn't care much for him either, and later I learned
that he was forever starting fights and backing down quickly when
challenged. Would you believe that one time in Italy Truman
Capote, using judo, threw Humphrey Bogart on his ass? Truman
loves me telling the story. The only person that I know that
Bogey could lick was his wife—not Betty Bacall, whom I like, but
the one before her. Even Oscar Levant challenged him and won,
and poor old Oscar got winded chewing gum.

There were many really swell people there that I knew, people
like John Wayne, Robert Ryan, and Jimmy Stewart. There is not
a nicer person than Jimmy Stewart anywhere. Cary Grant always
would have time to talk to the new actors on the studio lot and
ask them to join him in the commissary for lunch. Since I was
being paid by RKO for three years and was never in a picture,
they would ask me to travel once or twice a year and emcee the
opening of a new movie. I had great times on the road with Rob-

ert Preston, a first-rate gentleman, and Lucille Ball, who was a pal.

There were so many really fine people in Hollywood in the late forties, fifties, and sixties. I read so often now of the narcotics problem in Hollywood: many people are on cocaine and heroin. I know of many cases where filming actually has to be postponed because of drugs. This is very common. There are several new comedians who, I am quite sure, will not be around or even alive by the time this book is published. Maybe overdosing and the drug habit is nature's way of getting rid of a subculture that civilization wants to eliminate.

We lived in Hollywood for eight years, and I never knew anyone who used drugs. I never even heard a rumor of narcotics use all the time I was there, which proves how square, even oblong, I am. I only saw my first marijuana a few years ago at Malindi, Kenya, in East Africa. A little African boy would come around at four o'clock each afternoon on a bicycle selling fresh fish and marijuana to the British people who lived there.

I do recall that a friend of mine worked on a picture with the late Peter Sellers, who tried everything from Baum Ben Gay to cocaine. Sellers tried to get my friend to use some mild stimulant-aphrodisiac in brownies that Peter baked in which the main ingredient was marijuana. I gather you don't smoke a brownie, but eat it.

My friend was reluctant to get involved, but to be hip and adventurous he took home a few. He told his wife about his surprise and she too was curious, so the kids were sent away for the night. They locked the doors, turned off the phone, and got into bed before biting into one of Sellers' magic cookies. They waited and waited, and nothing happened! They just stared at the ceiling for the rest of the night, and the next thing they knew they were watching the "Today" show. That's about as close as I can come to exposing second-hand the mysteries of narcotics.

You will notice that many of the books written usually contain a confession that Hollywood stars were on drugs and licked the problem. Some are taking it up just so they can write a book about their wonderful recovery. If that is the criteria for a best seller, this book will not be one.

I was born with an edge on, and sometimes if I use a strong shaving lotion I get very talkative at breakfast. I find life and people and everything around me so interesting, I want to see them, hear them, feel them. Oh, I think two martinis before dinner never hurt anyone, but *chacun à son goût*, as we with a French dictionary always say.

Later, when I was on "The Tonight Show" and would spend some time visiting Hollywood in the sixties, I was well aware that Oscar Levant and Judy Garland were on something other than Chiclets. But honestly I never ever saw anyone smoke a joint or roach—or whatever the hell it's called.

Later, when my contract at RKO ran out and I didn't have a radio or television show, things became quite serious financially. Hans Conried, in addition to his acting, became a radio director. He hired Hy Averback and me to do daytime radio soap operas. The three of us always helped one another. After a fortunate and successful start in show business, my career fell apart, and even my friend Fred Allen referred to "my meteoric disappearance." It was a bad year or two. Trouble just seemed to follow me. When trouble wasn't following me, I was leading it!

Then one day I got a call to go to Twentieth Century Fox for a part in a picture. The picture starred Bill Lundigan, June Haver, and Frank Fay. I was happy to see Frank again as he could be very funny. I got the part, and Fay would always make me run errands for him.

He always called me "Chester"—why I do not know—and ordered me around. Somehow the campy way he carried on amused me. He would ask me to go the "apothecary" and get "the King" some aspirin. He would say the King had a terrible headache, and I would always fall into the dumb trap of believing him and scurrying around for aspirin. He would ask me to come into his ornate dressing room, and when I would walk in, he would caution me not to talk too loudly as he was baking a cake in the dressing room drawer and the cake "would fall." He referred to himself as "the King" and spoke always in the third person about himself. He was quite old then, at least to me, but he would say how upset his parents were because they didn't want him to be in show business.

He reminded me much of Bea Lillie in his pretensions. If Johnny Carson reads this, and I hope he will, this will interest only him. Johnny refers to himself as the Crown Prince of Comedy, in deference to my speaking of myself as "the King." Well, that whole act I took from Frank Fay, and now, Johnny, you know why you are the Crown Prince!

Frank Fay would have been very good in television as he was a handsome man, always beautifully dressed, and used a most literate vocabulary. He was so grand, he was funny. He was once married to Barbara Stanwyck, who is everybody's favorite girl. She must have been a saint to put up with him. He was an original, and yet no one ever speaks of him anymore. He has the honor, I believe, of having the longest "holdover" run at the Palace Theatre in New York—something like twenty straight weeks.

Our picture was called *Love Nest* and looked quite promising. Bill Lundigan, the male star, and I got on very well because he had been in the First Marine Division, and I had known him in the Russell Islands of the South Pacific.

I was to play the part of the sexy boyfriend opposite a new young starlet. She was a handful and very difficult to know because her status at the studio with executives had little to do with her ability as an actress. She was always late and never knew her lines, yet everyone was very careful in their relationship with her.

Since she was the object of constant sexual remarks behind her back and to her face, I felt some sympathy for her. It must be a bore, I would think, being constantly propositioned. To this constant barrage of priapic offers, she would reply in that strange, funny, whispering voice, "Promises, promises!" Later I heard Zsa Zsa Gabor use the same retort, "Promises, promises!" It must be a trade language that sexually attractive women use, meant neither as a put-off nor a come-on, neither annoyance nor acceptance—just drool, you silly boys! "I am only interested in a career."

She was never without a book on the set with the title turned out for all to see. I recall quite vividly that it was a book by Marcel Proust, a rather exotic French author much in vogue among the intellectually pretentious of the time. I found her "act" interesting, but must admit I was quite surprised that this sad, shy, arrogant loner became a star. She was, of course, Marilyn

Monroe. The secret was—and I am not certain whether it was
planned or luck—that what Marilyn later dazzled the world with
was something that "happened" only on the screen. On the set
she was just another Hollywood starlet, not as attractive as many
and not as likeable as most. Marilyn was like a caricature of a
woman, like the on-stage act that Carol Channing does; but the
talented Miss Channing is only pretending. Beneath Carol's
"stage presence" there is a real woman of theatrical experience,
charm, and intelligence. I fear that beneath the façade of Marilyn
there was only a frightened waitress in a diner.

After the picture had finished filming, I was then free to go
about my business of finding other work. I had only a four-week
deal with Twentieth Century Fox. The studio called me back and
asked if, without extra pay, I would pose for pictures of loving
with Marilyn to be used as still photos for advertising and publicity. Wanting to be co-operative I said, "But, of course."

It should have taken a few hours. Well, a few hours went by,
and she did not show—her usual "act." Then she arrived and said
with that silly voice, "Oooooo, I'm late." She then went directly
to the phone and talked to someone for another twenty minutes.
I have a low threshold of tolerance for unprofessional behavior
and finally said for all to hear on the set, "Tell that broad to get
her peroxide butt over here as I am leaving in half an hour."

She did come and we made the silly pictures, but I was cautioned by the photographer, "Come on, Jack, you'll simply have
to act like you like her. The pictures we have taken are not good,
and it's my job. Please help me!"

So I hugged and kissed her, bit her ear, breathed down her
neck, which was really her navel, left the set, and never spoke to
the poor darling again.

After Love Nest there weren't many film offers and only a few
in daytime radio that I didn't want to do. I was up for a few important pictures, but Jack Lemmon always got them. What I really became interested in was this new form: television. So I
spent my days building on my home—rooms, a nursery, brick
walls. I really enjoyed working with my hands and tinkering with
my beloved MG. Our home then was above Sunset Strip, and
while modest, it became a haven for my family and friends.

Sunset Strip at that time was an attractive part of West Hollywood; now sadly, with the invasion by rock stars and the *schlock-music* business, it looks like a drive-in Sodom and Gomorrah. The trouble with Los Angeles is that it has no center or feeling of community or culture. If the world was coming to an end and we were all asked to gather at the community center, it would have to be Nate and Al's Delicatessen. I wouldn't know where else to go.

I recall a bizarre weekend we spent in Las Vegas with Frank Scully and his wife, Alice. Frank was a writer and a much-loved liberal Catholic eccentric. He had lost a leg from a football injury and later a war injury, and had just been knighted by the Pope. He became a Knight of Malta, and to celebrate this honor I invited the Scullys to go with Miriam and me to Las Vegas. We stayed at a popular hotel, then called The Last Frontier. I enjoyed his company much, and we had a pleasant dinner. The floor show at the time featured a black singer, Arthur Lee Simson. He was a great showman and sang in a trick falsetto voice that was very flashy. He sang in many languages—Spanish, Hebrew, French—and then said, "And now for my Catholic friends, may I sing 'Ave Maria.'"

Splendid! How appropriate for my friend Scully. But then something happened that I still do not quite believe. As Arthur sang "Ave Maria" in the most reverent though perhaps hysterical tones, the lights dimmed and out came a dance team that cavorted in a blue spotlight. It was the usual ballroom-*cum*-ballet nonsense about a man chasing a girl in a white dress. (I always felt that in ballet, if the man ever really caught the girl, he wouldn't know what to do with her.) However, I was in a state of both laughter and shock: a dance team running around to the music of "Ave Maria"!

My friend Scully, not only a Knight of Malta but a man with one leg and one lung, had trouble breathing. Actually it was in such poor taste that it was hysterically funny. The manager of the dining room, Abe Schiller, a Brooklyn guy in a cowboy suit, came over later and asked us, "Did we enjoy the special treat for Frank?"

I gasped, "It was all very amusing, but didn't he think the sacred music and the passionate dance a little questionable?"

Abe was very honest and said, "You know, someone told me the same thing last week!"

Another story about Scully comes to mind. At his home I would meet many famous screenwriters and other press people. One lady was a very attractive gossip columnist. She was British, and her name was Sheilah Graham. She was a minor member of the Louella-Hedda school of journalism, but was personally very nice and quite a beauty.

When she left early one night, I asked Frank about her, and he told me in the most secret confidence that she had been the mistress of F. Scott Fitzgerald. He continued and made me promise not ever to repeat it, saying "that poor old F. Scott died in her house." (Nothing so shocking about that.) But he also said, "Fitzgerald actually was found by the ambulance drivers lying dead by her fireplace, when in fact he died in her bed." (Now we're getting somewhere.)

All ears, I gulped. "And what else?" "Well, when he died, Sheilah called me to come and help move F. Scott to the fireplace."

Now, do you gather what is so funny in a macabre way? If someone died in your bed, would you call a man with only one leg to come and help you move him?

I never, but never told this story because I had promised Frank. Years later Sheilah wrote a book about it, and it was later made into a motion picture. In the motion picture Fitzgerald died with his boots on by the *fireplace!* It must have been a rough move, like a stag movie made by Laurel and Hardy.

All my friends were doing well at this time; Hy Averback was acting, announcing, and later directing films. Hans Conried was a much-sought-after actor, and Jack Douglas was writing the funniest scripts in radio. But I realized that I had to make a move to the East where television was really taking over. We sold our house and furniture, and kept only the few things that we could pack into a station wagon. Miriam and Randy traveled by train, and I drove alone across the country.

Oh, before I forget, Hy spent a good part of the early fifties chasing girls up and down the Hollywood Hills, and then to rest he would come to our house and Miriam would cook a great dinner. The three of us were very close, and then one day he got married to a young lady who is the image of my Miriam. I mean at a distance or on a tennis court, they look like twin sisters. Her name is Dorothy, and now we are all together at least twice a year. We often make trips out to the Coast to see them. Well, one day on a visit Miriam became ill and phoned her look-alike friend, Dorothy, for the name of a gynecologist. Dorothy sent her to her own doctor in Beverly Hills, and on the examination table at a most unusual time, the doctor said to Miriam, "You remind me of someone." I won't go any farther with this anecdote, or I will need an antidote. (I hope I am not typing too fast for you.)

Please join me in New York.

7

Which Way Is The East Side?

The exodus from the Large Orange to the Big Apple is quite a culture shock for someone who was raised in the Midwest. The people and mores of the middle of America are not unlike the customs of the folks in California, or even in the part of the Army that I knew, but I was not prepared for the aggressive behavior patterns of metropolitan New Yorkers. After twenty-five years of living here, I am just barely able to cope with the New York syndrome. I knew then that we would have to live as close to New York City as possible because that was where the work was, and we looked for a suburb that contained space, a good school, and a sense of community that we were used to. We found it in a small village just a half hour from the city: Bronxville.

It was an easy commute, and when I would drive into the city, the problem was always where to park. In New York most of the garages are underground, and you enter on a one-way street and exit on the next one-way street. To this day, I never know whether I am going uptown or downtown, so I still frequently have to ask, "Which way is the East Side?"

Even twenty-five years ago, muggings and street crime were a problem in New York. I was not used to going into a clothing store only to find the doors were locked and the owners barricaded in and hiding behind their counters. There was a men's shop on Madison Avenue which I frequented and got to know the owner, George. One day I walked in to find the store surrounded by a few policemen. It was the most bizarre holdup I had ever encountered.

George had been behind the sweater counter when a young black kid walked in and asked the owner to reach up and get a certain sweater. When George turned around and reached for the sweater and brought it to the counter, he found himself staring into the muzzle of a revolver. He remained calm since this had happened before, and after all what is one sweater? But the young black wanted not one but the whole shelf. Okay, so my friend reached up and got the whole shelf of sweaters. The kid then wanted to march the owner into a dressing room and lock him up while he made his escape. The holdup man had a whole armful of sweaters and began to leave when another man walked in with a gun and took the sweaters and marched the first robber into the same dressing room with George. Two robberies in two minutes is a bit much, but that's the way of life in New York.

Another New York City story is about the time an off-duty policeman was driving on a side street when he saw three men with their legs spread and their hands reaching up against a plate-glass window. Obviously they were being held by a plainclothes policeman. The off-duty cop stopped his car, jumped out, and drew his revolver, only to be embarrassed when he learned that they were installing a large store window and the men were simply holding the glass up waiting for it to be secured.

A lady in the Bronx, according to the New York *Times*, has finally found a solution to the frequent burglaries of her apartment. At first, she had thought that by adding more locks to her door, she would eventually foil the thieves. Over the years, she had accumulated eight locks. But still her place was broken into. She went to a locksmith for consultation. But instead of selling her a ninth lock, he told her to leave four of the locks unlocked and four locked when she left her home. Since then she has been free from robberies. You see, when a burglar picks her eight locks, he is locking just as many as he is unlocking.

A few years ago my daughter, Randy, now a lawyer in Rockefeller Center, was held up by a crazy man with a pistol in an elevator at two o'clock in the afternoon. He made Randy get off on an empty floor and beat her with his pistol and threatened to push her out a window if she didn't give him her watch and pocketbook. Mind you, this was in Rockefeller Center at two o'clock in the afternoon.

So that's why I am now writing this from the country, well armed and fifty miles from the city. I am very much in favor of handguns being registered and licenses given to responsible citizens. If it's to be them or us, I vote for it to be us! There should also be a severe penalty for anyone carrying an unlicensed handgun on the street. And those people who have handguns in their homes have a responsibility to know how to use them.

When we arrived in the East, we knew very few people. I had been in New York a few times with a radio show I was doing called "Take It or Leave It," which later became "The Sixty-four Dollar Question." The producer of the program, Eddie Feldman, was a former New Yorker, and when we did the program from Manhattan, we were always invited to the home of his mother for a wonderful Friday-night Jewish dinner. There I met a fellow, quite a charming guy really, who was married to Eddie's sister, Esther. He really wanted to be in show business but was stuck selling fire insurance. I felt that one day he surely would find a place in our business—and he did! His name was David Begelman.

Begelman later became an agent with Freddie Fields. They were called Loeb and Leopold behind their backs and were very successful. This is the same David Begelman who is the main character in the book *Indecent Exposure*. He was found guilty of forging checks and embezzlement, but no matter, he later became president of MGM and United Artists. Now, that's Hollywood!

Twenty-five years ago there were wonderful shows on Broadway: *My Fair Lady, South Pacific, Mr. Roberts,* but for the last ten years I think the theater has been not only a bore but very often an embarrassment. I have a theory that the theater can exist only in a large, "vertical society"; if people live in stone caves on top of each other, they will go watch anything—frog-jumping contests, cock fights, discos; they will sit through some of the worst rubbish imaginable. If they could walk in the woods or on a beach, if they had a dog and could run on the country roads, "theater" would be unnecessary.

Miriam and I still see ten or fifteen shows a year, and I have not seen more than one or two that were worth the trouble. To go to the theater at forty bucks a ticket, to park a car, to walk the dirty streets, and then to sit for two hours and be bored—I have had it!

There should be a better system devised for reviewing Broadway shows. I think a *one-to-ten* rating might be helpful, simple, and honest for the average, intelligent commuter to evaluate his chances for the evening. For instance, a *ten* would be *South Pacific*, a chocolate-nut sundae, or an orgasm. A *one* would be Kabuki, dysentery, or a root canal.

Using that system, a recent Tony winner, *Dream Girls*, is a *five* —surely no more. I could not believe my eyes and ears when at the end of the first act of *Dream Girls* (because they had been conditioned by some critics), the audience gave a standing ovation to what appeared to be an epileptic fit.

A so-called mystery play, *Death Trap* was certainly a mystery to me, but it ran for more than three years. It was so dull that I resented the screams because they kept awakening me. The next play I saw not only had screams but gunshots and thunder and lightning. I tell you, it's very hard to get any rest in the theater anymore.

Broadway theater of late is as exciting and entertaining as watching a horseshoe-pitching contest. Television, if selectively watched, is far superior in entertainment, information, and even good drama.

Moving from one medium to another seldom works. I did not see *Nicholas Nickleby* on Broadway, but in all fairness everyone I know who saw it loved it. They really thought it was the theatrical experience of their life. I do not question their opinion. I did not see it because I objected to committing myself to eight and a half hours of sitting in the theater. Well, they are going to show it on television next year, but I can tell you now it will be a disaster. I paid three hundred dollars for the eight hours of tapes of the same cast made in London, and I had quite enough after twenty minutes. My wife insisted a few weeks later that we give it another try, and so we saw the next three and a half hours. With four hours still to go and unseen, I gave the tapes away. As the French would say, *Nickleby vaut le voyage!*

In the last two years, I have only enjoyed *Amadeus* and *Othello;* the other twenty evenings were painful. I see that I have digressed, but I feel better now that I have said a few words about the present theater. I am, however, surprised, when I bring up my feelings, at how often many people agree.

Miriam and I still very much enjoy going to the city once or twice a month, mainly to see a foreign motion picture and to have lunch or dinner at the Russian Tea Room or my old hangout, the 21 Club. I meet all my pals there. The owners, Pete Kriendler, Jerry Berns, and Sheldon Tannen, have been friends for twenty-five years. If you are not a New Yorker or have never been to the celebrated restaurant on Fifty-second Street, let me tell you that the ultimate status symbol for most people who eat there is to have one of the owners—Pete, Jerry, or Sheldon—kiss your wife, girlfriend, or mistress. If your ladies are not kissed, you are just not "in." I feel sorry for the poor woman who only gets a handshake or a smile—you must get a smack on the cheek! I just figured out how the custom began: When the boys lean over to give your companion a buss, it gives them time to figure out who you are!

When Miriam, Randy, and I first settled in Bronxville, all we could afford was a basement apartment, and I kept thinking: What went wrong? We had just left a modest but lovely new home in California, and here I was staring out the window and looking at people's ankles. I got to recognize our neighbors by their shoes. If you wanted to commit suicide, you would have to jump *up.* I did a few guest appearances on television shows, and a few of the New York critics began to write about me. After I had made one appearance, Jack O'Brian, an important TV critic, called my monologue, "the freshest comedy of the season."

Things were really quite serious with the Paars financially.

Then I heard that CBS was interested in me and asked if I would make an appointment to see them. I didn't have an agent but knew a very important one with a large agency. He worked me into his schedule, and I went to see him. I remember being told that he liked me but that really they could not handle my career. Sorry, but that was it! Can you imagine being turned down by an agent? I left his office dejected, and as I got to the elevator, he came rushing out and said, "Look, we were friends on the Coast, but you look beaten and no one wants a melancholy comedian. Don't keep that appointment at CBS. You are too discouraged. They'll never take you."

The one thing that can be said about me is that I never, but never, take anyone's advice; in all fairness, I never give any advice, either. I went over to CBS and was ushered into a room with a giant of a man; his name was Stone, and he was at least six feet six. He asked me who my agent was, and I said I didn't have one. He advised me that the matters to be discussed were complex, so I had better get someone. I remember saying, "You understand all that. I like you. I trust you. Money makes me nervous, and I am not really capable of negotiating. I need the work, and I think I'll be good. Whatever you think is fair will be fine with me."

The man at CBS, Lew Stone, was more than fair. I went from that one agent who turned me down to, I swear, in the same afternoon, a salary of two hundred thousand dollars a year.

It seems to be good sport to knock network executives, but you will find me an exception. I found most of them to be very decent and intelligent men. Contrary to my "difficult" image—that was an act—actually, most of them were and still are my friends. There was one great guy later at NBC. His name was Mannie Saks, and he was one of the kindest men I ever met in the broadcasting business. He was a homely little sliver of a man, with a very large heart. Mannie was a top executive at RCA when he died in 1959, and show business hasn't found anyone quite like him.

Once General David Sarnoff, then head of NBC, said in a discussion, "Anyone can be replaced." Then he thought for a minute and added, "Except Mannie."

Everyone liked Mannie because he liked everyone. He had no

former friends. Mannie used to negotiate million-dollar deals, yet
he was diffident and friendly and never too busy to listen to an
actor's problems. IIc was generous with his time and so generous
with his money that they called him "the fastest wallet at 'Toots
Shor's." Mannie's secret was that he liked to help people—
whether they were big stars or just trying to get their feet in the
door of show business.

Once, when he was flying to Hollywood with Milton Berle, the
comedian remarked gloomily that he had forgotten to take out
life insurance to cover the flight.

"Take half of mine," Mannie said, cheerfully, and endorsed
half his policy over to Berle.

Mannie was known as the man who couldn't say no. In a business famed for shin-kicking and elbowing, Mannie couldn't bear
to hurt a soul.

One night he was having dinner with a young actress who
wanted his advice on her career. Having work to do later but not
wishing to seem to give her the brush-off, Mannie made up the
excuse that he had to fly to Chicago later in the evening.

As they left the restaurant, he said goodbye but the young actress insisted that she accompany him to his apartment and help
him pack. Mannie had no recourse but to go to his apartment
and pack. He thanked her and once more said goodbye. But the
young lady insisted on accompanying him to the airport. Mannie
protested but to no avail, so together they took a cab to the airport, where she waved a cheery goodbye as Mannie boarded a
plane for Chicago. When he got there, he boarded another plane
and flew back to New York.

The program that CBS wanted me to do was a tough one, I
think perhaps the most difficult of any television show on the air.
They wanted me to go against Dave Garroway's "Today" show
on NBC, which meant three hours a day, five days a week, practically all ad lib. The reason was that this was before the perfection
of tape, and so the first two hours, from seven to nine, were sent
to the East and Midwest, and then at nine we had to do an extra
hour for the West Coast. It was a challenge all right, but I welcomed it. There was just one thing: I had to replace a friend,

Walter Cronkite. Strangely enough, Walter liked doing that crazy show, and I knew he felt badly about being replaced.

I called my mother in Indianapolis to tell her that I had a wonderful opportunity.

"What is it, son?" she said when she heard my voice on the phone. "Did you get a job?"

"I have a wonderful job," I enthused. "I'm taking over the CBS 'Morning Show,' the one Walter Cronkite does. They've offered me two hundred thousand a year! Think of that!"

"Don't sign it," she cautioned me. "There must be something fishy. Anyone who would pay you that much must be crazy."

I took over "The Morning Show" in August 1954. CBS kept a scoreboard to show how the switch from Cronkite to me was being received by the viewers. Under "Cronkite" they put the total of letters received expressing regret over his leaving. Under "Paar" they listed letters registering approval of my selection for the show. One day the producer came in sheepishly, handed me a letter, and said, "We don't know how to score this on the board." The letter said, "We enjoyed Walter Cronkite so much and hated to see him leave." And it was signed by my mother!

My mother was a most amusing woman. Many years later, when we first moved to Connecticut, she came to visit our new home. She was then in her late seventies. She always visited us on her birthday, and she really loved presents. She also was a great one for sending cards for any occasion. Since she had received some birthday cards from her friends, she asked me to take her to the local store to find cards that thanked people for sending cards. I did. Later my chum Joe Garagiola, the sports announcer, came to play tennis and have Mom's famous chili. After dinner she lay down on our *chaise longue* in the bedroom and said, "What a lovely sunset!"

Those were her last words, and she quietly died. It was so sudden, so unexpected, that now I can look back to that evening and think: What a wonderful way to leave us. No pain, no fright—just, "What a lovely sunset!"

At that time I often told the story of my mother writing to CBS about missing Walter Cronkite, because it was a most unusual true story. But then I received a phone call from a friend, the columnist Earl Wilson. He said, "As a friend of Walter Cronkite and you, I must tell you not to repeat that story. It's demeaning to Walter, and he is upset by it."

To this day I do not know how it's embarrassing to Walter, but I stopped telling it. Many years later, when Walter was on the cover of *Time* magazine and they naturally grilled him for anecdotes about his life, what did he tell them but the story about my mother. I never did figure that out, but let me quickly inform you what you already know: Walter Cronkite is just as decent and likable a man as he appears. I know of no one who has handled fame better than he.

It was on the CBS "Morning Show" that I learned how to talk with people and became quite good at it. If you were interesting, I was fascinated. If you were a poseur, I sensed it quickly, and as politely as I could I reached for your hat.

I might have made something of that show, but the hours were too tough. I had to get up at four in the morning, catch a five o'clock train, and start talking from seven until ten. When I had to leave the program, CBS tried to find other things for me to do, but it didn't work out. However, they were really very understanding and more than kind to me.

By now I had made a reputation as an Olympic conversationalist and now had to wait a year or so for the really big break by taking over NBC's "Tonight Show," which was like defending the Alamo five nights a week. It was to be exciting. You worked without a script or net.

8

"The Tonight Show"

There are many false stories about the history of the "Tonight" program. Now is your chance to hear it from the "horse's mouth," or from any other part of the equine anatomy you may prefer.

If you are referring to a late night program called "Tonight," then the first would be a variety show of music and skits that starred Steve Allen, not unlike Jerry Lester's "Broadway Open House." The title *per se*, possibly came from Pat Weaver, a very popular NBC executive who didn't invent programs but wrote great memos. But if you are referring to the late night program that became the most imitated show in television and that consisted mainly of conversation and personalities, then I am guilty.

I did not follow Allen as you might think. The last person to do the variety-type show was Ernie Kovacs; it had a short run and was abandoned by NBC as a format. The next program in that time slot was "America After Dark," possibly the lowest-rated program in television history. It featured newspapermen, columnists, press agents, etc., and was a disaster. Very few of our print brethren work out well in the television medium. There is a conceit in writing a column in a newspaper that dies when transferred to video. "America After Dark" lasted about six months and was losing listeners and stations on the network. When I was hired to fill the time, there was little hope of anything happening.

I certainly needed the work, but there was no ego involved. All I knew was that for an hour and forty-five minutes from 11:15 P.M. till 1:00 A.M. I had to do something. The NBC people had little interest in what I did, and all their suggestions seemed silly to me. Their main thought was to split the program into three separate half hours and to have a different game show in each thirty-minute segment. They also wanted to hire guests by the week as it would be less expensive: $320 a night, or $800 for the full week.

I was assigned the leftovers from the previous shows to produce the program. They were perfectly nice people but were not at all creative. I take little credit for suggesting and finally insisting that the only answer was to invent a conversation show. So my claim to fame is that all I did was to rearrange the furniture and introduce a davenport.

However, so as not to appear overly humble, I soon discovered that I was good with people. I had a naturalness, even a feistiness, and an honest curiosity about most things. I was a good listener and interested in what people had to say until they bored me and the audience. Then I had to, gracefully or not, get them off the stage.

Unlike some of the imitations today, I also believe I had a sense of the new journalism.

The program was described then as one hour and forty-five minutes of people sitting around trying to change the subject. I called it "a night light to the bathroom." I made it look easy. It was not.

The main problem was that the middle-level executives who were nominally in charge of the program had beneath them a lower echelon of producers, advisers, and associates who were frightened to death of the fact that they worked for NBC. I did not own or control the "Tonight" program, so naturally they didn't know whose instructions to follow. I would constantly be advised or would have my ideas vetoed by this middle group on the grounds that someone called *they* wouldn't like some singer, act, or author. *They* didn't think a program made up of a mixed bag of comedy, conversation, and music would work.

Who is this *they* that everyone is trying to please, I would ask? Finally, I wrote a memo to the staff and said, "As of now and starting tonight, *YOU* are to tell *THEM* that *I* am *THEY!*"

This is not to say that I was always right. I took chances. For instance, a trivia question. There is not, I am certain, one person in millions who could tell you who the on-air announcer was on the first of my "Tonight" programs. Give up?

It was not Hugh Downs—Hugh was the network announcer off-camera and was hired to do commercials, of which we had none in the beginning. You'll never guess . . . so I'll tell you. It was Franklin Pangborn. (Who is or was Franklin Pangborn? He's that gay little guy who plays desk clerks or florists or hairdressers in the movies.) I thought it would be a riot to have someone like him be the announcer. It was funny but only for shock. It didn't last more than two weeks because dear Franklin could not ad-lib in character. He was an actor who could only read lines. We had no script, so back he went to Hollywood. And then Hugh Downs took over, which was one of the better things that happened to me by good luck. He was the perfect opposite for me, and we never had an unkind word in five years between us.

There were many problems before the program went on the air, and the first was a director who was assigned to me. He came from the Ernie Kovacs show, but although he was talented technically, he did not understand what I had in mind. I overheard him one day say that he would "book the show," and I would just come in and do it. The first thing he did on his own was to suggest to the staff a guest who had the longest toenail in the world. The man had to walk around with a box over his foot to protect his fame. Of course, he was canceled by me immediately.

This director also had some small piranha fish (these are from the Amazon and can strip a cow in two minutes). He had them in a large bowl in his office and would feed them live goldfish. I knew then that this man and I would not be a team for long— like for no more than the next five minutes. It was the first time I had fired anyone, but I told him to take his headphones and leave our offices. The word spread that this Paar guy was pretty tough and impossible to work with. The next director, Hal Gurnee, stayed with me for more than twenty years and is still one of my best friends.

The program was scheduled to come from an old, spooky theater in a shabby part of Manhattan; it was like working in a rescue mission. The street and theater at that time of night, 11:15 P.M., were filled with winos who had fruit flies all over their heads. Then there were the poor, lonely souls called "bag ladies," who wander the streets with shopping bags and who sleep in doorways at night. The bag ladies would take up two seats—one for themselves and one for their outdoor furniture.

Guests were to be paid $320, union scale. Johnny Carson has had the good sense to keep it that way.

Most of the really hard creative work went into the monologue or opening comments on the news of the day. I think that Johnny Carson and I were the only ones really good at that form.

Practically all of the writing and hours of preparation go into the first eight minutes. I had three writers who remained with me for nearly ten years: Paul Keyes, Bob Howard, and the legend, Jack Douglas. Most nights the only written material went into about three pages for the opening. Johnny Carson has raised this to an art form and has become the best monologist in the medium.

The program was broadcast live each night for one hour and forty-five minutes, Monday through Friday, from the Hudson Theatre on West Forty-fourth Street. The Hudson was a broken down, depressing place, much too large for an intimate, conversational program.

The small staff I brought with me to the program were old friends and very loyal ones. There were about five of us who had to combat the lower echelon of NBC minor executives. One serious problem with the NBC people was that they simply didn't understand that people talking could be interesting and entertaining. They wanted movement, dancing, and burlesque bits. On that budget we could hardly afford half of the Smothers Brothers.

The main problem was with an executive who had previously "created" "America After Dark" and wanted to "create" something again. He was not well and would frequently go into what would be termed medically as epileptic seizures. This would usually happen in private. We kept it from the staff and NBC until it became so serious I never knew when an attack would be brought on by stress or by his drinking, which he was not supposed to do. How in the hell can you run a program of one hour and forty-five minutes of live television every night and not have stress?

Sometimes at two o'clock in the morning I would get a phone call from the executive's wife; she would berate me for upsetting her husband. I finally told her never to call my home at this hour again and that if her husband had a problem why didn't he quit? And she said, "He can't quit. He's an *executive*, and besides the show is a hit!"

Well, one night Miriam, the musical conductor José Melis, the executive, and I were driving up country from a late-night show. NBC had rented a Carey Cadillac, and I was sitting up front with the driver. Suddenly the most frightening scene took place. The executive began striking Miriam and José in an attack. We could not pull the car over on the West Side Highway as there is no way to stop. Finally, we found a place and parked, and by the greatest good fortune the driver was a former paramedic in the Paratroopers. He knew how to handle emergencies of this kind.

I knew then that this could not continue. The drinking and stress had to be brought to the attention of the network. I bring this up only because I got the reputation of being very difficult and hard to work with. This gossip came mostly from the troubled executive. He had nothing to do with the program and didn't understand it. When the early ratings came out and NBC knew they had something going, I went to the top brass and told them the problem.

The two heads of the National Broadcasting Company, Bob Sarnoff and Bob Kintner, could not have been more understanding. They said that they would withdraw network people from the show and that I should form my own staff and produce "Tonight." I never wished to own the program or have a package. I just wanted to make the decisions and hire new, bright people who understood this kind of extemporaneous programming. I

never asked for more money or any of the deals that are so common today. It remained that way until I left the show nearly five
years later.

We started with only about fifty stations and ended up with
nearly one hundred and seventy-five. The program became the
most successful program on NBC, and now Johnny Carson has
taken it to new historic highs in network programming.

In the second year or so, Bob Sarnoff, against my better judgment and wishes, changed the title to "The Jack Paar Tonight
Show." I never knew why the change was made (perhaps there
was a corporate reason) but had to accept it graciously since it
was presented as a compliment. I was not so insecure that I
worried about what the show was called but never referred to it
on the air as anything but "The Tonight Show."

In the first few months, the show caught on with the public
and the most difficult problem was to keep the New York press
agents from planting their usual phony stories and clients on the
program. I was tough with my staff in not being taken in. The
first encounter I recall was being threatened by an executive from
the *National Enquirer* backstage about co-operating with his
paper, as he said Steve Allen had done, by agreeing to mention
the scandal sheet on the air. I had him physically thrown out of
the theater. Since I had never read the paper or knew anyone
who did, I never felt any repercussions from his warning.

I do recall with some embarrassment an incident when a
Broadway press agent brought backstage a young, bearded British
actor who had written and was starring in a play. The play was
not doing too well. I liked the actor-writer but explained to him
that since our program had caught on, I had to be very careful in
booking the show. I wanted to be sure that he was amusing and
interesting since he was (then) unknown in America. I remember
saying to him, "What would we talk about?"

He replied, "I am sure I can think of something." He did and
has continued to do so for twenty-five years. He became one of
the most brilliant conversationalists in the English-speaking
world. The "beard" was Peter Ustinov.

A similar incident happened when we later did the show from
London. An actor unknown to American audiences came to the

studio theater and was very amusing to the audience but not particularly to me. The British laugh at the slightest nuance of English speech. An accent of a north or midland Britisher, an Irishman, Scotsman, or particularly an Indian sends a London audience into gales of laughter. There is no wit involved; it's simply the going from one accent to another, an effect which may escape the American ear. Well, this fellow was a big hit, and after the show I told him how grateful I was and that if ever I could help him in the United States to please call on me. He was wearing a rather shaggy sheepskin coat, and as I walked with him to the stage door, I was surprised to find him getting into a Rolls-Royce. That's how I first met Peter Sellers.

For the first two years, when the program came from the Hudson Theatre on West Forty-fourth Street, I had a private office down the block at the famous Algonquin Hotel. The Algonquin was, and still is, the gathering place of the theatrical and literary life of Manhattan. It is in this hotel's dining room that Alexander Woollcott, Robert Benchley, Dorothy Parker, George S. Kaufman, Marc Connelly, Tallulah Bankhead, and Oscar Levant would meet for lunch and formed the famous Round Table. All those of the above who were still living in the sixties later appeared on the program.

I usually had dinner there before the show, and one night dining with a few friends I found myself in an eyelock with Noël Coward. I felt awkward because I could see that he recognized me from television and was getting up to come to our table. I thought, "Dear God, I hope I am wrong." I had nothing to say at all to Noël Coward, so I looked down at the dinner plate only to find the brass buttons on his blazer cuff at the level of my coffee. Looking up I was embarrassed, flattered, and tried to stand, but he said, "Please don't let me interrupt your dinner. I just want to say that I am amazed how you do that program every night and I am addicted to it. We have nothing like it in England. I have become a fan of yours." He later came on the program, and we became friends until he died.

Noël Coward had the most idiosyncratic speech I had ever heard. It was so intimidating, and yet he was an unusually warm and gracious man. One would be a fool to ad-lib with him because with the slightest inflection, one raised eyebrow, and two words, he could make you laugh or scare you to death.

On the show one night I said to him, "I saw your motion picture *Cavalcade* three times, read your books and plays, and now just think here I am sitting next to you and about to sell some Bromo-Seltzer. Is that carrying democracy too far?"

"It does overstep at times," he replied in his cryptic, Morse code–type speech.

Some of my favorite Noël Coward stories are these: Chuck Saxon, the New York artist, lives near us here in Connecticut, and we are together often. He was a great fan of Coward and one day met him. Saxon was tongue-tied, as we all are, and said, "Mr. Coward, I so admire you, your work, especially your lyrics. I particularly like:

> '*Just one of those things,*
> *Just one of those crazy things,*
> *A trip to the moon on gossamer wings,*
> *Just one of those things.*' "

Noël said in his clipped speech, "Dear boy, you are quite mistaken. That is a song of Cole Porter. I did not write it."

And Saxon said, "Are you *sure?*"

Noël told me that he once entered a bar and thought he saw the back of an old acquaintance, David Rose, the composer. Coward sneaked up behind him and in perfect rhythm tapped with his finger on the man's skull, "Holiday for Strings." He beat out, "De-de-de-de-de-de-de-de-de-dum-dum." The man turned around, and it was not David Rose!

The last time I spoke with Noël was on the phone. He had called someone at a dinner party Miriam and I were attending, and when he heard I was there he wanted to speak with me. We talked, or rather I listened for a few minutes, and then he said, "Dear boy, I must tell you the wittiest dialogue that I heard last week in Hollywood. You see, Lucille Ball and Danny Kaye were rehearsing a television special and were not getting on. Lucy was on the stage, and Danny wanted to direct her from the control room. Lucy got angry and said to Kaye, 'Screw you! Who do you think *you are?*' And Danny on the talk-back said, 'You're full of shit—that's who *I am.*' "

We were lucky from the very beginning in finding new, fresh talent. Dody Goodman, for instance, the French pixie Genevieve, and Pat Harrington, Jr., who is now so popular on television's "One Day at a Time."

Dody was the first big hit on "Tonight" and had a great deal to do with the original success of the program. Dody had been a dancer in such shows as *Call Me Madam, Wonderful Town, High Button Shoes,* and something called *My Darling Aida* in which she played a cooch dancer and wore a large black diamond in her navel.

However, she seemed more like a bird-brained housewife than a ballerina as she came into my office to talk about the possibility of being on the show. She wore a black skirt, a demure, ruffled blouse with a black-string tie, and spoke in a distracted manner that defied description. I greeted her and we began to chat. To answer a simple yes or no, she would twist her mouth into a knot, scratch the end of her nose, and open her large blue eyes to the size of fried eggs. She began to tell me a long rambling story about a Cary Grant movie she and her mother had seen in her home town of Columbus, Ohio. The story had no perceptible point, but her Midwest twang and hesitant, naive manner were highly amusing in a baffling sort of way.

"Look, honey," I finally interrupted. "Just answer me one question. Are you for real? Or are you putting it on?"

She twisted her mouth, patted the top of her pink hair, widened her eyes, and said, "A little."

She was, it soon became apparent, indeed real, and the more she talked the more obvious it became that no one could have made up Dody Goodman. She came on the show my second night, and soon millions of TV viewers were asking each other whether this seemingly dumb blonde was actually real. Her hesitant delivery gave the impression that her picture tube was on but her sound wasn't. Dody never seemed to try to be funny; she just stumbled into it. The things she said really weren't particularly funny, but as she talked, fidgeting, fluttering her hands and smiling happily, she achieved a wackily endearing quality. It is not easy to explain her appeal.

Dody is very bright in her circuitous way to the truth. She is terribly witty, in a droll way, with a natural sense of the ridiculous. She is a tireless talker, and before long I began to feel like the announcer on "The Dody Goodman Show."

One night on the show, about a week after New Year's, she said good night in these words, "Good night, and a Merry Christmas to all. I know it's too late to say that, but I just thought of it."

Another night in the dressing room she said to me, "You have a speck on your eyelash."

I couldn't see anything but batted at my eyelashes to brush it away.

"You still didn't get it," she said, brushing at my left eye. I still couldn't see anything.

"Oh, mercy," she finally said, touching her forehead. "It's on *my* eyelash."

Dody feels that her cockeyed outlook on life may be inherited since, according to her, everyone in her family is a little odd. After Dody's success on the show, her family gave a party for her in Columbus. Mrs. Goodman danced with various young men. Finally she confided to one with a smile, "I'm Dody's mother."

"I know," the young man answered. "I'm her brother."

I first met Genevieve one summer night in 1957, when she came on as a singer. She sings charmingly, but I was more taken with her personality, which rubs off on one and lingers like the aroma of escargot. Once having savored her effervescent spirit, I largely dispensed with the singing, and then Genevieve did everything on the show from commercials to reading the baseball scores in which she referred to errors as *faux pas* and boo-boos. Just as captivating as her accent are the quaint phrases born of her unfamiliarity with the English language. She once told me that she had "crossed Greta Garbo on the street." Another time, while talking about an expected visit from her father, she said he was going to "take a fly from Paris." Her charming language-mangling had so endeared her to television viewers that I was certain she would become a big star. She went into summer stock and broke all records on tour, but then gave up her career for marriage.

The usual rumor has it that she was a fake and came from Brooklyn, which was unkind and untrue. She was, and is, as real as anyone I knew on the "Tonight" program.

When she was on tour, she would occasionally call me on the phone from wherever she was, and where she *was*, she never knew. Once I recall saying, "I'm in a meeting. I'll call you back. Where are you?"

"Oh, Jock, I am not sure. St. Louieee, I think."

"But where in St. Louis are you?"

"In 'otell."

"What hotel?"

"Jock, I do not know."

"What does it say on the telephone? (*Nothing.*) Are there any matches on the desk? Read them to me. (*No matches.*) Go to the bathroom and get the soap and read it to me."

"Okay, I find. Am staying at 'otell Avory."

I never did call her back that time. Recently she was ill and her husband, Ted Mills, wanted to call me from Washington where they now live. He later explained he could not find our number in her personal phone book. He had looked under "Jack," under "Miriam," under the "Paars." Nothing.

Later that night, when he visited Genevieve at the hospital, he explained he could not call us as we were not listed under any system he could figure out.

She said: "How stooppeed. They are listed under O . . . for 'Old Friends.'"

Ted had to buy his own groceries while Genevieve was in the hospital and tried calling the local Gristede's (a chain in the Northeast). He could not find any listing in her book and finally asked her why it was not listed under *Grocer* or *Gristede's*.

She said, "It eeze listed under *T!*"

"Why," asked Ted, "in God's name is a grocer, Gristede's, listed under *T?*"

Genevieve said, "There are two Gristede's in Washington. The one I call is under *T* because it's '*the* one by the fire station.'"

One day the phone rang at my office in the Algonquin Hotel.

"This is the U.S. Immigration Service," the caller announced. "We've been watching 'The Tonight Show.' Where can we find this Guido Panzini? We want to check on his port of entry."

The U.S. government, it seemed, had been taken in along with millions of TV viewers in a cheerful masquerade by a supposed Italian golf pro from Salerno named Guido Panzini. It was our most hilarious charade of the early shows.

It went on for many months and was completely ad lib. No matter what I would ask Guido, he could answer in the most perfect Italian accent, and while always very funny, he was just believable enough to fascinate the audience. He pretended to be a real golf pro who had sneaked into this country. He told the most, well almost, believable stories of conquests on the links and in the bedroom. We never went so far that people would know that it was one of the greatest put-ons since the Orson Welles "War of the Worlds" radio broadcast.

Guido Panzini was really an NBC salesman, a handsome young Irishman by the name of Pat Harrington, Jr. I used to meet him in the corridors of the network, and he would go into his impersonation. I talked him into going on the air with me, and he quickly became a TV favorite. In his first appearance, I asked him how he got into this country.

"Wassa captured in war," he said. "I learna English in war when serving on Italian submarine. We come up behind American warships and watch recreation movies that were showing on their rear deck. One time we getta so intrasted in double feature, we follow U.S. ship righta into Newport and getta captured."

He talked about his career as a golf pro, and I asked him the most difficult course he had ever played.

"Tanganyika Contary Club in Africa," he replied. "It goesa uppa side of Mount Kilimanjaro. Hardest hole issa third. Green there issa other side of pygmy village. If you short witha two iron, means pow!—blowgun dart inna chest."

Guido told of having a wife and three children in Salerno, and I asked if there was ever any hanky-panky with a handsome Italian chap like himself loose in New York.

"Mebbe a lidla bit hanky," he said, "but definitely no panky."

We used to carry on this interview at the bar of Toots Shor's

Restaurant on Fifty-second Street. One time late at night, some waiters were carrying out garbage to the street corner, and Guido howled, "Therea gozza the *hors d'oeuvres* for '21.'" (The famous restaurant next door.)

Pat left the NBC sales department and became a star on his own. Guido is now Schneider, on "One Day at a Time."

Elsa Maxwell was hardly a new face. She looked like Ernest Borgnine in drag but became a big hit on the first years of the program. Hermione Gingold, the British actress who was also on many of my shows, didn't care for Elsa and referred to her as "just another pretty face."

Elsa wrote a silly society column for the Hearst papers and was so serious on television when discussing the wealthy that it became funny; rather *we* became funny. She was not actually witty, just so brazen and outspoken that my look of astonishment sitting next to her became hilarious.

She was democratic only in the sense that she seemed to prefer old, half-assed, deposed royalty, rather than ruling sovereigns. "They need me more," she said stoutly.

She was scornful of the *nouveau riche* and accepted only the "*oldveau riche*." Elsa was a great name dropper and once told me on the program that she was a good friend of England's keeper of the Privy Seal. "What I can't understand," I said, "is if they have a privy, why do they wish to seal it?"

There is a much-quoted line of hers. When I mentioned on the program that her stockings looked wrinkled, she quickly said, "I'm not wearing any!"

One night I noticed that she had some notes for the program tucked away in her ample bosom. To tease her I snatched at her neckline to show the audience the concealed notes. Elsa jerked back, and her bosom quaked ominously. "Be careful," I warned, "you might start an avalanche!"

Elsa really had no visible means of support, but I felt that she was given donations by society figures for mentions in her column and on the program. Oscar Levant once called her "the oldest living woman on a scholarship."

She really was a harmless old fraud, but "our act" became the talk of television in the early sixties. She attacked people and governments, and there were many threatened law suits, but nothing came of them.

One night, just before going on, she whispered, "Ask me about _____." She named a socially prominent woman. After we chatted a few minutes, I complied with her request and inquired about the woman whose name meant nothing to me. Elsa ignored me. A few more minutes of talk passed, and again I inquired about the woman as she had asked.

"Oh, all right," Elsa said in apparent annoyance, "since you insist!" She then tore into her enemy.

Those early days of the show were as exciting for me as for millions in the audience, sometimes more exciting and even frightening for me, since there were several death threats. I mention them now but would never refer to them on the air, because the world is so full of crazies that it would only have encouraged new ones. I had a very loyal staff who did their best to keep anything worrisome from me, but on many an evening when I would walk on stage and take the usual bow, I would quickly scan the audience; if I saw policemen in the audience or some in the aisle, I knew that we had received some nut letter or phone call. (I am certain that Johnny Carson goes through the same routine.)

In the first two years of live broadcasts from the Hudson Theatre, our show discovered and presented for the first time to a national audience the following: Carol Burnett, the Smothers Brothers, Mike Nichols and Elaine May, Bob Newhart, Alex King, Shelley Berman, Phyllis Diller, Peggy Cass, Charlie Weaver, Don Rickles, Louis Nye, and many others.

I have a confession to make: Hundreds of young performers wanted to sing on the show or dance or do their comedy routines, but the big-status thing became sitting and talking with me. Many felt badly if they just did their acts and left to great applause but were not asked over to the davenport. There was no fixed rule about it, but we usually booked other people—actors, authors, scientists, or politicians—for conversation.

One night Harry Golden, a writer, came on. He was very interesting and amusing, and had a theory about racial integration. He explained that no one in the South objected to standing and talking with a black person, but one did not ever *sit* with them.

Harry called it *vertical integration*. I suddenly realized that in our year or more on "The Tonight Show," while there were black performers on, I had not actually sat down with one and talked. This may seem a strange thing to say now, but I do it only in the historical context. It just had not been done on any program or panel show that I knew of. And so I asked the next black singer to sit with me and talk. Please accept this in the spirit of describing the times and customs of early TV. In no way do I claim credit for an important social change.

You would never guess who the first black person was to be asked to sit and talk . . . and what a beauty she was and is. It was Diahann Carroll.

Later we were the first to introduce television to Nipsey Russell, Godfrey Cambridge, Bill Cosby, and Dick Gregory—all of whom could and did outtalk me, the King of white talkers!

9

Plumbing Can Make You Famous

After two years of live programming there came the advent of video tape. This made the show much easier to do, as we could tape the program at 8 P.M. and be home in bed when it went on. We also moved from the Hudson Theatre to the much more pleasant and professional facilities of Radio City studios. We were now in color. However, this meant that the NBC censors could preview what would be on that night. This was of no concern to me, since if something is offensive, it should be edited. There are slips of the tongue and bad judgment by myself and guests that are best removed. Also there is the real question of libel. However, I quickly point out that never in my years on "The Tonight Show" did anyone ever win an action in court against the program.

One night, in February of 1960, I read something that I thought was funny in an earthy, outhouse genre, yet rather sophisticated in its double entendre. When one thinks what is allowed on radio and television today, he will have to decide whether I should have had to go through the ordeal that I experienced.

I told a harmless story, the kind of story that could practically be read at a Wednesday-night church social. An NBC censor ordered the three-minute segment cut and replaced it with news bulletins. I never knew the story was cut until I got home and watched the show.

The next morning this incident became a front page story across the country, calling the silly joke "obscene"! The press had never heard the story, since all they knew was that there had been an edit.

Never having been a favorite of a portion of the press of the country, I took a beating in type because of the word *obscene*. I called NBC's president and asked him to review the tape. He did, said it was harmless, and that I was to forget it. I insisted that since he felt it was harmless or mildly questionable, I should be allowed to rerun the edited portion the following night so the audience could make a judgment. You see, the press printed the word *obscene* but failed to tell the full story.

I finally informed the network that they should think about my problem and let me know by 6 P.M. if I could rerun the three minutes. At six o'clock I was told by Bob Kintner, the president of NBC, not to be so thin-skinned and sensitive. He said it was a mistake to cut it in view of the trouble it caused, but their decision would have to stand. Actually, now I can understand their corporate view. It would have looked as if I was running the network if they had agreed to my request.

Still, my problem unsolved, I knew the only thing to do would be to explain my position to the audience that night and then walk off the show. I didn't know what I would do; after all, this was really the biggest hit I ever had. I was not, however, going to be pushed around by the press unfairly. By leaving the show, the real story would have to come out, and then I would have to look for a career somewhere else. I was no longer an unknown begging for work. The other choice would be that NBC could pay me and keep me off the air for a year or two. It didn't matter. As I have proven, I would rather stay home anyhow!

I admit that I have a bad temper and am emotional, sensitive, and unpredictable—I even puzzle myself! But I would like to think I would take the same stand if a friend of mine or even you, a stranger, were in the same exact circumstances, that I would yell and scream and defend you or him!

To make a "long story short," it's too late now, but you may have heard that I told the studio audience what had happened and that I was leaving the "Tonight" program. The only one who believed I would walk away that night was my assistant, Mitzi Moulds. She knew when I asked for my cuff links, which were locked in her desk. There were ten suits and some personal effects, but what the hell, I had plenty of clothes and pictures of my family. The cuff links, however, were special and personal.

The audience was stunned. Hugh Downs was nearly speechless; his eyebrows haven't come down yet. I had thrown away a half million dollars a year, but America had to be taught a lesson! (That last line was in jest.)

For days my home was surrounded by press cars, television crews, and police to protect the neighbors' property. I had many phone calls and talked to only a few. Bob Hope and Jack Benny called and said it was the damnedest publicity stunt ever in show business. They also said what a clever little devil I was, and asked if I would be on their shows the following week? This really hurt, as there was no thought of publicity. Besides, forgive me, being *unknown* was not one of my problems. During my many years at NBC, I never had a personal press agent.

While there were many, I imagine, who believed that it was all a charade, the truth was that I became quite ill. My wife knew we had to get away somehow, but for two days we could not open our front door. Finally, on the second night, we climbed over a back fence and got to a small airport in Westchester County, where a private plane of a friend flew us to Florida. The friend was building a new hotel outside Palm Beach, and the only people there were construction people. We lived in an uncompleted cottage and occasionally watched television, where the story continued, "Where is Jack Paar?"

I wanted to watch the "Tonight" program but was kept so sedated that I could never stay awake. It was not a very happy experience and, all told, was the most melancholy I had in television.

Well, one day, a man putting in telephone lines in the hotel in

Palm Beach recognized me and called the Miami *Herald* newspaper. We figured that there was nowhere else to run to, and besides we had Randy, who was getting quite disturbed by all this strange activity.

A day or so later, I was sitting out by the empty pool, wondering what I was going to do with my life, when I saw a large limousine pull into the driveway. I thought it was the press and began running down the road. Two men got out of the car and yelled, "Jack, we want to talk to you."

I recognized the two men as Bob Kintner and Bob Sarnoff, the top two men of the National Broadcasting Company. I felt very foolish, since I liked both of them, and walked back.

I was embarrassed to ask these gentlemen into our unfurnished, unfinished rooms, but I did and we all sat on the bed. Either Bob (Kintner or Sarnoff) explained that the National Broadcasting Company was not going to release me from the contract. I had become an important personality to the network, and in the past they had always been proud of me. They realized that I had honorably made my point, even though the means were a bit bizarre. They then said something that I did not know: Miriam, whom everyone loves, had phoned them and told them where we were hiding and that she was worried about my emotional state. They wanted me to go away for a while and forget the program. They did not want me back in New York for a few weeks. But then I had to return and fulfill my commitment.

I sheepishly said, "Where can I go? I'm already in Florida. Maybe, Cuba?"

They both said, "That's not a good idea!"

Sarnoff explained, "We have tickets and some money for clothes and expenses. We would like you to go as far as you can, where no one has ever heard of the 'Tonight' program."

I asked where?

They both said, "Hong Kong!"

And that night Miriam and I were put on a Pan Am flight to the Orient for two weeks. I later had to return to the program, and the night I did there was the highest rating the show ever had. I walked out on the stage, feeling happy to see all my friends in the audience, and said, ". . . As I was saying—"

Enough of this foreplay . . . Here's the silly joke that was the cause of it all!

An English lady, while visiting Switzerland, was looking for a room, and she asked her schoolmaster if he could recommend one to her. He took her to see several rooms, and when everything was settled, the lady returned to her home to make final preparations to move. When she arrived home, the thought suddenly occurred to her that she had not seen a W.C. (water closet) around the place. So she immediately wrote a note to the schoolmaster, asking him if there was a W.C. around. The schoolmaster was a very poor student of English, so he asked the parish priest if he could help in the matter. Together they tried to discover the meaning of the letters W.C., and the only solution they could find was the Wayside Chapel. The schoolmaster then wrote the English lady the following note:

Dear Madam:

I take great pleasure in informing you that the W.C. is situated nine miles from the house you occupy, in the center of a beautiful grove of pine trees surrounded by lovely grounds. It is capable of holding 229 people and is open on Sunday and Thursday only. As there are a great number of people and they are expected during the summer months, I would suggest that you come early, although there is plenty of standing room as a rule.

You will no doubt be glad to hear that a good number of people bring their lunch and make a day of it, while others, who can afford to, go by car and arrive just in time. I would especially recommend that your ladyship go on Thursday when there is a musical accompaniment.

It may interest you to know that my daughter was married in the W.C., and it was there that she met her husband. I can remember the rush there was for seats. There were ten people to a seat usually occupied by one. It was wonderful to see the expressions on their faces.

The newest attraction is a bell donated by a wealthy resident of the district. It rings every time a person enters. A bazaar is to be held to provide plush seats for all the people, since they feel it is a long-felt need. My wife is rather delicate, so she can't attend regularly.

I shall be delighted to reserve the best seat for you if you wish,

where you will be seen by all. For the children, there is a special
time and place so that they will not disturb the elders. Hoping to
have been of service to you, I remain

Sincerely,
The Schoolmaster

The "water closet" story is mild and not at all objectionable, in
my view; yet it caused such anguish to my family. When you consider what is being said in motion pictures today or on radio or
television, the "W.C." story is practically poetry. Here are three
actual items I heard this week of August 1982. They are nearly
verbatim and were taken down as quickly as I could get to this
typewriter to record them. In all fairness, none of the three are
salacious or meant to be objectionable. They were done on serious, "call-in radio programs" in the New York area. I will repeat
them, since I found them so very amusing and bizarre.

As I tuned in on ABC one morning, the discussion involved
two fundamentalist ministers. One had said that he was not
against sex between married partners, as long as it was normal
and not of a deviant nature. The other minister had remarked
that he was *against dancing*, whether the dancers were married or
unmarried. The phone caller asked seriously, "Did the ministers,
referring to deviant behavior, consider that sex *standing up* is
wrong?" And the ministers' reply I quote exactly: "Yes, it is
wrong, because sex standing up is inclined to lead to dancing!"

This very morning on WOR, on the Sherrye Henry program,
there was a discussion about male impotency—a sad but serious
topic. The doctor said that one way to check on a serious male
dysfunction is take the "stamp test." He went on to explain that
without being aware of it, a healthy male has at least three erections a night in his sleep. And as long as he has these *normal*
erections there is hope to cure his impotency. Since the man will
not be aware of his erections in his sleep, he is advised to take the
stamp test, to place a ring of postage stamps around his penis and
go to sleep. In the morning, if the stamps are torn at the perfora-
tions, there is hope! (Now this will not be believed by certain
people, but before they accuse me of making up this story, please

check with a medical man before writing me.) I have read about this test in medical journals. It just sounds funny.

Can you imagine a woman listening on the radio and wanting to help her marital problem by sneaking up on her husband when he's asleep and trying to put a ring of stamps on his "member." I don't know what he would think when he awakened, but I would feel that I was *unwanted* and was being air-mailed to the Mayo Clinic.

There is another fellow on WOR—his name is Bernard Meltzer—who gives advice with rabbinical authority on everything from investments or sex to aluminum wiring in the home. When he feels the person phoning in is particularly deserving, he also gives away T-shirts. Now mind you, not everyone has a problem that gets a T-shirt with "Bernard Meltzer" printed on it. I will try and re-create what I heard. When I tune in, a woman is crying and saying:

"Oh, Doctor Meltzer, I don't know where to begin."

"Now darling, you calm down and tell me your problem."

"Well, it's the usual story. My sixteen-year-old daughter is on drugs and has stolen many things in the house and sold them. Last week my daughter and her junkie boyfriend attacked me and tried to pull the gold necklace off my neck. They pulled so hard that the links were pulled out of shape, and it cut my neck. My daughter hit me, and her junkie boyfriend threatened me in my own home. My necklace is stretched several inches, and my neck is cut. My gold rings are now oblong. I am afraid . . . I don't know what to do. I can't go on like this. I am thinking of killing myself."

Mr. Meltzer says, "Now my darling, killing yourself is out of the question. And I'll tell you why after this word from *Levolor Blinds!*"

(He does a few minutes of commercials, comes back, and gives her some sensible advice that I have forgotten.) And then the woman says, "Thank you, Doctor . . . Would you send me *two t-shirts?*"

I was telling these stories to Gerald Green, a writer of unquestioned integrity, to see if what I wrote would be believed.

Gerald replied that they would be accepted by him, and then he gave me two more. There is a call-in radio show on ABC at night conducted by a woman sex therapist. The other evening a man called in to say that he could only make love wearing a bathing cap. He was advised by the good doctor to continue being himself and to find a partner who would accept his *aqua chapeau.*

Another young man with a more serious problem called to say that his dysfunction and embarrassment was premature ejaculation. Now this whole conversation was on the radio:

WOMAN DOCTOR: Well, you see, your problem is all rooted in your psychological makeup. There are ways to—

YOUNG MAN: Oh, Doctor, I love your voice . . . it's so romantic.

WOMAN DOCTOR: You must forget about my voice and listen to me . . . your problem is caused by a highly developed sense of anticipatory sexual pleasure. There are ways to—

YOUNG MAN: Oh, Doctor . . . Doctor, I love your voice. Please keep talking . . . *it's happening now!*

WOMAN DOCTOR: That's all right . . . relax. But really, you must learn to control yourself. There are ways to—

YOUNG MAN: Doctor, I love you . . .

WOMAN DOCTOR: Well, I *like* you, but *really* you must learn to control yourself. There are ways to—

YOUNG MAN: Please . . . don't hang up!

What everyone listening to ABC radio heard was the first radio rape, and premature, electronic orgasm. Radio, television and motion pictures have certainly come a long way from my censored "water closet" story. Twenty-five years ago on radio, you would not have heard Amos and Andy or Lum and Abner making love on the telephone. And our beloved Kate Smith would not even do it on an intercom.

10

Fidel Si,
Paar No

It was never clear to me why NBC wanted to do "The Tonight Show" from Havana, Cuba, during the revolution. It had something to do with RCA, the parent company, selling a great deal of equipment to the Batista government. I liked the adventure of it, as it would be one of the earliest remote broadcasts live from a foreign country. There was a video link between Cuba and Miami that made it all possible.

Miriam, Randy, and I had spent some time there on vacations and had friends in Havana. Varadero was one of the finest beaches in the Caribbean, and it was an exciting, different culture only ninety miles from Florida.

The program that we did there was a disaster. It originated in the Tropicana Night Club, and it never occurred to us that the audience would not understand English. There were very few laughs, and in the far distance one could hear explosions from revolutionary activity on the outskirts of the city.

From the moment we arrived, everything seemed to go wrong, and I never understood what the hell was going on. Only recently, when John Scarne wrote his autobiography *The Odds*

Against Me, published by Simon and Schuster, did I learn that it was more exciting than I knew at the time. Here is an excerpt from Scarne's book:

Several weeks later Jack Paar and his television crew deplaned at Havana's Rancho Boyeros Airport, where they were met by a welcoming committee composed of a number of Cuban officials and police officers. After Paar had received the usual Havana airport welcome afforded to visiting dignitaries, he was escorted to a waiting limousine. No sooner had Paar seated himself in the limousine than it began to pull away. Several police officers immediately jumped the moving limousine, yanked the driver from behind the steering wheel, and proceeded to beat him with their guns and night sticks. Minutes later the limousine driver was pushed into a police car and whisked away.

When Paar and his entourage arrived in the Havana Hilton Hotel lobby, I was there waiting. After we exchanged pleasantries, I informed Paar that I had reserved a suite for him on the fifteenth floor, just a few doors down the hall from my room.

Paar pulled me aside and in an excited tone said, "John, I had a terrifying experience at the airport. One of the men who met me at the airport escorted me to a waiting automobile which was to take me to the hotel. No sooner had I entered the automobile than two Cuban policemen pulled the driver out from behind the wheel and began beating him up." Paar hesitated a moment, then looked me straight in the eyes and anxiously asked, "You don't think the driver was trying to kidnap me, do you, John?"

"Jack," I replied, "I don't believe so, but I'll check later and try to find out the reason why the driver was beaten up."

"Okay, John. Call me later and let me know," replied Paar as he left to rejoin his group.

Minutes later, as I watched Paar follow a bellboy into the elevator, a friend, Captain Vega, of Havana's secret police, approached me and declared, "Your friend, Jack Paar, just had a close call at the airport." It was Captain Vega who related the airport incident to me.

After hearing the captain out, I asked him, "What was it all about?"

"Mr. Scarne," he said, "we have information that Castro's underground is going to do everything within its power to prevent Jack Paar from doing his NBC television show from the Tropi-

cana Night Club. It would be a great psychological victory for
the rebels if they succeeded in preventing Jack Paar from appearing at the Tropicana."

I nodded and remained silent as the captain continued. "The
driver whom we arrested at the airport was trying to kidnap Mr
Paar in order to prevent him from appearing at the Tropicana.
This same driver is a member of the rebel underground group
who snatched Juan Manuel Fangio, the Argentine world-cham-
pion racing driver, from the lobby of the Lincoln Hotel in downtown Havana. I have assigned a twenty-four hour round-the-clock
police guard for Jack Paar during his stay in Havana. Further-
more, I want you to promise that you won't say a word to Jack
Paar about the rebel plot to kidnap him. His knowledge of such a
plot would frighten him and possibly cause him to cancel the
telecast."

"I promise you, Captain, I won't mention a word about the
plot to Jack."

Several hours later I visited Paar in his suite and told him that
he accidentally got into the wrong car at the airport and that the
driver of that car was wanted by the police for a stick-up, and the
beating incident had nothing to do with his presence in the automobile.

"I'm happy to hear that," replied Paar as he heaved a sigh of
relief.

I spent the following afternoon with Paar and his police bodyguard visiting various sights of interest in old Havana, and believe
you me I was the most frightened of the trio. Paar and the policeman seemed to be having a good time as our guide pointed
out the spots of interest. I was happy when the sightseeing tour
ended and we returned to the hotel.

The day before the taping of the show I spoke to Paar in the
lobby of the hotel and asked him where his policeman bodyguard
was.

"Oh, the cop. He's at the swimming pool," he replied. "I'm
tired—I'm going upstairs to rest for a while."

As I watched the elevator doors close behind Paar, I got a feeling that trouble might be brewing. I took the next elevator to the
fifteenth floor and as I exited, I spotted Jack Paar standing near
the turn of the hall corridor. When he saw me, he said, "John,
there's two men in my room with guns!"

"Okay, Jack," I said, "I don't want you to take any unnecessary chances. Follow me to my room and lock yourself in, and don't come out until I come back and call you by name."

Paar nodded as he followed me down the hall corridor.

After Paar had locked himself in my room, I walked down the hall corridor to investigate. As I approached the entrance to Paar's suite, I noticed the door slightly ajar. I pushed my foot against the door and it swung wide open, revealing two men dressed in overalls, standing near the door's entrance, each holding a monkey wrench. They both appeared surprised to see me.

One of the men forced a smile and in Spanish said, "*Somos del Departamento de Ingenieria y nos enviaron a inspeccionar el servicio sanitario.*" ("We're from the engineering department, and we were sent here to check the bathroom facilities.")

"*Gracias,*" I said, as they started to leave. I remained in the hall corridor until I saw the two men disappear behind the closed doors of the service elevator. Then I entered Paar's room, locked the door behind me, and phoned the hotel's police security department, which, in turn, checked with the engineering department. I was quickly informed that no hotel employees were ordered to check the bathroom facilities in Jack Paar's suite. I phoned Paar's police bodyguard at the pool and asked him to come to Paar's suite immediately. Five minutes later the bodyguard arrived, and I quickly briefed him on what had taken place. He was still thanking me profusely as I walked down the hall corridor toward my room. When I approached the door, I knocked and called aloud, "Jack, Jack, it's me, John Scarne."

Paar wore a puzzled expression when he unlocked the door. "Jack, it was nothing," I said as I motioned to him to follow me.

As we entered his suite, he displayed a wide grin when he saw his policeman bodyguard sitting on the divan. Paar stared a moment, then turned to me and inquired, "John, what was it all about? And what were those two men with guns doing in my room?"

"Jack, those weren't guns you saw—they were wrenches. The two men were hotel maintenance men who were sent to your room to check the bathroom plumbing."

Today, as I reflect back to the summer of 1958, I don't think that Paar believed a word I said at the time, but like the old trouper that he is, he made me feel that he believed my white lies and pretended that he wasn't a bit worried.

The next day Paar taped his Tropicana television show. He left the following morning for New York City. I don't know what Jack Paar was thinking as his plane winged its way over the Atlantic, but I did know I was a happy man now that Jack Paar had left Havana. A couple of days after Jack Paar left, a hotel maid, while cleaning the hotel suite formerly occupied by Paar, discovered two .38-caliber revolvers under the seat of the divan.

Trying to do a television show in a foreign land, with technical problems and a language barrier, is never exactly easy, and when you throw in a full-scale shooting revolution it does little to simplify things. Nothing seemed to go right. We had hoped to have Ernest Hemingway, who lived on a ranch outside Havana, as a guest on the program, but he was tied up with a book. Later I learned that he was *reading* it—not writing it.

The stagehands spoke only Spanish, and I could hear them arguing backstage. A fight broke out in the wings with some of our NBC crew, and the noise came over the show on the stage.

"More *silenzio* back there," I shouted over the din, "or you won't be *amigos*." That was the best I could do.

Looking back on it all now, I shudder a bit, but come to think of it, all of this excitement is what made live television so different from TV today. When last have you seen anything of reality on the tube?

When Castro overthrew the Batista government in January 1959, I decided to go down to Cuba and get some film and perhaps interview Fidel. I didn't have any producers or writers but hoped to pick up a cameraman there. I got my pal, Jim Bishop, the newspaper man, to go along, and we two were among only a few Americans who were in Havana at that time.

We lived in great luxury in a suite of about seven rooms, with a grand piano, on the twenty-second floor of the Havana Hilton. The hotel was empty, and the staff was happy to have us as their guests. On the floor above us was the suite of Fidel Castro, and since there were no carpets, only marble floors, we would hear the boots of his aides marching back and forth all night long. I must say it was very exciting, and I felt it would be a great coup to be the first to talk to him on television. No one from American television could reach him, but I had an "in" with a lady member of his staff, an American-Cuban who promised that if I was patient she would arrange it.

Jim and I spent one night out at La Cabaña, a colonial-era fortress built by the sea, where they were keeping the prisoners of the Batista government. We were on the front porch of a cottage within the fortress where Che Guevara had his headquarters. What I remember clearly to this day is that it was a bright moonlit night. We were surrounded by the young, bearded *barbudos* with hand-held automatic weapons. A hundred yards from the front porch was the largest statue of Jesus Christ I had ever seen, perhaps two stories high.

Guevara was a handsome man, and he was visited by two or three beautiful women. Baseball players, actors, and musicians have their groupies, but I must say so do revolutionaries. These were not peasant girls but very sophisticated, well-groomed women.

The soldiers were reserved and well behaved. Looking like disciples with their beards and with the statue of Christ nearby, you could easily forget that you were involved in a revolution and not in some religious experience.

The beards on all the young men was a very clever ploy in that all of Castro's men could be immediately separated from the Cubans who did not participate in the revolution. There was no way a young Cuban could grow one in few days.

We talked to a Bishop Muller of Havana and asked him whether or not he knew if Fidel was a Communist. The Catholic Church is not usually naive in such matters, and Muller told us that he had known the Castro family for many years and that they were not Communists.

Jim and I also went out to the palatial Batista home and found the record player still spinning, not playing a record but still turning. The foyer of this magnificent house was lined with twenty or thirty suitcases, all packed with silverware and clothing that the former President could not get out in time. We went down to the wine cellar and found a humidor of the finest cigars, and we each took a handful and passed them around to the bearded soldiers who accompanied us.

A few days went by, and Jim, who has a fiery Irish temper, said the hell with this waiting around and flew back to the United States. Now I was left alone in this seven-room suite and frightened about what I should do. Every time the phone rang, I would rush to answer it, only to find out that each room had its own line and that I never could get to the one that was ringing.

At 2 A.M. that morning, I finally got the call and was told that Dr. Castro was on his way down to my suite for an interview. It happened so suddenly, when it finally came about, that I was momentarily at a loss for words as the rebel chief walked into my rooms, trailed by a group of his armed *barbudos*, many of them just youngsters from the mountains.

In my nervousness, I blurted out something about his being a good neighbor and living above me, and did he come down to borrow sugar?

The Cuban leader smiled and shrugged as if to say "Crazy *Americano*."

I had to arrange quickly to get a cameraman. I found a Cuban TV man in the lobby and had him sent up. In the meantime Castro and I talked. I wished that I could say it was something profound, but actually we talked about American television, "The Tonight Show," cigars, and how much I enjoyed coming to Cuba. I found myself in my usual role of sounding like Tarzan talking to Jane.

I told him that I had been out to Batista's home, which he had not seen yet and he said, "You want to buy? We sell for two million dollars. You have two million dollars?"

"No," I replied. "But I would like to get the Norelco shaving concession when things quiet down."

We talked of his son, nine-year-old Fidelito, and how he had missed him during his many months in the mountains. It was just two guys talking.

I had no reason to mention the previous kidnapping threat or what happened in this same hotel months before, as I didn't know about it until I read John Scarne's book.

Later on camera he said, "I am not a Communist." He said that he liked and admired Americans and hoped the United

States would understand that he was going to rid his country of the tyranny of the former government.

It was a good interview, perhaps even historic in the sense that I was in way over my head, but we ended up talking as two men talk. I stuttered and stammered, but it was real and honest, and I saw something of the man that I never saw again when he made formal speeches.

He was with me for more than an hour, and when he left, he wanted to look around my pad. He laughed when I told him not to drop his shoes that night as my bed was below his.

That's about all there was to it, but it certainly was a newsmaker for the "Tonight" program. I still wish that our country and his could have gotten on as well as we did. I hope to return one day. I like Cuba and its people very much.

11

Presidents Who Knew Me

The first U.S. President I almost met was Ike Eisenhower. I was thrilled by the opportunity as we had been in the same war and for several years we were *dress-alikes*. The occasion was an affair in Washington, and I was the master of ceremonies. The cast consisted of some very big new motion picture stars and some old favorites. The President knew some of the stars personally, but I am certain he had not heard of me. However, I got many laughs and was pleased at the opportunity of entertaining him. After this show, the stars were informed by the Secret Service that we were to stand backstage because the President wished to speak to each of us. We stood in a long line, and Ike came down talking to the stars, old and new. As he got to me, a photographer behind me shot off his flash camera over my head and right into the President's eyes. Ike blinked, grabbed me by the hand, put his other hand on my arm and practically gave me a manly hug. Then he said, "How very nice to see you again . . . *Conrad Nagel!*"

We knew Mr. and Mrs. Richard Nixon quite well and spent some time together down at the island of Key Biscayne, Florida. Randy and the Nixon girls were friends, and I liked Patricia and

Julie very much. The White House never had better behaved and more likable youngsters than those two. This has to be attributed to their parents.

The Vice-President, as I knew him then, was a little awkward socially, but he is not a man of small talk. Our talks walking down the beach, going to church, and swimming were usually about sports. The Nixon family came to our home in Westchester, and we had a family evening with Mr. and Mrs. Billy Graham, who were old friends of ours. Miriam is a gourmet cook and was nervous enough cooking for the Vice-President's family, but having the Secret Service peeking over her shoulder was especially unnerving.

Everyone wants to know about the mystery man, Bebe Rebozo. I knew him quite well. We would have breakfast many a morning in our bare feet at the local drugstore counter on Key Biscayne in Florida. At first, Bebe had a chain of laundromats in South Florida and was interested in politics. His first important friend was Senator George Smathers, a neighbor of ours who was very close to Jack Kennedy and was best man at Jack's wedding. Bebe also, as I recall, wore a wristwatch that was given to him by the then-Senator Lyndon Johnson.

Bebe is a respected and well-liked member of the Key Biscayne community. His name sounds like a Mafia character, but Bebe is not of Italian descent. He is a Cuban and a rather unusual one: a Cuban Baptist.

He and Richard Nixon became close friends. They are both rather shy men and found a loyal, lasting friendship. Bebe is Tonto or Sancho Panza; he screens all calls and keeps the nuts away even before the Secret Service sees them.

I was always pleased that after all the charges, all the innuendo, nothing was ever proved against Bebe. He was finally, completely cleared of all the gossip and scandal that was to follow the President.

If you believed the papers at the time, he was the owner of a large bank in Florida. I am sure you would have visions of tall buildings, marble, guards, big beautiful private offices. Well, now hear this: The bank is about as big as your local gas station. We kept an account at Bebe's bank for many years and would only go

there on Fridays to withdraw or deposit because it was the thing
to do on the island. You see, on Fridays you went in your bare
feet, and everyone got free popcorn.

In November 1962, Huntington Hartford, the wealthy A&P
heir, was opening a new hotel on Paradise Island in the Bahamas.
His public relations people offered my family a one-week vacation
there with no publicity or obligation since he wished to train his
staff with a few guests before the opening. It seemed like an attractive offer. We arrived at the beautiful new hotel and found
only five other guests there—the entire Nixon family including
the former Vice-President, Mrs. Nixon, Tricia, and Julie, plus
Bebe Rebozo.

We were, I am certain, surprised to find each other there. It
was particularly awkward as Richard Nixon had just lost an election to Governor Pat Brown of California a week before. This
was surely the most humiliating defeat he had ever suffered. After
all, he had barely lost the Presidential election against Kennedy by
only a hundred thousand votes. Much of that difference included
the questionable votes in what some thought was a rigging of the
count in the Cook County (Chicago) district of Illinois. But to
lose to Pat Brown in California by a million would be the end of
the road, or so everyone thought—including, I am sure, Mr.
Nixon.

He was a sad, depressed man, as pathetic a national figure as I
had ever seen. He was drinking heavily, and my heart went out to
his family. We ate together in the empty hotel, and then Miriam
and I decided to try and have the Nixon children join Randy in
whatever recreation we could plan. Mr. Nixon would sit and
brood and occasionally utter a few words of profanity, which surprised us. I had never before heard a vulgar word from him.

So I asked Bebe if he would like to join us that evening and
bring Tricia and Julie to see the native quarters of the Bahamas
where there was wild dancing and music. We knew that Mrs.
Nixon wanted to be alone with her husband because her heart
was breaking too. Off we all went and got a table down in front
to watch the local fun. We were outside on a beautiful moonlit
night.

There was a floor show of a sort, with the local Bahamians

holding a limbo contest. The limbo is a wild dance in which, near the end, you have to bend over like a banana and go under a pole without touching it. There were many good dancers, and our kids really laughed and applauded. Now the Bahamian emcee recognized me and winked. I winked back, and the next thing we knew he took the little blond girl sitting next to me out on the floor. She danced up a storm, equally as good as the local people, and then bent over and went under the limbo pole.

When the dance was over, he had all the contestants out on the floor, and because she was blond, white, and obviously a tourist, the local black people graciously applauded for her.

The emcee called our little blond girl out, thinking it was my daughter, Randy. He said, "Now, little girl, tell the audience who your father is."

And her reply was "My father is Richard Nixon, the former Vice-President of the United States."

Because there had been no publicity, as had been promised, no one knew that the Nixons or the Paars were in Nassau. What a gasp from the audience! He then gave her a trophy, an eighteen-inch wooden carving. The poor darling looked so pleased that she had done something on her own! But now what would her father say?

As we were returning to the hotel, Tricia said, "I want so to keep that award. I've never really won anything before." Bebe and I talked it over and figured that if she walked into their suite with the statue, in view of her father's condition, there could be trouble.

It was decided that I would keep the award overnight and try and explain it to the former Vice-President in the morning at breakfast. I am an early riser, as is Mr. Nixon. I found him sitting alone over coffee, and the dialogue went about like this:

PAAR: Good morning, sir. The kids had a good time last night.
NIXON: Good. Good. What the hell is that statue you brought?
PAAR: That's what I wanted to talk to you about. You see—
NIXON: Look's like a damn heathen statue to me. Whatever you
    paid for it, you got screwed.

PAAR: Well you see, I didn't buy it, and it isn't mine. It's
     Tricia's.
NIXON. What the hell did she buy it for? Goddamn pagan junk.
PAAR: It's not junk, sir. The young lady won it and should be al-
     lowed to keep it.
NIXON: How the hell did she win it?
PAAR: Brace yourself. Your daughter, Tricia Nixon, is the new
     "Limbo Dancing Queen of the Bahamas."
NIXON: I'll be damned. A Nixon finally won something.
PAAR: She won it fair and square . . . it's a good thing the dance
     wasn't held in Cook County.
(*Nixon laughed for the first time in three days.*)
NIXON: Of course she can keep it . . . you go tell her mother. I'll
     be damned. My daughter is the Limbo Queen of the Ba-
     hamas. (*He roared.*)

Now a guy like that can't be all bad.

Thursday of that week was Thanksgiving, and we all had a fine
dinner. With cigars we retired to a room which had a record
player. I had brought with me a recording written by one of my
former writers, Earl Dowd. It was, as you may well recall, called
The First Family, a funny but devastating series of sketches of
the Kennedys, particularly the President, Bobby, and Jacqueline. I
had not yet heard it. Most of us laughed, and here is what may
surprise you: Mr. Nixon walked over and lifted the playback head
off the recording and said, "That man is the President of our
country. Neither he nor his family should be the butt of such
jokes."

Since the next day was Friday, which was the night my prime-
time program was shown on NBC at ten o'clock in the States, I
inquired as to whether anyone in the Bahamas had an antenna
that could pick up Miami. (My programs were taped on a Sunday and always shown on the following Friday.) I was told that
an American golf-course architect lived out on a point in the bay,
and he had the only antenna that could get NBC in Florida. I
took a boat ride out during the day and asked whether I could
come over with my wife and daughter to see the program. He and
his wife were delighted. We promised to be there by nine-thirty.

Later during that day, Mr. Nixon asked me what I was going to do that evening. He wondered if his family could come along. I was sure they would be welcome at the little cottage and arranged for a boat to take us all over. When we arrived, I found that these nice people who lived there had made cookies and coffee. To them, a visit by a television personality in their home was a great event. Little did they know I was bringing visitors, including Bebe Rebozo.

I first walked in, explained that I had some friends with me, and asked if there was room? They said, "Of course," and then I introduced to these startled people the former Vice-President of the United States.

Now the punch line to all this is that I had really forgotten who the guests on that particular TV program were. The usual monologue went well; there was some singer, perhaps a sketch by Mike Nichols and Elaine May . . . but the main guests were the first television appearances on a talk program of Ted and Joan Kennedy.

That was awkward! And I still remember young Julie, a very political young lady even then at fourteen, saying, "He's the one who *cheated* at college!"

The surprise to everyone in the next six years was that this man, so badly defeated, was again nominated by the Republican party to run for President. He was on my Friday night program then. He had been on the "Tonight" program with me, and against his own judgment and that of his many advisers, I got him to play the piano. It was an unusual moment, with Richard Nixon playing a ricky-ticky tune that he had composed. Marshall McLuhan, the media analyst, had written in his first book that if Nixon had played the piano on the "Tonight" program in the 1960 campaign, he would have won the election.

The next time he appeared, I was asked over to his suite in the Waldorf Towers for lunch on the day of the appearance. I went up to his room and was told I could find him down in the ballroom. I went down, and there in the dark, empty, huge room was Richard Nixon practicing the piano. He knew a good thing when he was talked into it.

Later on in the program, we were both startled because in the middle of our talk his hand began to shake and a loud noise was heard. The Secret Service, always alert, jumped into the picture, and I was certainly puzzled. What had happened was that the alarm on his wristwatch had gone off.

It was on this same program that I used a ploy which I have used with many others. If you are sitting next to a guest on a television program, and you are in the middle of expressing a thought and see that your guest is about to interrupt, you quietly reach out and touch the guest's knee. It means WAIT!, as all TV people are aware. Well, I was talking and saw him about to interrupt, so I banged his knee, only to see him wince. It was then that we all learned, both TV and press, that the candidate had a serious knee infection which later turned into his serious trouble with phlebitis.

I did not see the Nixons again for several years, although I would occasionally get a note from him about something I had done on TV. One night on Key Biscayne, at the hotel where we had all gathered for many years, Miriam and I were entertaining some very important network officials. They had come down to get me to take over their late night program, which was then starring Dick Cavett. I had little interest in returning to TV and certainly did not want to replace Cavett. He had worked with me for several years, and in a sense I had started him on a career in television.

As we walked into the dining room with Martin Starger, president of the American Broadcasting Entertainment Division, and Lou Weiss, TV head of the William Morris Agency, we immediately saw Secret Service men whom we recognized. I knew the President was there with Mrs. Nixon, Julie, and the omnipresent Bebe. It would have been wrong to rush over and say hello to these old friends, as we would have been stopped by the Secret Service, and that would have been embarrassing for everyone.

They had finished their dinner, and the President got up and danced with Mrs. Nixon and then with Julie. Soon they were to pass down the aisle past our table, and I was certain they would stop and chat. Martin Starger and I changed places so that I would be right smack on the aisle and so that they could all meet the President.

Ah, there they came! We all stood. First there was the Secret Service, looking both left and right like predatory birds; now, the President, smiling but looking with tunnel vision straight ahead; then, Mrs. Nixon. Surely she would see Miriam and call the President back. Smiling but looking straight ahead, she whizzed by. Even Bebe had learned to keep moving looking straight ahead. Then Julie, with those pretty eyes looking like laser beams.

They all went by so fast, it was like a scene from *Chariots of Fire*.

Well, I was crushed after this big buildup. I was really standing there with omelet on my face. How could I explain? Starger and Weiss began to laugh and needle me about my pretension. I was actually a little hurt.

And then the door to the dining room reopened, Julie came rushing back, kissed Miriam, and said, "Give my love to Randy."

I never saw them again. Perhaps they have been sitting lonely in some restaurant, and I didn't see them. I have now learned to walk looking straight ahead.

Skipping some sad years with the Kennedys, which I will save for later since I knew them best, we come to Lyndon Johnson. I knew him only slightly when he was the Vice-President. He didn't like me, and why I embarrassed myself by being nice to him, I will never understand. The only reason that I can think he might have disliked me is that anyone who was close to the Kennedy family was anathema to him.

The first time I met him was the night before the inauguration of John F. Kennedy as President. The Ambassador, whom all called Joe, the President's father, had a private party at Young's Restaurant. He had rented the entire downstairs for a midnight supper following the gala that Frank Sinatra had staged. Only a select hundred or so were asked. We arrived early, and there were only a few people already there. Sitting alone with Mrs. Johnson was the Vice-President-to-be. The room was still cool from its emptiness. It got cooler. I thought: What the hell, I'll go over and introduce myself. "Good evening, sir, I'm Jack Paar."

He gave me his cobra look and said, "Yes, I know."

I tried again, "Did you and Mrs. Johnson enjoy the show?"

Lyndon said, "It was too long."

"Could I get you and Mrs. Johnson a drink?" I tried.

"We already have one," he said.

Well, I wasn't going to bring my wife into this atmosphere and thought: screw him. He's only the Vice-President. This happened at every meeting I ever had with him. The Johnsons were always alone in the Kennedy crowd. At supper parties at Hickory Hill, Robert and Ethel's home, they would sit by themselves scowling. Why in the hell didn't they stay home? Lyndon Johnson, among other things, was a *party pooper.*

However able Lyndon Johnson was as a consummate politician, and effective as he had always been in a personal eyeball-to-eyeball confrontation with fellow senators, he was a social disaster. His public speeches always seemed to be written by some writer who worked for Hallmark:

> *The President is here today,*
> *to wish you luck in every way.*

Years later, when he became President, I was doing a program from the National Archives. This is the block-long building that contains the most sacred documents of this republic. There are hundreds and hundreds of precious letters and thousands and thousands of feet of film, recording every event since the invention of the camera—for instance, Lincoln's Gettysburg Address, Brady photographs, and Franklin D. Roosevelt's personal letters. Everything that is considered to be of historic value is placed there. I had access to almost everything and the co-operation of some wonderful employees who worked there—mainly Dave Powers, who was one of President Kennedy's old Irish, Boston friends. Well, I discovered a lot.

Would you believe that Lyndon Johnson had placed his gallstone in a mason jar in the National Archives? Filming late at night in the lobby of the Archive building, I began my introduction to the filmed part, which was to be seen later on television. I chose that particular setting because the room had a great echo that was very dramatic. I mentioned in the introduction, almost in a whisper, so that officials who were watching me could not hear, "President Johnson has even placed his gallstone here in a jar." Well, the echo carried to the officials who were checking up on me.

The next morning I was asked to come and see the director of the Archives, and he said, "Surely, you are not going to use that story on the air. It will mean the job of everyone who has talked or helped you."

I said, "On that basis I will not, I promise you. But is it true?" He would not answer but replied, "They even have a piece of Lucy's wedding cake here."

When Lyndon Johnson became President and Robert Kennedy was the Attorney General, it is no secret that the two really disliked each other. Such a hatred is amazing when you consider their positions in the same government. Well, there was a famous meeting one day in the White House at the President's desk. Robert entered the Oval Office carrying a briefcase. Lyndon Johnson was anxious for the Attorney General to sit as close to his desk as possible. But so was Robert Kennedy. He knew that Lyndon was taping the conversation. But in Kennedy's briefcase was a new development of the FBI, an electronic device, a degausser, which was erasing everything that Johnson was recording. The score then was Johnson o, Kennedy o, but the Attorney General had his say, and no one to this day knows exactly what was said.

There is a book recently published entitled *The Sweetest Little Club in the World*, published by Prentice-Hall and written by Louis Hart. The author, who for many years was in charge of the Senate dining rooms, speaks frankly of shocking inside stories of senators and congressmen and states that Lyndon Johnson was not only AC/DC but a little FM.

This came as news, since I had always thought the most amusing story about him was written by a woman correspondent who spent a night on the ranch at the Johnson home in Texas. In the middle of the night, she heard someone enter her room and get into her bed, and a familiar voice said, "Move over, this is yo' President."

When Barbara Walters, interviewing Mrs. Johnson, asked her about Johnson's womanizing escapades, I recall Mrs. Johnson saying, "Lyndon was a lover. He loved everyone."

Did she mean *anybody?*

Mrs. Johnson surely must be a saint, as is Pat Nixon. So was Mamie Eisenhower. And Betty Ford is a swinging saint. Being First Lady of the land is a bouquet of unhappiness.

We got to know the Fords through our old chum Joe Garagiola, the sports announcer on NBC. He and President Ford became very close friends; and on the night of the election, when Gerald Ford lost to Jimmy Carter, you may be surprised to learn of the disparate group that stayed at the White House. In the private living quarters that night were Pearl Bailey, Senator Jack Javits from New York, and the entire Garagiola family—Joe, Audrey, the two Garagiola boys, and their daughter. That's a pretty good cross-section of America.

Miriam and I were asked to the last formal dinner that President and Mrs. Ford gave at the White House. It was a dinner honoring the President of Italy, and what a group that was. All I can recall is that we were formally dressed, the women in beautiful gowns, waiting at the top of the stairs to enter the reception room. The orchestra was playing, and each couple was announced on the public address system. Listen to the group and then try and figure what the Paars were doing there:

> *Mr. and Mrs. Joe Garagiola*
> *Mr. and Mrs. Mario Andretti*
> *Mr. and Mrs. Yogi Berra*
> *Mr. and Mrs. Jack Paar*

I didn't know anyone in the Carter administration, but what a collection of Al Capp characters that family was. We never before had anything like it. Brother Billy made even Margaret Trudeau look like a nun. He even moved his lips when he listened.

Nearly all our Presidents have had embarrassing children or brothers. As you all know, relatives can be a real pain even if you are not the head of state, but the Carter family convinced me that the next President should be an *orphan*, preferably a *gay orphan.*

The first time I met young Senator John Kennedy was on the "Tonight" program. He was, I believe, the first political figure ever to appear on an informal, primarily entertainment show. My first impression was of how attractive but thin he looked. We sat in my NBC office and smoked cigars. I always had a select supply of Cuban cigars. Jack, his brother Bob, and I preferred cigars of the finest quality and vintage. I don't believe that any of the three of us were ever photographed smoking one.

The senator came with his best and closest friend, Lem Billings, and we discovered that all three of us were born in the same year, even in the same month.

The program went well. The audience was very taken with him, since they had never before seen such a young, attractive senator. The next morning there was a great reaction, and his father called and thanked me. Then Robert appeared with his new book, *The Enemy Within*, and he was fascinating, since I got him to stick to the subject of the union-gangster connection. He was very outspoken, and a result of it was that both Robert Kennedy and I were involved in a $2,000,000 law suit brought against us by James Hoffa, whom Bobby had called "a gangster, thief, and crook." That kind of interview had not been done before. Bobby became a famous person overnight.

Later, when Robert received his legal notice of the law suit, he called at NBC and asked me if I had received notice. I stammered, "Yes, and I'm worried."

He said, "Why?"

I waited a few seconds and said, "What if *you* don't have your half?"

There were a few other legal suits that followed for alleged libel during the "Tonight" program. I never lost one.

Joe Kennedy took a personal interest in me and would phone often. I recall once, during my feud with Walter Winchell, the columnist, that he said, "Stop replying to Winchell on the air. He's dead as an important columnist. You are making people read him again. If you mention him one more time, I will come and kick you in the ass." And so I cooled it.

One time late in the evening, Miriam picked up our phone at home. The NBC night operator was calling. The operator explained that she was instructed that my number was not to be given out, but she had a problem. Miriam asked her to explain, and the operator said, "The President, the White House is trying to reach Mr. Paar."

Well, Mr. and Mrs. Sidney Carroll were visiting us, and we all ran to the five phones, so there was Miriam, Randy, Sidney, and his wife June listening in. With all that heavy breathing, President Kennedy surely must have thought I had emphysema. It was just a pleasant call about a program I had done in the South Pacific on the subject of World War II.

If you are of the opinion that my including a telephone call from the President of the United States is not a big thing but just an ego trip, you may be right! But now I can tell you that during his brief time in office, Miriam and I were never invited to the White House on a social occasion. I think it was felt by some of his advisers that I was too controversial, had made too many enemies in the press, and was too much of a maverick. Only once did I go to the Kennedy White House, and then it was through the back way, where I was hidden in the basement and then taken to Pierre Salinger's office until the President was free. It was nothing important, but I wanted the President to know that I had rounded up all the people who were involved in the PT 109 incident. I had found Reg Evans in Sydney, Australia. He was the brave "coast watcher" hiding in the mountains, surrounded by hundreds of Japanese, who tapped out the message to our Navy that Kennedy and his crew were safe and hidden on a small island. Also, I was bringing the little dark Melanesian, Ben Kevu, the native who carried the famous coconut to Evans, and who had never even had shoes on before, to the United States for a program. That was about all there was to it, but my wife always thought it would have been nice if I had been able to walk in the front door of the White House like other citizens.

After the Bay of Pigs disaster there was a group formed to try and raise money for what was called "Tractors for Freedom." Castro had said that if the Americans would supply so many hundred tractors, he would release the captured prisoners. The committee consisted of Milton Eisenhower, Walter Reuther, and Mrs. Eleanor Roosevelt. Since someone was needed to raise the money, I was picked. I had to get permission from NBC. I worked very hard and hammered away every night on the air for contributions, something that is really not my style. We raised millions, but I took a beating from the press and the Congress and was accused of acting on my own in violation of the Logan Act. This is the law which states that no private citizen can negotiate with a foreign government. No one defended me until Mrs. Roosevelt came on the program and wrote in her column her admiration for my courage. What no one knew was that I was asked secretly to do this by President Kennedy!

I was disappointed because there was an expression, "When the going gets tough, the tough get going." Unhappily I found that "when the going gets tough, you're on your own." Anyhow, if you were interested, now you know.

And now we come to Camelot. This word was utilized by the journalist Teddy White, who in the first interview with Jacqueline Kennedy at Hyannis Port, used the analogy of King Arthur's Court. I knew no one who belonged to Camelot, if indeed it existed at all. John F. Kennedy certainly would not have been a part of this mythical group. Perhaps some people, mostly Mrs. Kennedy's personal friends, became legends in their own minds. In understanding the Kennedys, one must always remember that they were first and were always very classy Irish politicians. They were raised to seek and use power. There is not a doctor, scientist, dentist, or osteopath among them. They are a charming, interesting group of people like no others I have ever met in the real world. They make their own glamor in the basement, and it's catching. You must beware or you are off on an ego trip that may change your life and, if you are a professional journalist, may discredit your objectivity.

I may surprise you with this observation, but hear me out. A recent television program was "Brideshead Revisited" by Evelyn Waugh. I found the family it portrayed in many ways to be much like the Kennedy family. First you have the mother, the Catholic matriarch Rose, a brooding presence but not the most beloved parent. As in "Brideshead," Joe Kennedy, the father, while an unfaithful husband, was a beloved father to all the children (there was also the similar figure in the TV show). The Ambassador, as I called him, was the drive and the cement of the Kennedy family. The children adored him. And the main character in "Brideshead," the Charles Ryder character—the young middle classmate of Sebastian, who when once he visited the home never got the taste for wealth and elegance out of his system—was very similar to Lem Billings, Jack's closest friend.

You also have the Catholic sister, in "Brideshead," who will not get a divorce because of her faith. I never saw anybody in the Kennedy family, and I have the greatest collection of Kennedy home movies and walk around carrying a teddy bear as in the story, but there is a Teddy! Now follow me carefully. This story, "Brideshead," was written in 1945 and was set in the period between the two great wars. Has anyone else pointed out, however fleetingly it passed by in the story, that the children of Ryder were named Caroline and John John? Not Caroline and *John*, which could have odds in the hundreds, but Caroline and *John John*. (Now you're talking about coincidental odds in the thousands.)

There is no great meaning in any of the above, but I think it's fascinating, especially for those who knew Lem Billings. He met Jack Kennedy at Choate prep school, and our young President in his youth was a wild and crazy guy. Lem was the more conservative student, although later he was the craziest of all the Kennedy group. He became, in every way but blood, a Kennedy like Ethel, Robert's wife. She is more of a Kennedy by osmosis than some of the real sisters. The men who were lucky enough to marry three wonderful girls, Eunice, Pat, and Jean, are not in the contest at all.

Peter Lawford, the actor, was eliminated in the semifinals. Steve Smith, who married Jean, takes care of the family business, but Sarge Shriver is hardly ever seen in the family gatherings. I have dined with Eunice many times over the years and visited her at her home in the compound at Hyannis, and I have never even met Sarge Shriver. Miriam and I have been invited to Teddy's home on several occasions, but his wife Joan never appeared at dinner; nor was her absence explained, though she was in the house. Jacqueline Bouvier was an honorary Kennedy. She could play on the course but never could join the club. She remains to me one of the most interesting women of recent history.

Lem Billings is missing from many of the biographies about the

On Guadalcanal
with the
1st Marine Division.

Randy at five years old.

Scene from *Friendly Island*, with David Wayne and Bill Lundigan.

The publicity still from *Love Nest*.

WUB016 PD HYANNISPORT MASS JUL 8 1223P EDT

JACK PAAR NBC INC

1960 JUL 8 PM 6 53

   30 ROCKERFELLER PLAZA NYK

DEAR JACK MANY THANKS FOR YOUR GENEROUS WIRE IT LOOKS AS THOUGH

THE ONLY CONTRIBUTIONS THAT THE KENNEDYS HAVE MADE TO YOU ARE

A TWO MILLION DOLLAR LAW SUIT FROM JIMMY HOFFA AND LARS DALY

HOWEVER WE'RE FOR YOU BEST REGARDS

   JACK KENNEDY.

639P

JOSEPH P. KENNEDY

Hyannis Port
Massachusetts

December 12, 1960

Dear Jack:

I am today in receipt of a telegram which you sent
from Honolulu on November 9. It was mixed up with Jack's
45,000 wires, and I finally got it here at the Cape on
Friday.

I want you to know that I have come to the
conclusion that you are one man that I know who should
always follow his heart and not his head, because while
I listened to the show from Hawaii in which you opened
the envelope announcing your choice as President, I
laughed heartily, because I don't know anybody who did
more, indirectly, to have Jack elected than your own good
self. I know that you didn't do this deliberately, because
you have protested time and time again that you have to
stay neutral. But if we had had five more Jack Paars in
the United States—neutral as they must be—we wouldn't
have had to wait almost 24 hours before we knew we were
elected.

So at this time, I thank you very much for your
thoughtfulness in sending the wire, and for the great
"neutral" help you gave us in the campaign.

And please don't ever change your format on your
show. People follow a lot of one-show-a-week programs,
and I have yet to meet anybody who started looking at
your show who doesn't become an adict.

With my warmest personal regards, in which I know
all the Kennedys join me.

Sincerely yours,

Joseph P. Kennedy

Mr. Jack Paar

Jack Paar and friends.

Peter Ustinov.

Alexander King.

Randy in 1966. (*Credit: D'arlene Studio*)

With Miriam campaigning in Detroit for Bobby Kennedy.

Kennedys, yet there was no one closer and more devoted to the family than he. He came from a middle class medical family in Baltimore. He met Jack at Choate, and they remained the closest of friends until the President's assassination. Nearly every weekend, he spent with the family either in Bronxville, New York, Boston, or on the Cape. I believe he may have had an unrequited love for their sister Kathleen, "Kick," who was killed in a plane accident in Europe.

Lem was a big, broad-shouldered man with the damnedest, silliest voice, which did not go with the body. When Jack went into the Navy and got his commission, Lem tried to follow but was turned down because of his eyesight. He joined the British Red Cross and drove an ambulance through their North African campaigns. Later he got a commission in the United States Navy, probably through the intervention of Joe Kennedy with Secretary of the Navy James Forrestal. He came from a Republican family and was extremely patriotic.

Everything he said was funny, not necessarily witty but hilarious with that voice and his laugh. After the war he held silly jobs with advertising agencies, such as being the account executive for something called Fizzies, which was a powder one poured into a glass of water to make a carbonated fruit drink.

Lem drank too much, which was a concern to us all. By this time he was also very close to Miriam and Randy and had the greatest gift of anyone with children. We all loved him. He was in many ways a child himself. Many weekends were spent with us either in our home in Bronxville or here in Connecticut.

After the death of the President and later Robert, Lem gave up playing sports with the Kennedy children. He would no longer wrestle with the boys or play the mixed, boy and girl touch-football games. He explained why: "There are now thirteen kids without a father (Bob's eleven and Jack's two). I can no longer be their best friend. They've got to respect me." He loved those kids, and he could be and was tough in the years that came later.

Lem died last year, and his funeral was in a cathedral packed with some of the most distinguished people in the country. They cried and laughed as many spoke of him from the altar. Andy Williams followed the casket, yet again singing, "Ave Maria." Although Lem was not a Catholic, some of the Kennedy children, now grown men and women, spoke; and just to repeat some of his escapades made everyone in the church really roll with warm laughter. You see, the Kennedys don't cry. I have been with them in sad situations but never, never saw a tear. Oh, I am certain they do at times, but not in front of nonmembers of the blood family.

One time Lem was in the Italian Alps skiing. He had had too much wine for lunch, and as he was waiting to get on a lift, he stuck his two pointed metal poles hard into the snow. They went through both his shoes by mistake, actually piercing the leather and the skin on his two feet. Well, he was in pain but too embarrassed to say anything and began to move around leaving tracks of blood in the snow. The Italians were alarmed: Where was this blood coming from? Lem, feeling like a puppy who had missed the paper, kept saying, "Not me! Not me!" and walked away, looking like Charlie Chaplin but trailing blood on the white snow all down the path. He walked to the hospital but was in bed for a week.

Senator Ted Kennedy is beloved by his sisters and Ethel. In a family gathering he is not at all like the serious, no-nonsense Kennedy you see on television. He is a very amusing man and can hold his own on the fastest track with witty people. He does impressions and has a routine of conducting the Boston Symphony that's first rate. He does side-splitting impressions of his grandfather, Honey Fitz, as an Irish politician. And some of that loud, unnatural, old-fashioned oratory that has unconsciously crept into his delivery in real life comes from those impressions.

He is a firm, old-fashioned father, who is very strict with his children and, when he needed to be, with Ethel's. He's tough.

Joan, his former wife, can be an absolute beauty. But whatever her or their problems, she was just not accepted by the real Kennedys. Once, when Ethel had broken her foot skiing and was outside on a veranda with two telephones ringing from people all over the country, I sat and watched. A few of the staff and some family members sort of waited informally in line to talk to her next about important assignments they had been given. These assignments mainly had to do with a tennis tournament which

Ethel was producing. Each one reported. At the end of the line I noticed a rather nervous-looking girl I did not know. She had a slight twitch, and when she got closer, it turned out to be Joan. I had known her quite well, but I didn't recognize her. She reported. Her only assignment was to find out what movies were available for the weekend. She read her list and sadly walked away. I was touched.

A few years ago we were asked to spend a weekend at the big, beautiful family home on the Cape with Pat Kennedy Lawford and Lem. Miriam and I were given the big bedroom on the first floor. This, I was told, was Jack's room, where he slept as a teenager and as President of the United States. Well, now come on, that's a moving moment, and both my wife and I were very touched—really moved! We then went to Ethel's home for dinner, a few hundred yards away, and when we returned much later that night, we were told that the electric fuse had blown in our room. We believed them. They had actually gone back earlier and removed all the bulbs from the lamps so that there was no way one could see. We brushed our teeth in the dark and then tried to get into bed and found we had been "short-sheeted." This is a prep school trick where you fold the lower sheet back to the middle and then up to the top. There is no way you can get into bed, and if you don't know the trick—and we didn't—you can spend ten minutes trying. Only the screams of laughter from some of the Kennedys listening outside the bedroom door indicated that there was a joke going on starring the Paars. I pleaded with them to come and help us, but they all went on to bed. So if you read how chic it was to be in *Camelot*, that is the real story.

The Kennedys and their friends are all great game players. After a dinner the games begin. They can be charades, word games, or usually at Hyannis Port, something called "Sardine." I never understood the point of it because it goes like this: All lights are turned off, and half the group hides anywhere—under a bed, in a closet, under a table, etc. The other half tries to find you, and when they do, they pack themselves in or under or whatever with you. Well, I was not about to play a game in which wherever I opened a closet I would find Arthur Schlesinger, Jr., and jam in with him. So I went out and lay down on the dock facing the house with my after-dinner Havana.

It was a dark night. No lights were on. I looked up, and on the dark roof hiding behind the chimney was Rafer Johnson, the great Olympic champion. Rafer, as you may know, is a handsome black man, but on a dark night on a dark roof hiding behind a chimney, surely he had to be the winner. Besides, it would be impossible to get out on that roof unless you were a good athlete.

I didn't want my wife to play because playing this very game was how the first Mrs. David Niven was killed in Hollywood. She opened a closet door, stepped in, and found that it was the staircase to the cellar. She was killed in her fall to the basement. I was labeled a party pooper.

The Kennedys never used vulgar language or even told a sexy joke. It was not considered socially acceptable. Ethel, in some ways the most interesting member of the clan and certainly the most active, had the habit of stopping any remark, however well intended, with a full glass of wine, California to be sure, right in the kisser. I have seen many people get the Napa Valley salute: Lem, Steve Smith. One night even Andy Williams got a spritz from the Gallo Brothers.

Not long ago, in a small private dining room at the 21 Club in New York there was a small gathering which included Vitas Gerulaitis, the tennis champion, his mother, my wife, the governor of the state of New York, and a few others. I don't remember what he said, but Hugh Carey was awarded the Golden Inglenook Prize. The governor of New York, for heaven's sake! Dripping in this shower of Chardonnay, he simply took off his tie, hung it over the chandelier, and the luncheon went on. That's class! Now understand, this has nothing to do with drinking. I have never seen any Kennedy intoxicated; it was just our Ethel being playful.

Once out on the Kennedy yacht, Arthur Schlesinger got a whole bowl of cole slaw over the head, which spilled over onto his tall, Junoesque wife, and she was picking celery out of her bosom for minutes. It goes with the territory!

We were at Hickory Hill the night that Arthur Schlesinger and Supreme Court Justice Byron White got dunked in the pool in their evening clothes. I sat next to that great lady, Alice Roosevelt Longworth. It was a beautiful setting of tables by the pool and candlelight on each table. First, you must understand that in my home, because my wife is so diet-conscious, we never have cream or butter. Well, I didn't have my glasses on, the wind blew the candle out, and I ate just by putting my fork into the dish before me. It was delicious . . . a beef ragout, perhaps—I had to guess since I couldn't see—a salad, maybe, and then my fork came up with something I had never had. It was pure ambrosia. I said to Mrs. Longworth, "I can't see, but what am I eating that is so unusual?" She said, "For the past five minutes you have been eating my butter!"

When I was asked recently what were the toughest interviews I ever conducted, I replied readily that the toughest was with the late Joy Adamson, the lion woman, talented beyond belief as an authority on animal life in Africa. She was a really fine writer and a superb artist. Her paintings of African tribes are among the best ever done, and her book *Born Free* is a classic. But because of her drive, she simply would not reveal a single aspect of her personal life. She would appear on the show with only one topic to discuss: her own ambition to raise money for her fund. Nothing would deter her from that, and you got nothing, but nothing, in an interview.

Next would be the Kennedys, any Kennedy. They are, as a group, just about the most interesting, articulate, informed, amusing of living-room raconteurs, but you will never learn on television what they are really like. They are extremely cautious and dull on TV.

Off camera, they are the best company you could wish for. All are very natural, kind, and generous. I have always thought they didn't project their much more likable real personalities in interviews. Robert, once discussing the problem with me off the air, said that their reason for not projecting was that they all peaked politically at the top when they were very young and did everything to avoid appearing youthful. That may be the best reason, but Eunice and Ethel also are not themselves on television.

A case in point: In the 1979 Democratic primaries, when Senator Ted Kennedy was running against Carter, there was that di-

sastrous interview on television with Roger Mudd. Unknowing
people who were for the senator felt that Roger Mudd had "murdered" him. It wasn't murder, it was "suicide." Roger has been
for some time a very close friend of the Kennedys. I would meet
him at many gatherings of their close friends.

Other important people who were frequently at Hickory Hill,
Bob and Ethel's home and the real center of the Kennedy fun-
and-games social life, included Ben Bradlee, Roland Evans,
Walter Cronkite, David Brinkley, Teddy White, Sander Vano-
cur, George Stevens, and always Art Buchwald. Incidentally,
Buchwald has been a great help to Ethel in any problem which
needed a fatherly touch with the children after her husband's
death.

Mainly it was Lem Billings who acted as a father figure. He
had a small apartment building on the East Side of Manhattan,
and it was usually filled with Kennedy kids who were spending
time in New York. He took young Robert Kennedy, Jr., on a
month-long trip to East Africa as he (Lem) had been sent, many
years before, by the Ambassador to take Robert Kennedy to
South America when he was a teenager. Lem would frequently
bring Bob and Jack's fatherless kids to our home in Bronxville because Miriam, coming from Hershey, had some secret "top of the
line" chocolate that the kids loved. Also, Miriam makes just
about the best chili in this hemisphere.

Caroline and John came for a weekend because I had made
some films which they had never seen about their father's adventures on the PT boat in the South Pacific. They were thrilled because I had brought back some seashells from the very small island to which their father swam in the rescue of some members
of his crew. I gave young John all the films I had taken, and now
he has the only record on film that exists.

Bob Kennedy, Jr., was about fourteen when his father was
killed, and I was asked to stand with him as an honorary guard at
his father's casket. Lem wanted me to help divert the young man
as much as I could from the tragedy, so I promised to get him the
lion cub, which he raised for about a year at the little zoo which
his school had in Millbrook, New York. Lem, Miriam, and I
would go up to the school to visit him, and once I spoke to the

students about Africa and showed some film. Bob Kennedy, Jr., was married last week and now works in the New York prosecutor's office. There is a feeling that of all the Kennedy boys, he has the greatest potential to succeed in politics.

The President's son John, who to my knowledge was never called "John John," also wanted to go see some lion. It was arranged that we could go out to one of our safari-park places in New Jersey and drive our car around, as many of you have done, with lion running loose within the fenced area. We went in the Secret Service car early on a day when the park was closed to the public. Something happened that thrilled the boy. A lion actually attacked the car and chewed a hole in the tire. We were stuck in the middle of the park with a flat, surrounded by lion with no one to help us. Good thinking—we used the Secret Service radio to ask that someone come and push our car out of the park. "Ten-year-old John Kennedy, Jr., was surrounded by lions in New Jersey." This was a pretty strange news bulletin on the radio that day, and it became the Tricia Nixon story all over again. This time, Lem had to explain to his mother.

There is no one who knows Ethel Kennedy who doesn't love her. She laughs, sometimes I think to keep from crying. She lost her father and mother in a plane accident, as well as her brother, who crashed into a mountain; and her sister-in-law died at the dinner table on a chicken bone which stuck in her throat. Both her beloved Bobby and her brother-in-law, the President of the United States, were killed by madmen.

Ethel has raised eleven children and is a great earth-mother type. I once did a network television special called "Three Remarkable Women." For this project, I picked my good friend Mary Martin and filmed a week with her at her home in Brazil, I spent a week in Africa living with Jane Goodall and her husband in the bush, and I filmed for days at Hyannis Port with Ethel and her brood. It was a great experience.

Ethel comes from a wealthy family. She was raised a few miles from us in Greenwich, Connecticut. Although her maiden name was Skakel and she is of Dutch descent, she looks more Irish than the Kennedys. The Skakels even had their own plane. Once a relative of Ethel's, a very obese and heavy lady, went into the lavatory on the airplane. It took some doing of twisting and turning to get her in, but once inside she had forgotten the combination of body turns to get back out. There was no way. They had to land the plane at the nearest airport, and mechanics were called to remove the door.

At Hyannis the family members—Eunice, Jean, Teddy, and Ethel—all have separate homes and are protected from the public by a fence. But in front, the open water is fair game for anyone with a boat who wants to come and gawk. There is a regular tourist boat where people pay to stop offshore while a lecturer on a public address system points out the various homes and gives the history of the Kennedys. Of course this sound carries into the compound and is hard to live with.

One day Ethel, three of her children, and I were sailing in a small boat. The boat tipped over in front of the compound when the dumb tourist boat came by. We were trying to right the boat when the announcer went into his usual talk: "If we are lucky enough, we may see a real Kennedy come out of one of their homes." The audience on the tourist boat kept staring in anticipation while twenty feet from them four card-carrying Kennedys were struggling in the water.

I would often go walking with the kids outside the compound fence. There would be hundreds of people trying to see over the six-foot barricade, and the then-smallest of the Kennedy boys would go over and say, "If you want to see a Kennedy, come here." They had made a peep hole in the fence and practically sold tickets. The public never knew that all those freckles belonged inside the compound.

Robert Kennedy was always my favorite in the family. I admired his courage. In the last months when he was running for President against Eugene McCarthy in the Democratic primaries, he asked me to meet him in Indianapolis. I went out to Indiana and was told when I arrived that he would arrive later that night by plane. First, before coming to the hotel we were staying in, he had to stop and make a speech outside at an open basketball court with an all-black audience.

George Stevens, Jeff Greenfield, and I went down to the hotel dining room for dinner an hour before the news broke that Martin Luther King had been shot in Memphis. However shocked we were and ashamed that our country yet again had turned to violence, our concern then was "How can Kennedy face a black audience that hadn't yet heard the news?" We knew he could not be talked out of appearing, and we rushed up to his room to tell Ethel the sad news and to ask what should be done. She just said, "Bobby can handle it."

It was his greatest moment. He went before the cheering blacks and said quietly, "Put down your banners for my campaign. I will have nothing to say tonight about my running for President. I bring you the sad news that Martin Luther King has just been assassinated." I have never experienced such a dramatic moment. The people on the basketball court were stunned but silent. It could have been one of the angriest moments in history. It was not. The candidate quietly spoke to them of his own brother's shooting and said that this new violence was not to be turned into a racial confrontation. He asked them to believe that justice would be done.

We had breakfast the next morning, sitting on the floor of his room. There were not enough chairs. I was then told what they would like me to do for them since I did not wish to get involved in speaking or appearing. That part of politics I don't care for, nor would I be good at it. I really was an observer of all this, not a participant.

What his public relations people wanted was for me to tape, on video, ad lib, the toughest questions we all could think of. Really mean, aggressive, grilling questions in a studio setting like "The Tonight Show." Just Bobby and me.

The point of this remains a mystery to me. That kind of approach was not mine and certainly not with someone I liked. If I had any talent for interviewing, it was oblique—a kind of naive softspoken approach which is natural for me. Besides, I had no wish to be on television.

I agreed but wanted to know why. I was not a political person. What was the purpose of trying to *embarrass* a friend? The publicity people said that Robert felt most comfortable with me and that he was going to try under pressure to give good, solid answers. They would take the best of these pieces of tape and make commercials. Not a bad idea really, but not one I enjoyed. We did it in a studio that morning, and I never saw Bobby again. The tapes were never used because he was killed in Los Angeles.

The day after Robert Kennedy's death, I was in a daze. As I mentioned earlier, NBC sent a car out to the country to pick me up, and without knowing the purpose, I went along. You see, all regular programming had been canceled, all commercials were taken off the air, and there really wasn't much for the television camera to "see" in the aftermath of such a tragedy. So I went into an empty TV studio and talked for two hours ad lib on Bob. I have no idea what I said.

The day of the funeral I shall never, never forget. After the service at St. Patrick's, invited friends—perhaps a hundred or more —left the cathedral to go to Pennsylvania Station to board a special train and accompany the Kennedy family and Robert's body to Washington. As I was going down an escalator and making a turn to go to a lower floor to the train, a reporter I knew yelled at me, "Did you know that they just caught the murderer of Martin Luther King?"

Not really understanding the impact of what he had said, I motioned with my fingers to my lips not to continue because the woman in front of me by a few inches I believed to be Mrs. Martin Luther King. We got on the train, and Miriam and I, as usual, tried to find the quietest, least-crowded part. We went into an empty car, and there sitting alone was Mrs. King. She is a very attractive woman. We sat down next to her, and I asked, "Did you overhear the reporter's words to me on the escalator?" "Yes," she replied, "but I still don't know what they mean."

I said to Mrs. King that a strange series of coincidences was beginning to disturb me. I told her I was with Bobby in Indianapolis the night her husband was killed, and I was in the hotel room when he spoke to her on the phone and offered to send the family plane anywhere to take her wherever she wished to be. And then I happened to be standing right behind her as the announcement was made that her husband's killer had been found. I offered the thought that my name was Jack, my dead brother's name was Bobby, and the President was born in the same month of the same year as I was. We both served in the same part of the South Pacific. Both of us had lived in Bronxville, New York . . . I was just making small talk, really.

She looked at me—she has a beautiful smile—and said something like "Dear God, what more can happen to us."

At that very second there was a loud, shrill, screaming sound such as I had never heard before. It was like a whistle, but a whistle is a whistle . . . what was *this*? It seems that by some strange mechanical phenomenon, if it's really important and one pulls hard enough on a cord and there really is a danger, everything is amplified.

Mrs. King, Miriam, and I looked out the window and there, as our train was going south, a train racing north was going by a station. A woman fell on the track, and we saw her leg from about the middle of the hip fly into the air. I will never forget it because there wasn't a drop of blood. This haunting memory still makes me wince.

And before the journey was completed, we saw another tragedy from our train window. For the whole three hundred miles to Washington, the tracks were lined with hundreds of thousands of people waiting to watch the funeral train go by. Something *had* to happen. A man who had climbed on top of a railroad box car to get a better view of the funeral train was electrocuted and burned black as we sped by.

I was shaken by the whole experience. I feared that what should have been a tribute to a unique, misunderstood, and good man was turning into a circus. Goethe, the German poet, said something about "the secret of all genius is knowing when to stop."

The funeral train arrived in Washington, and the passengers, some of whom were in a rather partylike mood, were to go on to Arlington National Cemetery for the burial. Miriam and I went directly to the airport and flew back to New York.

This has gone on longer than I thought. I've perhaps told you more than I should have, more than you really want to know. I am not anxious to run into Ethel. I would not want to meet her, the loose cannon on the Kennedy deck, if she were armed with a

glass of Chablis. But if I do, I hope that it's a good year and I
have an umbrella.

Shortly after I finished writing this chapter, the newspapers re
ported yet again rumors about Marilyn Monroe and Robert Kennedy. There was gossip about a secret diary that Marilyn allegedly
kept and someone allegedly has, but it has never been produced.
If such a diary exists at all, it may be explained by stories that
whenever Marilyn Monroe met Bobby with many others at the
Lawford home in California and he was talking informally about
politics, she—poor, tragic, flaky Marilyn—would sit on the floor
and make notes about the conversation. I have been told this,
and it seems so odd, but knowing Marilyn Monroe it was the
kind of pretentious, pseudointellectual thing that she might do. I
had heard it discussed more than once as odd behavior, but then
I had always found her rather bizarre.

Of course, all the Kennedys knew Marilyn. They knew everyone and were great fans of theatrical, literary, and sports people. I
recall that once, after Robert Kennedy had written a book, the
publishers had a cocktail party at the 21 Club for the book's
debut. There were many people there from the worlds of politics,
entertainment, and sports. I was talking to Robert when he noticed a famous sports figure. I never saw him so overwhelmed and
anxious to meet the man. It was Frank Gifford, who incidentally
is a first-class guy in every way. I was there when they met, and
Bobby was thrilled to meet Gifford. How pleased he would be, I
am sure, to know that last year his son Michael married Frank's
daughter Vicki.

Judy Garland once told me a touching story of meeting her old
friend, Jack Kennedy, after he became President. They had
known each other in Hollywood, and later Judy rented a house at
Hyannis Port near the Kennedy compound. Judy walked into the
Oval Office, and there sat her friend, now the President of the
United States. The emotion was too much, and she embarrassed
herself by sitting down and sobbing with pride. She said, "It was
my biggest moment, my best scene, and I blew it."

12

Dujy Landgar

You have probably never heard of a young singer with the strange, gypsy name of Dujy Landgar. Well, she was trying out for an Off-Broadway show when I became interested in her. She was a charmer and looked like a wet sparrow. If she weighed one hundred pounds, at least ten pounds were her eyes. She had her hair done by the North Wind and was a sixteen-year-old card-carrying darling. And she could really sing.

Well, she wanted so very much to be on television and be discovered. I was taking a chance because this was not the "Tonight" program, where one is supposed to take chances and help young performers, this was my Friday night prime-time program with a real budget. I decided to put her on, but there was this one catch: I had to call her mother, whom I knew, and get her permission. Her mother was not anxious for such exposure of her daughter so soon but was willing to grant permission if I would agree not to publicize her or mention her name until after she sang—and then only if she was really good. I agreed.

The young lady was thrilled. This was on Monday, and we began to make special musical arrangements for her; the show was to air a week from Friday. My staff took over and looked for a special dress for her gamin personality.

Now we come to Thursday. She had fallen and broken her leg the night before. "Well," I said, "wait a few months and tell her

I will put her on when she feels well enough and can walk. No, tell her we can preset her behind a curtain, and as soon as she can stand and bow, she has a date."

A few hours later I was told that the youngster was heartbroken and would die if she wasn't on next Friday. I have always been a sucker for a sad story. (Leaky Jack I was called.) A broken leg I could cope with, but a broken leg and a broken heart was too much. I told the director, Hal Gurnee, and my associate, Paul Keyes, to work it out. We could get a dress on her somehow and put her in a garden setting sitting on a bench. By then I was a nervous wreck.

Sunday, the day of the taping, I went to the studio and found her in a wheelchair wearing blue jeans which they could not get off because of the cast on her leg; it was broken in such a fracture that it had to stick straight out. There was no choice; she had to go on "as is."

As usual, I was sitting quietly in my dressing room before the program, a must for me because much of my work was ad lib and I had to think about each moment of a program beforehand. There was the added problem of how to introduce an unknown in a wheelchair, wearing blue jeans with a leg sticking out like a crazy statue. I heard a scream; it was really one of agony. I ran to the hallway, found my assistant Mitzi coming out of the ladies' room, and said, "What in hell is going on in there?"

Mitzi, always the calmest of my group, explained that they had taken little Dujy to the bathroom, and the toilet-booth door had closed on her broken leg as they were lifting her on the "john."

Well, she went on in the great tradition of gypsy singers, was a smash, and the audience loved her.

Are you ready? Have you guessed? Well, I took it on myself without asking her mother and came right out after her song and said, "Dujy Landgar is more or less a backward spelling of a famous name. This is Judy Garland's daughter; her real name is Liza Minnelli." She cried and laughed and was wheeled offstage by a nurse. A starlet was born.

Her mother, Judy, and I had been friends for many years through thick and thin, mostly thin. Everyone knew of Judy, the singer, possibly one of the greatest entertainers of our time, but what I discovered was her ability as a conversationalist. On Judy's first TV appearance with me, we *talked* more than she sang, and that was a side of her which was my discovery. On the basis of that one appearance, CBS gave her a program which was to feature her talking. It wasn't the success it should have been because we both learned that asking and kidding and loving and initiating a conversation is not the same as answering. Judy, on the air, was not a self-starter. She was what we in show business call a "counterpuncher."

Whenever she was on a downer and I could get to her, she would come on and be hilarious. I once did a big important special with her where she didn't sing at all. We just talked.

Judy was very funny offstage as well. Never bawdy, it was rather a grand manner that she had; and at times you would have thought she came from a high social background rather than her "born-in-a-trunk" backstage upbringing. I recall a few lines from her . . .

We were speaking of a well-known actress who was known for her bed-hopping, and I said isn't so-and-so a *nymphomaniac?* Judy said, "Only if you can *calm her down.*"

She told me that when she was a young star making a children's picture which became a classic, *The Wizard of Oz*, the dwarfs were very fresh and sexy with her. She also said that they were usually drunk and that you had to capture them with butterfly nets. One Munchkin said to her, "I would like to give you a sexual experience that you'll never forget." And Judy replied, "Well, if you do and I find out about it—"

She did an imitation of Marlene Dietrich that was very amusing. Once, at Noël Coward's home in London, Marlene had just returned from a tour of Europe; she had an album she wanted to play for them. Well, not many people are anxious to hear an album of Dietrich's singing, but Marlene only wanted to play the applause after each recording cut. Dietrich would say in that deep voice of hers, "This is me in Munich." After the applause on the recording, she would pick up the head and move it to the next applause, "That was me in Berlin." Then she would move the recording to the next applause and say, "Listen to me in Moscow."

Judy had many stories about her days as a teenager at MGM Studios in Culver City. By law, Mickey Rooney, Elizabeth Taylor, Deanna Durbin, and Lana Turner had to spend an hour or two a day with a teacher in a class on the lot. Unlike you and I, when we raised our hand in class, when Mickey and Lana would raise their hands, it only meant, could they go outside and smoke.

Judy always spoke warmly of Rooney but didn't care for Liz Taylor. She said on the air that Elizabeth had a terrible speaking voice, which she has. (I have heard Richard Burton refer to his then-wife's vocal equipment as a "fishmonger's voice.") Judy always felt that the beautiful Liz was badly mannered. Deanna Durbin disturbed Judy because "Deanna had only one eyebrow that went from ear to ear."

Miriam, Randy, my daughter, and I were with Judy the night in London when Liza announced her engagement to Peter Allen. He was a nice boy, but I did wonder about the marriage as they seemed unsuited for each other. There were three of the Allens— the father, who was their manager, and two brothers. I just never believed that they were related. They, the "Allens," seemed strange to me, however much I liked them. We took them all to dinner and had a few bottles of the "bubbly" to celebrate. Liza married Peter, but it didn't work out for whatever reason.

Judy could be the most difficult talented person in show business. Many TV shows would not touch her because of her unreliability. She would always refuse to come out of her dressing room. You had to beg her. She would not come to rehearsal. But that was only when shows were taped and she knew she could get away with it. But why? When shows were live, she would appear seconds before her appearance and give everybody a mild cardiac attack. To this day, I cannot figure the reason for it.

I will now give you an hour-by-hour account of My Date with Judy.

10 A.M. Scene: Judy's home in Westwood. Jack Haley, Jr., the producer for a Wolper special that I was doing, and I arrive at Judy's house. We are taken into a living room in a medium-size Hollywood home. The living room has obviously had a party the

night before, as there is a motion picture projector with film all over the floor. After a half hour, Judy enters in an old-fashioned dress, sweet, but wearing a great big broad floppy hat, the kind that Janet Gaynor wore in pictures.

11 A.M.: Judy is very sweet at first but has a strange look in her eyes. She asks to speak to me alone. The two of us go into her den, and she says, "Get rid of that guy! I have never met him before, but I hated his father." (His father was Jack Haley, who appeared as the Tin Woodman with Judy in *The Wizard of Oz*.) I try to tell Judy that she is being rude to young Haley, and I am embarrassed. Poor Jack said nothing to disturb her and indeed is anxious to get out of the house because he feels the enmity. I beg Judy to be polite to him, and she and I plan to go to the Brown Derby for lunch. I know that Jack is ill at ease, and this will be a way of breaking off the pending hatred on her part. I don't know what it is all about. Young Jack and she had never met, but she hated his father and now hates him. Young Haley leaves in a taxi and leaves the car for me. (What is strange about all this is that later Liza marries this very man, Jack Haley, Jr., and it's announced that they were all old family friends.)

12 noon: Somebody comes to her door, serves a summons, and reclaims her only automobile. The week before this she was given notice to vacate her home because the mortgage company was reclaiming the house. She tells me all of this, still wearing that ridiculous hat, and says, "Oh, well, behind every cloud . . . there is another *cloud*."

12:30 P.M.: Judy and I are driving down Sunset Boulevard and stop at a light. A great big stretch limousine pulls up to our right with dark, funereal windows. The window on her side of the limo comes down, and there he is, *The Man*, no doubt about it. The voice says in a Southern country accent, "Good afternoon, ma'am. I'm Elvis Presley. I just want you to know you are the greatest entertainer in the world." Judy is very grand and says, "Thank you."

At that point I lean over across her and say, "Hi, Elvis, I'm Jack Paar." The dark window goes up, I am sure almost faster than usual, and the car speeds off. Judy thinks that is really hilarious.

I can see that she is so pleased by this great compliment to her and at my embarrassment. You see, show people are like puppies —they love compliments. If actors had tails, they would be wagging them most of the time. Love me! Love me!

1 P.M.: We arrive at the Beverly Hills Brown Derby. She makes a great "entrance," mixed only by the waiters' reaction and sense that she has been there before under "dramatic" circumstances. She orders vodka and tonic. I have white wine.

1:30 P.M.: Judy doesn't want to order food but has a few vodkas to relax. This is unusual for Judy, as she most often drinks Blue Nun wine. I get worried and think if there is going to be a problem, I had better get my wife there. I call and leave word at the Beverly Hills Hotel to tell Miriam, who is shopping, that it's *May Day!* Join us.

2 P.M.: It goes on that way until about 3 P.M. Now at no point is Judy anything but regal. There is hardly room in the booth for me, Miriam, who joins us, Judy and that crazy voile sombrero. She doesn't want any food, but how about another drinkee-poo?

3 P.M.: We tell her that we must go back to the hotel and ask if we could take her home. She insists on joining us. We leave the Brown Derby and drive to the Beverly Hills Hotel. As we arrive under the canopy and park the car, Judy sees James Mason getting out of a car. She yells, "Jimmy," and rushes to meet him.

Mason is a very civilized man and a cool cat if there ever was one. He sees Judy out of the corner of his eye, senses a reunion he doesn't wish for, dashes, and disappears into the lobby. (As an observer, I wish to point out to you this irony: In their picture together, *A Star Is Born*, it was Judy who was the young sober actress and James, the drunken director, who was the problem.)

4 P.M.: Judy wants to eat. We call room service, and she wants a "tossed salad"—which, after another vodka and tonic, she begins to really toss. There may be a little on the chandelier to this day. None of this, you understand, is crazy drunkenness. It's with the sweetest look and the best manners of anyone in the room. It's just a euphoric, happy time! Judy always has class, and it even shows then.

5 P.M.: I am called down to the Polo Lounge of the hotel for an interview and must leave my wife alone with Judy. Judy begins to

tell Miriam her troubles and wants to borrow ten dollars and a raincoat as she had lost hers. Miriam gives her both. Judy tells Miriam that tomorrow will be a better day, as she is going to Twentieth Century Fox to audition for an important part in the movie version of *Valley of the Dolls*. She then begins to speak very frankly of sex, which scares the hell out of Miriam. Miriam goes to a phone in the bedroom and calls her friend, Dorothy Averback, and says, "*May Day!* Judy is here. Come right over."

6 P.M.: I return from the Polo Lounge and explain to Judy that we have a dinner date at La Scala with old friends, Mr. and Mrs. Paul Keyes. Judy wants to join us.

I do not want this and make up a story that it wouldn't be fair to her, Judy, since this dinner is obligatory and would be, I said, with two of the dullest people on earth. They would bore her beyond all endurance. "No," I plead, "I can't do this to you, darling . . . dull, dull . . . boring people."

Well now, let me explain that the Keyeses are old, dear friends. Paul was with me for nine years, five on "Tonight" and nearly four on my other shows and specials. He always traveled with me through North Africa, the Soviet Union, and Europe. When I more or less retired from television, Paul went to the West Coast and wrote first for Dean Martin, then wrote and produced "Laugh-In." He now writes for and produces the Frank Sinatra shows. He has won Emmys for his writing and producing. It was Paul who said in an interview, "I love Paar; I've fought my way out of three countries with him."

So as Miriam and I enter La Scala with Judy, there is no way to let Keyes know "we" now have a problem. I say "we" because I always include my friends in my problems. It keeps them young and on their toes. They are delighted to see Judy as they have never met her and do not know she is well on her way to a major headache, to say the least.

Judy, still the perfect lady but bombed, opens the conversation by looking them straight in the eye and saying, "Mr. and Mrs. Keyes, I believe are your names. Tell me please, *why are you both so dull?*"

I could die. There is no way to explain to Paul that it was an excuse to avoid bringing her. They are stunned because they don't know she has a liquor problem, that I have made up this story; and besides they have never met before.

She goes on, "Everybody uses my best friend, Jack. All the dull people in the world, all the boring people use poor, wonderful Jack. And Miriam," she says to my wife, "sometimes you're boring. Please try not to be. Work on it. We must save Jack from dullness."

Miriam gets Judy to the ladies' room, and then I am able to explain to Paul and his wife my dissembling, my lie actually. When they return from the loo, we order spaghetti with an Alka-Seltzer sauce. Paul and I are thinking of various ways we could get her home. I didn't drive to her house that morning, Haley did, and now I cannot remember an unfamiliar part of Westwood; Judy refuses to tell me how to get there. When a person is devoted to a cause, when she has started a campaign to stamp out all the dullness in the world, she doesn't want to go home.

9:30 P.M.: We all get in Paul's car and start down toward the ocean on Wilshire Boulevard. This certainly is a move in the right direction. As we are going down the boulevard, Judy screams, "Stop, I want out. I know somebody who lives in that building."

We are delighted because now we can get information about where she lives or deposit her safely with whomever lives in that building. She runs across the street, I run after her, and she tells me that Sid Luft lives in this apartment. Sid Luft was her former husband and the father of Lorna and Joe, the children of Judy and Sid, half-siblings of Liza.

Looking on the mailbox board, I cannot find a "Sid Luft," but she insists she knows he lives here. "Please leave and go back to your dull friends." Then, very grandly, she turns on the Garland charm and says, "You've been very charming. It's been a lovely day."

Day!—dear God, I thought it was the whole month of October. I know that Judy has at least the ten dollars that Miriam gave her if she wants to take a taxi. So I go back to the car and watch this great, great star who is now auditioning for a part in a *schlock* picture the next morning.

Judy now goes around the building, down an alley, and into a

U-shaped courtyard. We pull our car in, and there is Judy looking up at four apartment floors; she begins to yell, "Sid . . . Sid . . . *Sid!*"

Windows begin to open. People stick their heads out, and in our car headlights we see her take off her crazy hat, look up at all the windows, and say, as she makes a deep theatrical bow, "It's me. I'm Judy Garland!" (CUT AND PRINT!)

I have seldom witnessed a more dramatic moment. When I returned to the room that night, I went to take an aspirin and found that our entire supply of traveling medical supplies was missing. Judy was found the next morning, safe and well, sleeping on a pool table at Twentieth Century Fox. She did not get the part.

Months later, we received this telegram. It read:

I KNOW THAT MOTHER WOULD WANT YOU TO BE AT HER FUNERAL. PLEASE COME AND DO NOT WEAR ANY DARK, SAD CLOTHES. DO YOU HAVE A YELLOW SUIT?—LOVE LIZA

13

Kings, Klowns, And Knuts

Alexander King. I first met Alex in January of 1959. He was a frail but fierce little man with the air of a delinquent leprechaun. He was a friend of Sidney Carroll, the writer, and Al Hirschfeld, the artist; and they asked me to put him on the show as he had written a book called *Mine Enemy Grows Older.* It was not selling well.

I was a bit startled when I met King backstage. He was a fragile man, about sixty, with a wispy mustache, a jaunty bow tie, a gentle smile, and a satanic gleam in his eyes. Then he sat down with me in front of the camera and began to talk.

Rambling along in a stream-of-consciousness style, he was by turns witty, irreverent, poetic, outrageous, and vitriolic.

He had absolutely no inhibitions about himself. He talked freely and colorfully about his four wives, his drug addiction, and his varied careers as an artist, playwright, and editor, peppering his talk with invective and tipping over idols with obvious delight in his careening conversation.

Overnight he talked himself into being a national institution.

His book, which had sold 6,394 copies when he came on the show, sold 26,000 copies in the next week, shot to the top of the nonfiction best-seller list, and remained there for nearly a year. Alex could talk entertainingly about almost anything because practically everything seems to have happened to him. Born in Vienna, he spoke five languages, had traveled extensively, and had had an outstanding number of adventures and misadventures. On the show he regaled the audience with accounts of serving as a midwife in North Africa, being jailed for stealing art from the Metropolitan Museum, serving as an editor of *Life* magazine, wearing nothing but pink ties for thirty years, and nearly dying a half dozen times from a formidable array of diseases.

His books, like his conversation, are grab bags of reminiscences, opinions, invective, and bizarre and improbable tales that sometimes strained credulity but were never dull. "I notice," a friend told him, "that you didn't ruin your autobiography by putting your life into it."

Many of his most colorful remembrances are of his days in New York's Greenwich Village. One night he was coming home to his apartment when he saw a newspaperman that he knew slightly getting out of a cab with a big, homely dog. The man went into his apartment, leaving the dog to wander off down the street alone.

Indignant, Alex knocked on the man's door and asked, "How come you just walked off and left your dog?"

"He's not my dog," the man protested. "I never saw him before."

"He must be your dog," Alex insisted. "I saw him get out of the cab with you."

"I know," the man admitted. "I was coming home, and I saw the dog and thought to myself: What chance does a big, ugly dog like that have of getting a ride in a cab? So I hailed a cab and gave him a ride around the block."

Ironically, at last when he could afford anything he wanted, his health was so delicate that he could only eat rice. Yet he was happy. "I love to get up in the morning," he said. "I'm so delighted I'm still alive."

Once when he came to the show, his face had a particularly

ruddy glow, and I remarked how healthy he looked. "I stooped over to tie my shoelace," he said, "and all the blood rushed to my head."

Alex was extremely fastidious and had a fetish about washing his hands frequently. One night before the show, he washed his hands, and then we went down to a drugstore to get a cup of coffee. A grimy-looking workman spotted Alex and said, "Mr. King, I'm a great fan of yours. May I just shake your hand?"

Alex, recoiling from the grimy outthrust hand said, "Just hug me."

Noël Coward, when on the show with him, remarked on how well he used the language. "I have to," said Alex. "I'm an immigrant."

I told Alex that I was giving him a silver tongue on the anniversary of his first appearance. "Good," he said. "I can use it for a shoe horn."

His last wife, Marge, was thirty years younger than Alex, and he adored her. He insisted on dressing her in little-girl outfits, usually Scottish tartans with a tam. This will sound crazy, but Marge used to come to the show with Alex, and in the center stage without accompaniment she would perform drum solos. Don't ask me to explain it—you had to be there!

My favorite story, which in a way has become part of the language, was his adventure on a return to Austria after his great success as an author. He was visiting a little village that he knew in his youth. A man came down from the top of a nearby mountain when he heard that Alex, a local boy who had made good, was dining at a small café.

The old Austrian, who had lived as a hermit in a little shack, spent his life as an inventor. He grabbed Alex by the arm and made him accompany him to his little workshop. After a long climb they got inside, and the man showed him a strange machine. When you pushed a certain lever, a wire would pull a small piece of wood onto paper and leave a mark. The hermit said, "Isn't it wonderful? You must help me patent it, and we will both make a fortune!"

Alex then realized what the crazy hermit had done. *He had reinvented the typewriter!*

Tallulah Bankhead. I knew her near the end of her life and liked her enormously. My first impression was how short she was, considering her fame as one of America's finest actresses and her reputation as a *femme fatale.* She had been a raving beauty, and her outrageous wit scared most people. With me she was a very sweet, frightened lady and terrified of television. She was on the program many times, and before a show she had the rather off-putting habit, obviously an old theatrical custom, of hugging me and slightly spitting on my neck. I always thought we could have skipped that.

She had a house near me, in Pound Ridge, New York, and while it's of medium size, it has enormous landscaping with many expensive trees and bushes. The owner of the nearby garden nursery, where I hang out, told me that every Monday morning she would suddenly appear with several men of all degrees of masculinity and would point out the new trees she wanted. In other words, after a rousing weekend, Tallulah only asked for a tree or two in repayment.

The legend of Tallulah always mentions her habit, in the middle of an evening party, of excusing herself and returning, a few moments later, naked. There was no mention made of it by her guests, since they were used to it; but there she stood the rest of the evening, completely nude. As she got older, everything was a little droopy or, as David Niven says, "Like beagle's ears." Her friend, the British actress Estelle Winwood, finally said, "Tallulah, dear, why must you do that? You have such pretty frocks."

I obviously never heard Tallulah say this, but the remark I am told she made from the booth in a ladies' room is hilarious. She could not find any toilet paper in her stall, so she asked the lady in the next booth, "Darling, is there any tissue in there?"

"Sorry, no."

"Then, have you any Kleenex?"

"Afraid not."

Then Tallulah said, "My dear, have you two fives for a ten?"

Oscar Levant. He was the most outrageous and difficult person I ever worked with, and yet year after year I would visit with him either at his home in Beverly Hills or in his suite at the Algonquin Hotel in New York, I would go like a missionary. I was trying to save him from himself.

After "The Tonight Show" caught on, there were many imitations of it, and one was Oscar's show on the West Coast. He knew I was in Beverly Hills and called me at my hotel. He said, "I know you are in town, but don't ever telephone me. I don't take calls." Then he hung up.

Later he insisted that I visit him but told me only to come at a certain time. The time was not convenient, but he insisted I was to be there promptly at 7 P.M. Like a fool I went, and the reason was apparent when I arrived. He wanted me to see his program, which was taped and then playing on his set. I sat and watched, and on the program he went into a witty, mean, outrageous attack on me! I still do not know the reason for his vitriolic "friendship," or why I put up with him.

I am sure I did it because his show was only local, and he was very interesting to watch. The only way I could get him on the network and let the nationwide audience see Oscar was to take the abuse.

The first time I was asked to his home in Beverly Hills, when I rang the bell, the door opened slightly, and a maid asked nervously who I was. I said I was Jack Paar and that I had an appointment with Mr. Levant. She looked at me suspiciously, let me in, then locked the door, and put up a heavy chain. From upstairs I heard Oscar shriek, "Who's down there?"

"It's Mr. Paar," the maid squeaked in fright.

"Who let him in?" Oscar demanded. "I want nobody in this house but family."

He then shuffled in, clutching his heart, and told me all about his problems. "I've lost my voice," he said gloomily, "and my memory is completely gone . . ." He then proceeded to remember everything he'd done for the past thirty years. He also remembered to tell it to me.

"I'm in the middle of a terrible emotional breakdown," he said. "It's my fifth in two years."

The truth was that Oscar Levant, the one-time great concert pianist, had become a drug addict. He would tell you that himself and did so every hour on the hour. But still he could be very funny.

He always slumped in his chair, like a deflated balloon, his rumpled blue suit hanging loosely on his sagging figure. He looked like a reject from a Fellini movie. His lips were like inner tubes, flat from kissing a mirror, but I insist that he was an original. He could be a brilliant conversationalist, but you had to put up with his nonsense.

Ordinarily I didn't meet ahead of time with people who were going to appear on the show, but it was obvious that in Oscar's case it would be a wise precaution, since for him *living* was just a sideline. All his life he had been fighting off a case of wellness.

When I would go see him, I would stay perhaps an hour or two and then would explain that I had to leave. Oscar would say, "You call that a visit?" He was really lonely, and I saw through all that craziness.

I do recall some of his witty but scathing remarks . . .

About Leonard Bernstein: "Lenny uses music as an accompaniment for his conducting."

Of Perry Como: "His voice comes out of his eyelids."

"The worst thing about having a mistress is those two dinners you have to eat."

On women's movies: "Where the wives commit adultery throughout the film, and at the end of the picture their husbands beg for forgiveness."

When he appeared on our show, the studio audience was on the edge of their seats, to recoin a phrase. They knew it was a lion-tamer act and anything might happen.

He shuffled on stage, sat down like an accordion inhaling, and began aiming jibes at everyone in sight, including me. "I'd like to welcome you tonight," he announced, "on behalf of the mentally deranged of Southern California and the outpatients of all the mental hygiene clinics." He then declared that he was a graduate of several of these institutions.

I noticed that his hands were trembling. "What is this?" he said. "And I'm supposed to do surgery."

Oscar seemed to take particular glee in insulting people from our show. "I took Elsa Maxwell to a masquerade party once," he said. "And when I tore off her mask, I found I'd beheaded her." He then declared that Zsa Zsa Gabor had "discovered the secret of perpetual middle age" and that she was "doing social work among the very rich." I reminded Oscar that Zsa Zsa had said that Oscar was brilliant, but that "there is a fine line between genius and insanity." "I've managed to overcome that fine line," he growled.

I mentioned Dinah Shore, who is renowned for her wholesome sweetness.

"I never watch her," Oscar said. "Doctor's orders."

"Doctor's orders?" I echoed, thinking warily of his hypochondria.

"Yeah," he said, fangs showing. "I'm too diabetic."

He also told me of the time that he and his wife were guests at a large formal dinner at the White House. As they were saying good night to President and Mrs. Truman, Oscar turned to his wife June and said in a resigned voice, "Now we have to have them over to dinner."

At one point I called him "dear friend." Then, remembering his aversion to friendship, I added, "Does that offend you?"

"You're getting close," he said.

Despite the verbal carnage wreaked by Oscar, critics hailed his appearance on the show as one of the highlights of the year, and I invited him back for a return bout.

The next day he called and said he would be unable to come on the show unless I would send him some sleeping pills. "My wife won't give me any," he whispered. Accordingly, I dispatched a member of my staff with two Nembutal tablets in an envelope. He rang the bell at Oscar's house, a hand reached out and snatched the envelope, and the door slammed.

My emissary had scarcely returned and explained this to me when the phone rang. It was Oscar. "Your friend didn't come in the house," he complained. "We have an old gypsy tradition at our house that no one is ever turned away at the threshold. He must come back."

I sent the confused operative back to comply with the hospitality of Oscar's gypsy tradition. Oscar greeted him quietly and led him into the living room. "Now you have crossed the threshold," Levant said grandly. "It's been a pleasure. Goodbye."

When Oscar Levant died, I thought of the line that was found on a tombstone: "I told you I was sick."

George S. Kaufman. He would appear on our program only on a Wednesday! He explained that that was the day he had his hair done. This is amusing only if you remember his priapic hair, which looked like it was in a constant state of passion. He is famous for his great contributions to the theater as a playwright: *You Can't Take It with You, The Royal Family, Dinner at Eight,* etc. He also scripted many of the Marx Brothers' movies, and many of the lines attributed to Groucho were actually written by Mr. Kaufman. He is one of only three critics of the theater who actually wrote hits later when he switched to playwriting. The other critic-authors were George Bernard Shaw and T. S. Eliot.

I was also on the other end of his life before he died. I best remember his advice to me: "You should try everything in life with the exception of incest and folk dancing."

He was always very amusing and really enjoyed being on the "Tonight" program. He always came more or less prepared, and I would in this case just sit and listen. He remains the most quoted man of his time.

I hadn't heard from him for a few weeks, and then I got a phone call; he said he would like to appear the following Wednesday. We were delighted.

When he arrived at the studio looking very ill with his former wife, Leueen MacGrath, the actress, I became concerned in our brief meeting backstage. His walk was unsteady and his speech was slurred. I went to Leueen and asked to speak with her privately. I said, "My dear, George is drunk; surely we don't want him to appear that way. How can I cancel this appearance tonight?"

Leueen firmly replied, "You must not! He knows exactly what he is going to say and will manage it." Then choking up, she continued, "George has had a stroke. He knows he is dying, and he

thought your show was the best way to say 'Goodbye' to everyone."

I think now in retrospect, it would have been better if I had not
known the truth. I could have managed with a friend who had
been drinking, but I was not trained for this ultimate experience.
I sat very still and listened, and he was very moving and amusing.
When he finished, without my speaking but with tears welling in
my eyes, George said, "And now it's time to get the hell out of
here!"

Those were his last public words. It had a deeper meaning to
me because my own father, who drank too much, had a serious
heart attack later in life and spoke strangely. It would anger me.
Slurred speech had always meant alcohol to me. As George was
speaking, I thought of my own father and how much more understanding I could have been. Damn! Damn! Damn! I kept thinking. I wish I could have done many things over again.

The next day, the New York *Times* remarked about the bad
taste of Jack Paar, putting on the air a man in such condition. It's
one of the few times I did not reply to the press. There was nothing to be said . . . but if you remember the program, now you
know the story.

George Burns. If it's true that good guys finish last, it must be
because they live longer. George is just about the favorite of everyone in show business. He is also responsible for showing actors
that on a talk show true stories about the business can be funnier
than all the written material.

I played a small part in that. It was on an early "Tonight" program when George was to appear. I met him in the NBC Hollywood parking lot and said, "How is Jack Benny?"

He then told me some stories about Benny that were really
very funny. I asked what he planned to do that night on the
show, and he said that his writers had written some material for
him. I suggested that he forget the written material, since it never
works sitting down, and that he tell stories about his days in
vaudeville.

He did and was an instant hit. He became the funniest racon-
teur of theater stories I ever heard.

Jack Benny and he were the closest of friends for thirty years.
While Benny became a superstar hero in radio, he was always
dominated by Burns in a strange relationship.

Jack could be very aloof and cool, but only because he was very
shy. He was also very naive for such a great star, and George
would tell stories about Benny's enthusiasms for very simple
things. It was not uncommon for Jack to say in the locker room
of Hillcrest Country Club, "This is the greatest glass of water I
ever had," or "These towels are the finest in the United States."

When Jack signed the biggest contract in the history of radio
with CBS, his friends waited for him at the Country Club's restaurant.

Benny, after the signing, drove from Hollywood to Hillcrest
and walked, in that campy way of his, to the comedian's round
table. He was all smiles and said, "What a great day it has been!
I drove all the way from Hollywood and Vine in twelve minutes,
and every light was with me!"

George would do outrageous things to Benny. Burns would pull
his big Cadillac across the street from the front of the Brown
Derby and wait for Jack to come out. Benny would see George
and, dodging traffic to cross the street, would rush to meet him.
Burns would wait just long enough; then he would put up the
electric window and drive away. This would make radio's greatest
star fall down with laughter, standing there in the middle of Vine
Street.

It was not unusual on a Sunday night for Hy Averback and I,
just after we had broadcast the radio program "Take It or Leave
It," to get in my car and stop at a light. Benny, who appeared on
NBC the same night, often would pull up at the same traffic
light, see us, and ask, "Where are you guys going?"

We'd say, "Chasen's or the Cock and Bull Restaurant."

And Jack would ask if he could come along. He was the least
pretentious of men. I loved him.

Benny was not mannered offstage, but still he had that strange,
androgynous swinging-arm walk that many of us imitated for

campy laughs. One day he was walking down the street, and Phil
Harris was behind him. Phil said, "Put a dress on Jack, and you
could take him anywhere."

My favorite show business story comes from George Burns. It
takes a bit of an explanation for those of you who do not know
the era or customs of vaudeville. The performers were all nomads
who lived for twenty or thirty weeks of the year away from home,
if they had a home at all. The billing at most theaters would
change on a Friday, and all of the acts would head for the next
town by train late on Thursday.

A railway center like Chicago would find in its waiting room or
bar many acts coming and going, all of them more or less
acquainted with each other, having played "a date" together
somewhere in the past.

Sitting at the bar was a great star, whose name I forget, but he
was alone. Into the bar came a little, second-rate dance team,
Mary and Herman. They saw the great star, were thrilled, and
walked over and said, "You may not remember us, but we are
Mary and Herman. We opened the show with you in Cleveland.
Could we buy you a drink?"

The star said, "No, thank you. I wish to be alone. You see, I
just heard I lost my mother."

And Herman said, "Ah, we know how you feel; we just lost our
trunk!"

Groucho Marx. It was always good for the program to have
Groucho Marx as a guest, but to tell you the truth, he bored me.
You could not have a conversation with him—at least I never
could—on or off the stage. It was a tiresome monologue, consist-
ing mostly of puns. If anyone ever needed editing, it was Groucho. His great success on radio and television was just that. They
would tape sometimes two hours of that quiz show of his to get a
half hour for air. Over an hour of the show would be written by
ten writers, and the writers were always referred to as "staff" on
the closing credits.

Groucho was not, as you would assume, a favorite among his
peers. He was neither known for his wit nor his kindness. I will
say, I did laugh at his funny walk, given to him by George Kauf-

man, in movies. That bent-over gait was amusing. He walked like an arthritic banana.

George Jessel. The Hillcrest Country Club was on Motor Avenue in Los Angeles; it was the gathering place of the great comedians and comedy writers of the past thirty years. It was to a great extent Jewish, in retaliation for another country club that barred Jews. We lived just down the street, and I would often be invited there by some of its members. It had, and I'm sure it still has, the best luncheon food on the West Coast. Whenever I was there, in the dining room would be the Ritz Brothers, Danny Kaye, Benny, Burns, Groucho, Danny Thomas (a Catholic), Phil Silvers, and many more.

These great comedy stars would usually gather around one comedian when "he was on a roll." I think that most members will agree that George Jessel, practically unemployed, was the leader of most laughter!

Jessel had a funny, flowery turn of phrase and adventures that convulsed his peers. If ever I saw a crowd gathering around a certain table, it always meant George was the centerpiece. This went on long after he was a star anywhere. He had been broke ever since I knew him, and he was often a guest on "The Tonight Show." I had to be careful because he would often try to lead me into business deals that were not strictly kosher. They might have been kosher, but they weren't *strictly* kosher.

I remember him in vaudeville when he was a big star and befriended him. Somehow I gave him my unlisted home phone number, and that was a mistake. He would call me several times a week, always in the morning around 9 A.M. The conversation would go something like this one, "Hello, sweetie. This is George. I'm in Saginaw, Michigan. Is there anything I can do for you? Look, sweetie, say hello to my good friend, Sandra."

A few days later there would be another phone call, "Hello, sweetie . . . This is Georgie. I'm in Toledo, Ohio. I just want you to know where I am at all times, in case you need anything. Say hello to my new friend, Mary Jo."

I finally figured out what this little weekly charade was all about. Those phone calls were made from bed, and he had the

local tootsie in the kip. Since my name was an important one at
that time, perhaps it impressed the local hooker. Maybe it even
helped Georgie get a discount.

If you didn't know Jessel, you would not believe some of the
stories about him. He had a poetic, theatrical speech that was
great fun to listen to, and along with George Burns, he was an
original phrase maker. Later he went crazy with that ridiculous
uniform and medals and posturing and looking for a Communist
under every bagel; but damn, he was fun!

My favorite story about Jessel concerned his early marriage to
the beautiful Norma Talmadge. She was unfaithful to him, and
once George caught her in their bedroom with another man. Jessel got a gun and shot at the lover as he dove through a window. He missed. Later in court, the judge asked him, "How could
you miss hitting a man so few feet from you?"

Jessel replied, "I missed because I'm a Jewish comedian and
not Tom Mix!"

Later the comedian had a hard time getting over his broken
marriage to Norma. He really loved her, but there seemed little
hope for reconciliation. They had a very large house in Palm
Beach, Florida, and George bought an expensive necklace as a reunion gift. He knocked on the door of his former home. The slot
opened, and Norma said, "What do you want? It's over."

Jessel offered her the necklace and said, "I bought this for you.
Please accept it and let's make up."

She took the necklace through the slot, looked at it, and gave it
back, slamming the little door closed.

Georgie seemed crushed, but waited a moment and then rang
the bell again. When Norma reopened the little slot, the heartbroken comedian said, "Do you mind if I use the pool?"

14

Lords, Ladies, And Laughter

The British are like chimpanzees. They look like us, they can do many of the things that we do, and they are great fun to watch. Just listening to them and observing their strange behavior has always been great entertainment. I fear also that, like the chimps, we like and enjoy them more than they do us.

The British cannot climb trees any better than we, but they certainly do many things superbly well. As eccentrics, we are not in the same league; also their tolerance for the bizarre surpasses ours. I have read the Sunday-only London *Observer* for twenty years and more recently the Manchester *Guardian*'s weekly overseas edition. Long ago I came to the conclusion that they really don't care much for us at all. Their press, and some of it is very good indeed, needles Americans on practically every page. And yet London is my favorite city, and I treasure the friendship of many there.

I believe that as actors they are the best in the world, certainly the best among those using our common language. I further confess that most Shakespeare plays, with the exception of *Hamlet* (starring Richard Burton) and *Othello* (starring Sir Laurence

Olivier), leave me puzzled. I have little idea what is going on up there.

Shakespeare's plays are to me much like a concert of bagpipes. I can never tell whether they're good or bad.

On an early visit to London, Hans Conried and I went to the theater and had difficulty following the action on stage. It was a minor Shakespeare play and frankly was boring. I suggested we get out of that theater as quickly as possible, but even during the interval (the British word for intermission) Hans was concerned because we met Mr. and Mrs. Raymond Massey in the lobby. (Massey was Canadian.) Hans said, "If we don't return to our seats, the Masseys will notice, and it would be very unprofessional." Clearly Hans also had had quite enough of this production, but I prevailed and we left. Hans continued to worry about what the Masseys would think.

A few days later, I got a call at my hotel, and it was Mrs. Massey. She explained that she had been trying to locate us at all the hotels and to apologize for *their* behavior. I asked, "What behavior?"

And she said, "Raymond and I never returned to our seats after the interval, and we were certain that Hans and you had noticed."

And yet I had something to do with bringing three London productions to New York by my nightly praise of the shows I had seen on several trips there. They were *Beyond the Fringe* with Dudley Moore, Peter Cook, Alan Bennett, and Jonathan Miller; *Stop the World—I Want to Get Off* with Tony Newley, which ran in New York for several years; and *Oh, What a Lovely War*, which was a lesser hit on Broadway.

The *Beyond the Fringe* group appeared on my program many times. I never would have thought at the time that little Dudley Moore would become a big romantic motion picture star.

It was Jonathan Miller, about whom I really believe the word "genius" can be used without hyperbole. He excels as a comedian, a director, a writer, a doctor with a doctoral degree in Pathology, a wit, and a conversationalist; I never met anyone with such talent. Recently I saw him on TV with my old protégé,

Dick Cavett, and it was a concert of words—so beautiful, informative, and hilarious in the most intellectual and creative sense.

He is so honest and funny about his own fears that he makes us all seem rather brave and courageous. He said, "My greatest fear is that I will be tortured by an enemy who wants me to reveal secrets that I do not know."

I have had frightening dreams like that, too, in which I am tied to a tree, and Ethel Merman keeps singing in my ear!

"The Tonight Show" would fly to London for two weeks each year. Our programs there were the most interesting and stimulating that we did because everything was new to us and we had so much to talk about. Once we would get the hang of British speech patterns, it was great fun. They were wonderful audiences because they had not seen a television show like ours. The commercials alone would make them roar. There was no one on their two channels at that time who was as uninhibited and informal as I appeared.

They had never seen television commercials, and our show was the Yellow Pages with music. I heard a lady remark, "He's quite funny for a salesman."

Later there were many imitations of "Tonight" in England; they are now referred to as "chat programs." A few years ago, I was asked by the BBC to appear on a program called "Tonight." I thought that they would be interested in my views of London, their social customs, and our differences. I was prepared for the same courtesy that I had always shown the many English actors and writers who appeared with me in the United States.

Well, I was mistaken. They had two hosts who kept offering me drinks. It is the custom there that they have an open bar, and people drink in the Green Room (a theater waiting room). I never drink before a program and thought it peculiar that they didn't want suggestions from me on what topics I thought would be interesting in view of the similarity of our programs, even down to the title, "Tonight."

These two guys, who talked like hairdressers, made me feel unwelcome and uneasy. You can never tell about the British; gays in England are practically a cottage industry. I should have been sus-

picious because one said backstage, "For far too long, officials at
the BBC have said, why can't we get someone like America's Jack
Paar. And now we have you."

Well, perfidious Albion (which means I should have listened
to Napoleon), it was a setup, and I sensed hostility the moment I
went on the last half hour of their program.

They, who had made no notes while we talked backstage, suddenly whipped out little file cards and began firing rather nasty
questions. I could not figure out the point of all this because
BBC officials had begged me to go on the air with them.

Well, America, I didn't let you down. After a few moments,
one of the designer-hosts said, "Didn't you once flounce off your
show?" They were referring to the leaving of the program over
the censorship incident. I was prepared to discuss that with them,
but I didn't like the word "flounce." And so I said, "Americans
don't *flounce*; the only flouncing one sees is in the hallways of the
BBC and at your Admiralty." (They had just had a gay naval
officer defect to the Soviet Union.) I continued, "Americans walk
like this. Good night, gentlemen." I did my John Wayne walk
and left the stage, leaving them with twenty minutes to fill. I
don't know what they did, as I went directly to a taxi. Perhaps
the two guys exchanged recipes.

Sir Hew Weldon, who later became head of the British
Broadcasting Corporation, and Miriam and I often have dinner
when he is visiting in our country; he is a delightful man who is
very close to the royal family. He told me a funny story about the
day of the investiture, when Charles became the Prince of Wales.
It was a splendid ceremony that lasted many hours with all the
horses, carriages, feathers, and carrying on that only the British
can do. (Incidentally, on such a small island, where do the British store all those crazy costumes?) The BBC naturally video-
taped the ceremony and ran an edited version for one hour and a
half that evening.

But a few days later, the royals—as Sir Hew always refers to
them—wished to come to the BBC to see the video tape of the
pageant. In those days there were no tape facilities except in the
broadcasting headquarters.

Sir Hew got everything ready in a small studio but was not

prepared for the large group that came: "Ma'am Darling" (the Queen Mother), "Lilibet" (the Queen of England), Princess Margaret, Prince Charles, Princess Anne, Prince Philip, uncles and aunts, and various children. It was far more than expected, but Sir Hew arranged for a light afternoon tea.

As the royals watched the taping, they had their own *lingua franca* for commenting on the proceedings. It seems that the monarch's family have a way of scoring, as in a sporting event. Here are a few examples:

"Very nice posture, Charles; score ten for Charles."

"Lady Worshipper . . . Oh, dear, an apple-green dress. Down five for Lady Worshipper."

"Lord Lorthmore with his mouth open. Bad show! Down six for Lorthmore."

"You look lovely, Lilibet, nice smile and manner. Score ten for the Queen of England."

I found all of this charming, providing a wonderful inside view of the royal family. Then Sir Hew found that they didn't wish to see just the rebroadcast, but wanted to see the entire taping. That would take many more hours. He quickly arranged a light supper for the gathering. When it went on into the evening, he knew he had to get wine and a light snack. This was beyond his catering skill, so he called his wife to come and help.

Mrs. Weldon had more food sent in from a London restaurant and did the best she could, but when it went on into the late evening, she went into a small panic. At that point Mrs. Weldon whispered to her husband, Sir Hew: "Darling, don't these people have any *castles* to go home to?"

I had an experience on my first visit to London that I shall never forget. After dreaming about it, I sometimes still awaken at night in a cool perspiration.

What happened was that I arrived alone ahead of my staff on a weekend. I was thrilled to walk away the evening by myself. Everything I saw—every street sign, every church, literally *everything*—was a thrill to me. I didn't have to know where I had been—I could find that out later—but as you know London is the greatest "walkabout" in the world.

I returned to the hotel about 10 P.M. and found a note under my door. It read, "My car will meet you and Mrs. Paar at 6 o'clock P.M. and carry you to Leatherhead in Surrey. Black tie. Lord Beaverbrook."

I knew, of course, who he was, since I know more about England that I do about my own country. Lord Beaverbrook was one of the most influential men in England and the publisher of the *Daily Express*, one of the largest newspapers in the world, with a circulation in the millions.

I was certainly not going to go for many reasons. I did not have evening clothes, Mrs. Paar was not with me, and I am not at ease in surroundings beyond my ken or control. Tommy Cochran, my associate, arrived the next day and said, "Whether you like it or not, you are going. I will call Beaverbrook's staff and inform them that Miriam is not in England, but I will accompany you."

Tommy is always prepared with evening clothes and anything else that might be required anywhere. Cochran, who was with me on all my shows for nearly twenty years, has clothing and uniforms for any occasion. In a moment, he is ready for weddings, funerals, and in Rome, when he met the Pope, he was better dressed than His Holiness. Tommy is so Catholic that he goes to mass all Sunday morning; in fact, he keeps going until Luchow's opens. If there isn't a *mass* scheduled anywhere, he finds a clean Italian movie.

Well, since he was in charge of protocol on "The Tonight Show" and to keep me out of trouble, I agreed to go. I wore just a dark suit and a somber tie. Off we went. I was scared to death because frankly I don't like the unknown or any social challenge.

A Rolls-Royce (would the plural of that be "Rolls-Reese"?) "carried" us to Lord Beaverbrook's weekend home in the country, an hour from London.

There I was introduced to Lady Dunn; Lord and Lady Balfour (his father authored the Balfour Declaration, which created the state of Israel); Mr. and Mrs. Michael Foote (the present head of the Labor Party); and a Lady so-and-so (who, I learned, was Beaverbrook's mistress). She was pretty elderly to be a mistress, but what the hell, I thought, whatever makes a man happy . . . Maybe knitting turns him on.

Beaverbrook was a gnomelike man and very serious. I could not figure what I was doing there or why there was a dinner in my honor. They all grilled me on American politics and wanted to know all about Fidel Castro, whom I had recently met in Havana. Still, why me? There was either some mistake, or else they thought the "Tonight" program was a powerful influence in America, something I never claimed or wished. If that had been true (which it was not), there would have been a terrible responsibility that would have destroyed my reputation as an unpredictable personality.

To this day I am not certain. Surely NBC did not arrange such a soiree. NBC couldn't be that influential in England. My best guess is that it was probably a favor to Joe Kennedy, the former Ambassador to the Court of St. James's, who was an intimate of Lord Beaverbrook. The Kennedy boys' father was a big fan of the "Tonight" program.

The noble group wanted to know how I could fight with the press in America. How could anyone challenge Walter Winchell and survive? It was easy, I said.

As I would answer their questions in my frank, rather unprofessional manner, I could hear them whisper, "It's incredible." "I simply cannot believe my ears." They apparently expected Eric Sevareid or Joe Alsop; what they got was an uneasy young man who stuttered, although in Britain stammering is an almost acquired affectation—a sign of aristocracy. Maybe they thought I was an abandoned royal left on the doorstep of the *Mayflower*.

Tommy Cochran was worried, as when he once forced me to go to a party of Elsa Maxwell's where he insists that I said, on meeting the Duchess of Argyle, "I wear your husband's socks."

After dinner, as we were chatting over brandy and cigars, Lady Dunn announced, "Mr. Paar, I hear you're a genius. Say something funny."

I explained that I had always felt a special fondness for the British and that one of my great-great grandfathers had deserted at Valley Forge. I commented on the British love of tradition and old monuments, and told how one man tried to get me to take an hour's drive just to see an eighty-year-old Coca-Cola sign.

As I tossed off my little sallies, I was getting no great reaction from the guests. Lady Dunn looked particularly bleak. Still I plunged valiantly on, determined to wring a laugh from my little audience.

I mentioned the British fondness for titles. We didn't have that sort of thing in America, I reminded them, although we did elevate Elvis Presley to sergeant. This drew a slight smile from one of my titled listeners. The reason Americans don't have customs like being knighted, I explained, is that you couldn't get anybody to kneel down in front of someone holding a sword.

"You don't seem very fond of the British," Lady Dunn remarked, as I sputtered to a stop.

"To the contrary, I love the British! Who else sent a Hallmark card when you lost India?"

I reminded them that America joined England in both great wars. One of them said, "But you came in rather late!" "Perhaps," I stammered, "you start your wars too soon."

I was on a roll now . . . I continued, "We could communicate in a common language, though your speech is certainly more euphonious than our flat accents. But," I said, "I have always felt if you awaken an Englishman in the middle of the night, shake him, and surprise him, he would speak just like us."

At that, Lady Dunn and the rest of the distinguished guests finally all roared with laughter.

We left at midnight, and hurrying back to London before the Rolls turned into a pumpkin, I asked Tommy what he thought. He said, "Well, as a peasant you were a hit. However, I still think someday you'll be beheaded."

Turning now from the ridiculous to the absurd, we later had the famous—in England—"Goon Gang" on the radio shows from London. They were a kind of middlebrow Three Stooges. There were four of them—Harry Seacome, Spike Milligan, Michael Bentine, and Peter Sellers—but only the last traveled well. The others never made it in America. Although they used many old American jokes, they were quite inventive with an Ernie Kovacs kind of humor. They became the paradigm for the present Monty Python group.

British humor then had two speeds—either Noël Coward, Bea Lillie, and Joyce Grenfell, or comedy so low and boring it could never be accepted in America. The English have a penchant for men dressing up as women. In any English sketch you can always expect someone to say, "He dropped his knickers," and this causes great laughter. And goosing a nun is high comedy.

We see the best of English theater on Broadway, and certainly their television dramas are better than anything we do here. But if you could see their daily television fare—on the whole ours is better produced, written, and performed. At that time, for instance, can you believe that the biggest hit and longest-running musical in London was *The Black and White Minstrel Show?* I kid you not!

What was not known about this simulated minstrel show was that the music, with some rather great deep-baritone voices, imitations of our black voices, was pretaped. There was a live orchestra in the pit, but the singers were on tape. This meant that the orchestra had to follow the taped voices, and the actors on stage had to "mouth" the words that were on tape. Well, the night I saw the show there had been some electric power trouble in that part of London, which slowed the tape down slightly. Only a professional would have noticed, but I understand things like that; it became hilarious. The orchestra was trying to stretch the notes and the tempo; the singers were trying to slow their mouth motions down. Most of the audience thought it was a comedy effect, and it was one of the funniest moments ever to those who knew what was happening.

When I first met Malcolm Muggeridge on our "Tonight" shows from London, he was a dashing charmer. Malcolm had been the former editor of *Punch*, the British humor magazine not unlike our old *New Yorker*. He was quite a ladies' man and could win medals for drinking. Miriam and I would always go out to Robertbridge and have lunch with him and his saintly wife, Kitty. Now Malcolm is practically a stoic. He became the most sincerely, intellectually religious person I have ever known. He has had great influence on my life and thinking.

Our show was involved in an international incident that was not known in America. On our program in the States, Malcolm had said that the monarchy was an anachronism; the Queen made silly speeches, and the whole ridiculous charade should be abolished.

Well, it really hit the fan in England! There is a famous club in London, the Garrick, whose membership of literary, theatrical, and political personages is the *crème de la crème* of the United Kingdom. A membership trial was held to expel Malcolm from the club. NBC released a transcript of the broadcast to the committee without my knowledge. I would not have, as it meant offering non-legal testimony against a friend. Anyway, who do you think defended Muggeridge in the trial acting as his defense counsel? Robert Morley! I do wish I could have seen that. It never got to a judgment because Malcolm resigned with a very witty speech, and he and Robert Morley walked out of the kangaroo court together. I miss all the fun!

My dear friend, Muggeridge, was once a teacher in India and was enrolled to help by any means he could think of to cut the birthrate in that melancholy and mostly illiterate country. The plan that was devised was a string of colored beads to be worn as a necklace.

The beads were to teach the Indian women the "rhythm method" of birth control by different colors. There were so many green beads for the safe sexual period, four red beads for the menstrual period, then fourteen green beads again until the fertile period, followed by four orange beads to warn of conception, then back to green.

It took some explanation by Malcolm. It was like setting a clock—you had to teach the women to get in sync with their own body's nature cycle.

The Indian ladies loved the necklaces but believed the beads in themselves had some mystical, medical magic and began to change the beads around to make more pleasing color patterns.

Well, the birthrate zoomed, and my friend had to get out of the sexual jewelry business. Score eight points for the *Kāma-sūtra*.

Malcolm's father was a member of Parliament. His wife, Kitty, was related to the Webbs, who were the founders of the Socialist movement in England, although Muggeridge had little use for politicians. He told me he had voted only once in his life. That intrigued me—what made him vote the one time?

"Well," he said, "I just had to. There was this one candidate who had been committed to an asylum and upon discharge was issued a certificate of sanity. Well, now, how could I resist? What other politician anywhere has an actual medical report that he is sane? I simply had to support him!"

Before the war, my wistful friend was one of Britain's most respected journalists and in his twenties was a correspondent sent to the Soviet Union. Actually, he went as a believer in Communism, but in three months he became a confirmed anti-Communist and stayed another two years writing coded dispatches, exposing what he found to be an evil system.

He looks upon life as an *opéra bouffe*. His own experience is a comedy of errors. For instance, in the Second World War Malcolm was in British Intelligence (MI6) and was assigned to a neutral African country to spy on a German officer, who later turned out to be the secret agent of another branch of British Intelligence! More ironic still, the man in charge of Muggeridge's unit later defected to the Soviet Union—the notorious Kim Philby!

I recall at the time when there was so much in the press about President Kennedy's sexual activities, Malcolm claimed that most politicians are "positive rams." He told me that a former Prime Minister, David Lloyd George, who was a "wham, bam, thank you, ma'am" advocate, and whose chariot was always on fire, had said, "Love is all right if it doesn't take up too much time!"

Robert Morley is just about the most constantly amusing man I have ever met, and yet it will be very difficult to write about him. It's his manner and attitude that I enjoy. He does not deal in anecdotes or epigrams, but anyone who knows him will tell you he is the best companion ever. It's his understated speech and eccentric views that make me laugh.

He lives in Henley near the Thames River and likes to play croquet without a ball. I can't explain it, but I have played with him. You simply walk around with the mallet and make strokes at *nothing*, and he tells you whether you have gone through the hoop or not. He insists that one of the greatest disasters in the world was the invention of the ball. Robert explains, "If you give a ball to a child, the child will quickly throw it away, which is the proper thing to do. We force balls on children. Very harmful."

He is a chronic gambler and constantly in need of money.

Morley is wonderful on a stage but doesn't take acting seriously. However, he enjoys selling tickets. He told me, in that soft manner of his, "I simply enjoy seeing people buy tickets for my shows. When they come to the theater, I don't care what they do. They can eat chocolates; they can kiss and cuddle, fall asleep; they can come late, leave early. I don't care. I have their money! I am there if they need me."

He is a fine writer. He wrote *Edward My Son*, which became a big hit on stage and screen. He does all his writing in a covered gypsy wagon parked on his back lawn.

His good friend, actor Peter Bull, who looks like Robert, (together they weigh close to five hundred pounds), were naked and about to jump in a pool one day. Robert said to Peter, "Oh, Bullie, what a shame Rubens is not here to paint us."

I have known Robert for twenty-five years. I attended his son's wedding and the christening of his first grandchild, where Noël Coward was the godfather. Through Robert I met Bea Lillie, who lived nearby. Many nights in London, Robert, Bea, Gladys Cooper, and I would have dinner. The first night we dined, Robert let the restaurant owner know that it was his birthday. We were not given a check, and I really believed it was his birthday, but he did the same thing every night in a different restaurant. Robert said, "Even if we get a check, there will be a bottle of champagne sent to the table. Restaurant owners enjoy making a fuss."

Robert loves to cause confusion, and whenever he can, he starts a small confrontation between others and then sits back to watch the fun. He did it to me often. Once he insisted that I put a man on a "Tonight" show from London with him whom he had read about. It turned out to be very difficult to handle for me, but Robert thought it was hilarious. You see, the man *really* believed his theory that the world was flat and had founded a Society of the Flat Earth. When I discovered he was a seriously deranged person with maps and charts, then I didn't know what to do. I can kid a kidder, I can handle drunks, dope addicts, egoists, but there is no sport in shooting down a man with a belief.

When I once told Robert how proud we Americans were to have a man walking on the moon, Morley believed it was nonsense and one of the great publicity stunts of all time. I said, "Surely you saw the pictures with our men on the moon."

Robert replied, "You can do anything with a camera."

Later, when I was on with a weekly prime-time show, I went to London without writers or a producer because all I was planning to do was make a tape with Judy Garland. But when I got there, Robert talked me into doing a whole hour from London without my staff since he and Judy would help me put a show together. It seemed like a good idea because the costs wouldn't be much more, and then I would have a complete hour-length show from London and not just an insert for a program in America.

We hired a big orchestra and theater; a large audience of British people came to see us. I had plenty of material for an opening monologue; then Judy would sing, and we would talk with Robert and his guest. There was no script or written words. Well, Judy was high on everything the night of the show: from "uppers" to a little wine and perhaps Vick's VapoRub.

When I first saw Judy that night, with that crooked little smile she had when she was in orbit, I knew it was going to be a difficult but fun evening.

Then Robert Morley came, all smiles because he had managed to get Winston Churchill's Mad Hatter son, Randolph. The younger Churchill, more than anyone I can think of, really suffered from being his father's son. He was a first-rate journalist, a courageous soldier (he and the writer Evelyn Waugh parachuted behind the lines in Yugoslavia during the war), and an astute politician, but sadly he was an alcoholic. He drank four scotches an hour, and although he never appeared drunk, he would become very mean and combative. He was fascinating in a Monty Woolley kind of way—irascible, insulting, interesting.

It was a dangerous hour. I honestly believe that almost anyone else would have canceled rather than go on. But I had learned that reality is what makes television, and the only trick is to let the audience know in some manner that "there are problems on this stage tonight." And if you have the trust of an audience and can convey to them that they are seeing a real "event," they will go along, and it will become an experience for everyone. It turned out to be a marvelous show.

One thing about television—I found this out after the invention of video tape, which allowed us to see our work after the fact—is that a given show is never as good as you think, but it's also never as bad! It's never as bad, because those are live human beings up there, and when their stories die, their acts don't work, they can't hit the notes, they become *us!*

Morley's most outrageous behavior with me was to ring up at my hotel in London and say, "You simply must bring Miriam to the country tomorrow. You can take Gladys Cooper and me to lunch at a rather good, expensive restaurant I've already picked out. And then, we will all go off to a school where I am speaking to the children."

It was a wonderful lunch, and off we did go to this upper-class school. There were several hundred teenage children and the faculty sitting on a grassy hill. And Robert spoke amusingly for half an hour (he's great with young people), and then he said, "And now my big surprise for you dear young people. We are so lucky to have with us this afternoon an outstanding American. He is an intimate of the powerful men in the United States and is considered by many to be a possible choice for high public office. A man of unquestioned Liberal credentials. My friend Jack Paar, who will explain to you 'what the Americans are trying to do in Viet Nam.'"

I made an absolute ass of myself by trying to explain what I didn't believe in myself. It was so terrible. Gladys and Miriam had a wonderful afternoon hiding behind a tree listening. No tree could hide Robert, but he found it roaringly funny from behind a bush.

Bea Lillie, the great comedy star, was a pal of mine. She is now in her late eighties and has been out of touch with the world for ten years; she still lives as I write this. Mary Martin, when in England, always tries to see her, but Bea has forgotten everybody. She was so wonderful on stage and yet had such a tragic personal life. Bea Lillie was really Lady Peel, having married Lord Robert Peel. Bea would explain, "I'm *Lady* in my own wrong."

Her husband died, and then her life became her son. Bea Lillie was a favorite of the royal family and an intimate of Churchill. In the Second World War, her son went into the British Navy and was assigned to a minor ship. The boy was quite content, but Bea would have none of it. With her connections, she had him transferred to an important ship. It was immediately blown up, and the boy was killed. She never recovered completely from this tragedy.

The word *camp*, a show business expression, has taken on an androgynous, epicene, homosexual meaning, but its original theatrical definition was someone whose "act or manner" was so outrageous, *outré*, outside reality, that it became high comedy. I always thought that Bea Lillie was the original "camp." Jack Benny, Frank Fay, or more recently someone like Paul Lynde have been considered "camp." However, in the case of Lynde he may have had a problem. My good friend, June Carroll, the singer and composer, traveled with Paul in *New Faces*. When he misbehaved, she would caution him, "Paul, if you can't be a gentleman, at least be a lady." Lynde was one of the best-ever sketch actors in farce.

Auntie Bea, as we called her, practically invented the genre. We were good friends, and I knew her stories and lyrics by heart. It was a good thing I did, because in her later career she became very forgetful in the middle of a routine and would fake a pause with a twinkle in her eye that said, "Help me!" This would break us up; we both knew the problem, but the audience, who didn't know, would laugh at our laughter. Bea lived with a guy whose name was John Phillip, a former dancer I believe. He had, some of us thought, a Svengali-type control over her. When Bea and I did shows together, just sitting and talking in London or New York, Phillip would crawl on the floor below the camera lens and make gestures at her like a lion tamer. It frightened many of us, but it kept her attention, however strange it must have appeared to the audience in the studio. We all worried about their relationship, but when the going got tough and Bea became senile, it was mainly John who took care of her. So score ten points for John Phillip.

Back to Robert Morley, whom many of you will know better as the spokesman for British Airways. Robert is married to the daughter of one of the most beautiful women in the theater in England or America, the late Gladys Cooper. I knew Gladys when she was in her seventies, and no doubt about it, even then, her face was the most beautifully sculptured I had ever seen. Your first reaction had to be: what a classic beauty she must have been in her youth! Pictures of her then will convince you. We would meet out at Morley's home, and the first time we met in the rain at Henley, she was wearing a Courrèges yellow raincoat, hat, and boots. At seventy she was a knockout.

However, my story about her is that she and Robert, her son-in-law, were inseparable. They were always together, in America, in Europe, in the Orient, or at any of the gambling tables of the world. His wife, who was her daughter, was seldom included. Gladys and Robert were the best friends of all the "in-laws" I had ever encountered.

When Gladys turned eighty she was appearing in a play at the St. Martin's Theatre in London. On the night of her birthday, the theater was full of course, as she was a great favorite of the English.

Well, about twenty minutes into the show, a butler walked onto the stage carrying a silver tray with a note. Gladys was stunned because it was not in the script, but being a true pro, she took the envelope and read, "Stop this play at once!"

You see, Robert had bought out the entire theater and filled it with her friends, and a great birthday party then filled the stage. Those two were crazy about each other, and I believe they even asked "her daughter/his wife" to join them.

Morley on the TV commercial for the airline always says, "British Airways will take care of you." I am sure they will, but I hope that British Airways takes care of Robert. He's rare and quite a wonderful man.

Another English beauty, whom I met through Robert and Gladys, was then in her seventies, and her name was also Cooper (no relation). She was Lady Diana Cooper, a very witty, eccentric woman of noble lineage. She was the wife of Duff Cooper, a British statesman and writer who was best known as the United Kingdom's Ambassador to France. She is really a legend in her own time and in the thirties, forties, and fifties was considered by many as one of the most handsome women in Europe.

Like many of the nobility, Duff Cooper and Lady Diana were

always on the edge of bankruptcy, and yet they always had at least two servants and a driver. I never knew how they managed, but she was quite interested in "how would one go about getting on one of those curious quiz shows in America where they gave you sixty-four thousand dollars or something." I said I was quite certain they would be delighted to have her.

Lady Diana said, "I'm sure they would let me win because, dear boy, they must be 'winkled' [rigged]."

"No, Lady Diana, I am certain they are not." (How little I knew. They were, it turned out, "winkled.")

She knew absolutely everybody in England and France. She would dine with Winston Churchill, all of the premiers of France of the fifties and sixties and was one of the most influential women of her time. She found the former King Edward VIII, then the Duke of Windsor, and Wallis Simpson quite common. She now is in her late eighties, but at eighty-two she had several auto accidents. She parks her car wherever she wishes and simply leaves a note on the windshield: "Dear Constable—Don't be upset. I am off to the dentist's."

Sadly, as it happens, she is now quite forgetful. A few years ago, at a garden party, a lady approached her, and Lady Diana rushed by, only to realize that it was the Queen Mother. She hurried back to the lady, did an arthritic curtsey, and said, "Sorry, ma'am, I didn't recognize you without your crown."

When her husband Duff Cooper died, she and her son John founded an annual literary prize to be given in his memory each year for distinguished writing in England. Annually, the presenter at the ceremony would be a person from the royal, literary, or political milieus—for example, Princess Margaret, Winston Churchill, or Evelyn Waugh. At the last presentation something terribly funny happened, and I quote briefly from the biography of Lady Diana written by Philip Ziegler:

> The worst gaffe at prizegiving came, however, from Diana herself some years later. Robert Lowell, who was to present the prize, suffered a serious nervous breakdown and was taken to a mental home. A substitute was arranged. Then at the last moment her son was told that Lowell had discharged himself and was on the way to the ceremony. At all costs he must be kept

away from any kind of alcohol. John rushed to the spot, to find
Lowell, on his third glass of champagne and talking to Diana.
"Darling," said Diana brightly, "I've just been telling this gentleman how the principal speaker has lost his marbles and been
carted off to a loony bin!"

Richard Burton has a conversational magic because of his
voice, vocabulary, and manner, but one cannot believe everything
he says. He is a great guest.

We were the first to get Richard on a "chat show." It wasn't
easy because his then-wife, Elizabeth Taylor, didn't care for me.
Judy Garland, on my show, had said some unkind things about
Liz and their days together at MGM, and I had said what became a much quoted line: "Elizabeth Taylor should get a divorce
and settle down."

Richard had just opened on Broadway in *Hamlet* but had
recently been quoted as saying some silly things, possibly when he
had been drinking, that were quite defaming to Sir Winston
Churchill. His press agent, John Springer, had arranged for Richard to be given an honorary degree at Fulton College in Missouri,
where Sir Winston had made the famous "Iron Curtain" speech.
Burton repeated a portion of the speech on our program and
spoke a tribute to Sir Winston, a rather high-type publicity ploy.
Richard gave his fee for appearing on TV to the college; and
then, not to be outdone, I matched it. So the whole thing cost
my show fifteen thousand dollars. I want you to know that I am
also a "fellow" of that college. At the moment I wish I had the
fifteen thousand and could give it to the Animal Fund.

I was surprised, when I first met him on a Sunday afternoon, at
how much softer, more vulnerable, and more likable Richard is in
person than the aloof Burton you know from stage and films.

Well, he was a wonderful guest after we supplied a few vodkas
and he got over his fright of being on TV without a script. He
told me how sometimes during the performance of *Hamlet* he,
out of boredom, would change the direction of the play and stand
on a chair on stage and do the famous soliloquy.

Elizabeth had warned him he was only to do the "Churchill
speech" and not to sit and talk with "that Jack Paar." And when
Liz warns you, you had better listen! Well, the studio audience

loved him, and I was enchanted. Finally I got him not only to do the prepared speech, but we sat and talked on camera, and finally he got up on a chair and did the soliloquy. (There is a picture of this in the book.) It was a smashing show, and we were certain to have a big rating.

Now this is important. Richard Burton's appearance was not on "The Tonight Show" but on a program that I did later in prime time on a Friday night. While the show was seen on Friday night, the taping of the program was done on Sunday night because Johnny Carson used the studio, the best NBC had and my old one, five nights a week. If I wanted that studio, I had to pretape on a Sunday. This story will have no point unless you remember that it was taped on Sunday for a Friday-night viewing.

On the Monday morning following the taping, I was excited knowing that I had a first, a most unusual program, when the phone rang at my home. It was Richard Burton. He couldn't have been more charming, but he said, "I just want you to know that I have been on television many times, but never have I had such reaction as last night's. I have wires and phone calls from all over the country. Thank you so much for having me, and Elizabeth loved it!" (She had stayed in the hotel.)

There was just one thing . . . that program wouldn't be seen on the tube for five more days!

David Niven, at a party or in an informal gathering in a living room, is one of the most amusing and skilled raconteurs I have ever heard. He can dominate a room and outtalk just about everybody. But on television on a conversation show, he becomes a basket case. It is not just the moment he is in front of an audience, but the day before—he goes to pieces and actually becomes ill. However, his two books of autobiography are certainly among the best recently written. I will not repeat any of his stories here because they are classics and have become well known.

Miriam and I spent several days with him at his home on Cap Ferrat in the South of France. Most surprising was to find the debonair British actor excusing himself to drive his then-young daughters off to their French school; David Niven ran a car pool in a Volkswagen station wagon!

We laughed for many days at his stories about his experiences in the Army. He was the first British actor to leave Hollywood and join the British armed forces in the Second World War. At the time of our visit, he was very upset because a book had just come out—a biography—which claimed that his friend Errol Flynn was not only a Nazi collaborator but a bisexual. David was livid at the accusation because he lived with Flynn in Hollywood for some time and felt it reflected on him. Flynn was a handsome fraud, I always thought, but the innuendo (not so subtle really) surprised me because I knew Flynn slightly, in Havana during the revolution, where he always had a sixteen-year-old tootsie in tow. However, his heroic escapades as reported by the press at the time were quite untrue.

I remember a line of David's about Errol. David said, "You could always count on Errol Flynn. He always let you down!"

There was a whimsical reference to the Flynn affair by Burt Reynolds last year. We attended a dinner in honor of Burt, and when accepting the award, he said, "I know that when I am dead, they will probably say unkind things about me. They will say that I was a Nazi and that I had an affair with Charles Bronson. Well, the Nazis don't mean anything anymore, and Charles Bronson has never returned my phone calls."

15

My Daughter, the Lawyer

We were told by our doctor that our child to be born would be a boy, and so we picked a name, Andrew, after my grandfather. When the baby turned out to be a girl, we changed Andy to Randy, and the name has caught on as a feminine noun.

When first I learned that we were to become parents, my pioneer instinct was to build a nursery, since I wasn't working anyhow. I am never happier than with a saw and two-by-fours; I still think that the sound of a nail going squarely into wood is one of the great pleasures in life. I have built many extra rooms on this house, Long Barn, and did all the construction, electrical work, placing of tile, the installation of sinks, bathtubs, etc.— everything but the final plumbing hook-up, which is beyond me. But at our home in California, above Sunset Strip, we had a useless porch over a garage. I did a good job and still drive by to see my work whenever I am on the Coast. There was just one small thing: The roof of the garage—the floor of the nursery—had a two-inch pitch for rain drain-off. I never could figure out how to correct that, since to the eye it looked quite normal. But when we brought Randy home and placed her in her crib at night, only to find that by morning she would have rolled to the lower side of the slanting bed and be trapped there in the clutches of gravity. I am sure that even then the infant realized that her life was going to be interesting and downhill. This may account to this day for her ability as a good skier.

It is always surprising that if anyone recognizes me at all and discusses my television career, the first question usually is whatever happened to Randy? I had forgotten that my daughter played an important part in my conversation on television. She usually traveled with her mother and me, sometimes appearing on camera in my filming of travels through Europe, Cuba, the Soviet Union, the Orient, and Africa. She chose a career in law, mainly I feel because she didn't wish to follow in her father's heavy/controversial footsteps. We always were very supportive of Randy, but I think she would have made an excellent television journalist. However, she is now a very successful trial lawyer in the city, and she is married to a fine young man from Darien, Connecticut, Stephen Wells.

When one spends most of his life speaking extemporaneously for many hours a night, naturally one's only child becomes a frequent subject, much I fear to her regret and embarrassment. However, she had many advantages growing up in the environment and company of some of the most celebrated people of the past twenty-five years. She would sit backstage or have dinner with Judy Garland, Liza Minnelli, Peter Ustinov, or Robert Morley; she was friendly with the Nixon daughters and all of the Kennedy clan. When her school insisted that in order for her to miss class during our travels, she would have to have a tutor, it was "Charlie Weaver" who would help her with her lessons. In our home, she would sit at the feet of Alexander King as he wove his wonderful stories. She has seen a good portion of the world and developed a curiosity like her father.

The melancholy side of such a young life is that it separates you from your peers and turns you into a loner. When her young classmates were having "sleep-in's" or playing rock records, Randy was either by herself studying or off on a trip with us to some exotic place. And "how are you to keep them down on the farm after they've seen Nairobi!" Why listen to endless recordings when Frank Sinatra would send her tickets for his concerts, or Ed Sullivan would invite Randy and her friends to come to his theater and see the Beatles? I can recall an incident in Hawaii, when we were in the same hotel with Elvis Presley. I did not know him but was friendly with his famous manager, Colonel Tom Parker. Parker wanted to arrange for her to meet Elvis, and she said in some embarrassment, "No, thank you, sir, I must study."

Elvis later sent her a saddle (for what reason I do not know as we never had a horse), but still she grew up a very modest, shy personality. She never liked any special attention and thought the fuss sometimes made over her father was silly.

Her mother, who is responsible for her upbringing and good manners, recently for the purposes of this chapter, reminded me of some stories about Randy when she was growing up.

Her first funny remark—and when she is funny, it's usually because it's quite logical—was when we first moved to Westchester, New York, and her mother drove her to the city. When she returned, she told me that she had seen a "fairy." Wanting to go along with her fantasy I asked, "And what did the 'fairy' look like?"

"A fairy looks like a *boat!*" she assured me gravely.

When she was five years old, she told us that she wanted her own mirror because, she said, "I'm tired of making up in *door knobs.*"

On her first trip to England, she was very familiar with the English from watching the early television shows, and her first reaction was, "All these people talk like Robin Hood."

José Melis, a Cuban-American, was the musical director of all my television shows and a pal from the Army. He had a son, Michael. Michael was a wonderfully personable young man but was a hyperactive boy, quite prone to trouble. Randy adored him, and he was her first "best friend." Well, one day he was in serious trouble, and the principal of the school had dealt a very severe punishment. We learned that Randy, in tears, marched into the main office and asked to see the principal. She said, "Michael was being treated unfairly, and whatever the charges, he didn't do it!"

The head of the school knew full well who Randy Paar was, but when she asked how Randy knew that Michael was innocent, Randy said, "Because I'm his sister."

When her mother later asked her why she would say that Michael was her brother, Randy said, "How would they know!"

She was an outstanding student, but when she was eight or nine, we learned that she was kept after school for misbehaving in class. It seemed she was caught talking during a study period and was disciplined by having to "saddle-soap" fifteen baseball catcher's mitts. Her mother asked her what was she talking about in class?

She explained that she and her friend were discussing Barry Goldwater!

Her mother taught her the value of saving and the young lady, finally, by Christmas gifts, birthdays, and a few chores, had accumulated seventy-two dollars in change, which she kept in a cigarbox. She would count out this money several times a week and if she miscounted and ten cents was missing she would go into shock. She really wanted to buy a one-hundred-dollar savings bond. I told her mother that I couldn't go through this scene twice a week, so why not just give her the twenty-eight dollars. Miriam said that she would not be "given" any money, she must earn it! A few nights later, Miriam says that after guests left, I called Randy and said, "Empty the ashtrays, and I'll give you twenty-eight dollars!"

Randy also is extremely sentimental, particularly about animals. She once had two little turtles who became quite a nuisance to us because whenever we went away on vacation we had to leave them with someone, and turtle-sitters are notoriously difficult to find. Then one of the turtles died. We buried him with full honors in a matchbox in our garden, after I had rejected Randy's proposal that he be buried at sea in our swimming pool, since he was amphibious.

Shortly afterward, when we were leaving for a vacation in Florida, I suggested to Randy that we take the surviving turtle to the neighboring creek and turn him free. At this she protested strenuously that the turtle would catch cold. Patiently, I explained that turtles don't catch cold. She then complained that the turtle would be lonely if turned loose in the creek without his late companion. I remained adamant and decreed that the turtle must go. With long faces, Miriam and Randy drove away on their sad mission. When they returned, they reported that the turtle had been dutifully deposited in the creek. However, they had first gone to the pet store and bought two other turtles. They then released all three together, so our erstwhile turtle would not feel rejected.

When any pet or wild creature died, Randy was disconsolate, and I was ordained by Miriam to assuage her grief by conducting last rites for the departed. On one occasion I was pressed into service for a double funeral. Her friend Michael Melis's goldfish had died, and Randy had found a dead robin in our yard. I built two little white crosses, and Randy tenderly wrapped the bodies in Saran Wrap and aluminum foil and then placed them lovingly in an envelope. "That's so the ants won't get them before they arise," she said. I then spoke a few words of eulogy, we joined in a little prayer, and the deceased were laid to rest near the swimming pool. This cheered Randy up immeasurably, and I have since been expected several times to deliver these eulogies. I had sort of become the George Jessel of the animal kingdom. Randy's concern for birds extends even to those being prepared for the table, as we discovered once when she found Miriam stuffing a turkey and sewing it up. That night, while we were in bed, Randy slipped downstairs and cut the strings with a scissors, evidently to ease the bird's discomfort. The next day, when we were eating the turkey, I offered Randy some stuffing. "I don't want any," she said, "and I don't see how the turkey stands it either."

When Randy reached school age, we discovered we had to take a stand on her method of upbringing. There were two schools of thought, we learned, on how to raise children. There was the Jean Kerr or "treat 'em firmly" school. Jean, a Westchester neighbor of ours, believes in the old adage of "whap 'em first and argue afterward." On the other hand, there was the progressive or "let 'em do what they want" school, typified by James Mason and his then-wife, Pamela, who were also friends of ours. Their then-six-year-old son, whom they called Charley Poo, smoked cigars, wore

a straw hat, and loved to listen to old Harry Richman records. He
has since grown up a charming young man, who is now an aide to
President Reagan at the White House.

Their daughter Portland, who was a friend of Randy's, learned
to swim when she was six months old and had been learning
other things at a correspondingly early age.

Portland once came to visit us, and Randy showed her through
our house.

"How many bathrooms does it have?" Portland asked casually.

"Four," replied Randy.

"Oh," said young Portland, in a voice dripping with disdain.
"We have six."

There was a long silence.

"I think we have two more in the attic," Randy said, "but I've
never bothered to go up there."

In raising Randy, Miriam and I tried to steer a middle course,
somewhere between the airy abandon of the progressive Masons,
who had Portland's childish crayon drawings hung in gold frames
in their magnificent Hollywood home, and the iron-handed rule
of Jean Kerr and her distinguished drama-critic husband, Walter.

Miriam and I reached a very practical compromise on discipline:
she did it all. Since I had always thumbed my nose at authority, I
approached the role of parent with trepidation. The idea of telling anyone, even a five-year-old, how to shape his destiny, when
my own seemed to have been sculpted by Picasso, seemed incon-
sistent. I felt that spanking a child could result in serious misunderstanding, a feeling that is borne out by a story told me by Gerald Peters, a Canadian entertainer.

Peters has a daughter named Sally, who was quite a handful.
On one occasion, when she was five years old, she was particularly
naughty. She was soundly paddled with a hairbrush and ran crying upstairs to her room. Her sobs gave way to silence, and Peters
became worried. Going quietly upstairs, he opened the door to
her room. Sally was standing in front of the mirror, her little skirt
held up, looking back over her shoulder to inspect the damage
from the spanking.

"Well, I hope you're satisfied," she said bitterly. "You've
cracked it."

When we moved from the West Coast to Bronxville, New York, my television work was either early in the morning (the CBS "Morning Show") or later (the late-evening "Tonight" program), so I became a weekend father. I tried my best to think of interesting, fun things to do to get Randy's attention. One of my better ideas was to secretly use Scotch tape and put giant dynamite caps, the size of a half dollar, to all her croquet mallets. When she and her young friends would wham a ball, the explosion, while safe, was thundering. There was no doubt in her mind who thought up that diversion. I was a big man for about an hour!

We always tried to take Randy with us on my travels in search of stories for the "Tonight" program. We would often run into trouble with the Bronxville school authorities about her taking two weeks off from class, but they finally consented if she would, upon return, address the student body on her experiences. Following one trip to Germany, Spain, Gibraltar, and then down to North Africa, she had to go on the stage at the school assembly and tell of her worldly knowledge. Miriam and I were in attendance. The little girl walked out and simply said, "What I learned . . . is that if you want to get a cuckoo clock, the best buys are in Munich."

That was it!

It becomes quite a problem for a father who works on television early in the morning or late at night to get enough sleep. It is also very difficult for children, who must spend much of their time tippy-toeing, whispering at what, to them, are normal daytime activities. My friend Jim Hartz, who did the "Today" program, had to be off from his home every morning at four-thirty. His children were severely disciplined if they made any noise before ten o'clock. On a Saturday morning, Jim could sleep as late as he wished, and no one was to make a sound. The children would make their own breakfast and then quietly go outside and play a silent softball game. This Saturday morning, the kids decided to fry bacon. They were ever so quiet, but then a fat fire broke out, engulfing the kitchen. The kids very quietly went into his bedroom, lightly touched their father's shoulder, and whispered softly, "Dad . . . Dad, the house is on fire!"

After the revolution in Cuba was over, I would often take my family to Havana. For many reasons, it was a very interesting place to be; there were hardly any tourists in those days, the hotels were empty, and the Hilton people would always give us the big penthouse suite at a reduced rate because they wanted to encourage tourists, and I would always film and talk about life there on television.

At the time, Castro's wife, from whom he was separated, ran a dress shop in the Hilton lobby. We got to know her and their young son, Fidelito, who was Randy's age. They were the only children in the whole hotel, so naturally they played and swam together.

It was a strange scene, with these two little kids playing in the pool, while two bearded bodyguards were lying on the verandas in swimming trunks with a white towel over their laps. In each of their laps under the towels were two machine guns. There was always the threat of a counterrevolution, and the little boy would be a possible kidnap victim.

When it came time for them to leave the pool, his nurse called to Fidelito in Spanish to get out. However, he was enjoying his swim and made no move to obey. Then one of the guards asked him in English to get out. Stubborn as his father, the nine-year-old youngster kept right on splashing around in the water. I decided to try a little of my fractured Spanish on him.

"*Adios* to *aqua!*" I yelled.

He hopped out.

On one trip to Cuba, Miriam, Randy, and I decided we wanted to go to a typical Cuban restaurant. We didn't want to go to any of the tourist-type places, so we enlisted a cousin of José Melis to act as our guide. He took us to an obscure little restaurant in the old section of Havana, where we planned to invite heartburn by sampling various fiery Cuban dishes.

Our guide had to go on to another date, so we found ourselves minus an interpreter in the restaurant which had only Spanish-speaking waiters. By a combination of fractured Spanish, acquired watching old Leo Carillo movies, and much violent gesturing, I managed to get us a martini and a lethal combination of black

beans, onions, and rice served by a waiter who must have operated a flame thrower under the Machado regime.

Finally came dessert. I was linguistically exhausted, and willing
to retire on my laurels of having successfully ordered our main
course, but Randy insisted on dessert. I finally consented on the
condition that it be something simple like ice cream. With a sigh,
I summoned our waiter and resumed my arm-waving.

"*El cremo . . .*" I tried. "*La cremola? . . . el bovino? . . .
la chilly cremo? . . . el mucho cremo?*"

I finally shivered and went, "Moooo."

Suddenly the waiter's swarthy face broke into a grin.

"*Si, si, Señor,*" he beamed. "*Helado.*"

From his smile of recognition, I decided I'd hit the right cate-
gory.

Now for a flavor. Chocolate seemed the simplest, so I began to
try to order that in my scrambled Spanish.

"*El chocolate?*" I said. "*El browno? . . . tres chocolate? . . .
une darko?*"

The waiter broke into another smile of recognition.

"*Ah, si, si. Helado de chocolate. Si.*"

"No, Papa!" wailed Randy, as the man headed for the kitchen.
"I wanted peppermint stick!"

I was often given credit, most of it undeserved, for discovering
and helping new talent. There was much too much talk about it
by our friends in front of Randy, and she got the idea that anybody who appeared on my show was a "discovery." I was in the
bathtub one evening, and Randy yelled, "Come quickly. The
man you discovered is on the television!"

I had no idea who it could be, but had enough vanity to dry
myself quickly and rush to see who this great "discovery" was that
had found employment on another show. It was H. V. Kalten-
born, who was then nearly eighty years old.

Randy always had a level head and could needle her father in
strange ways. Once we were being driven in England past Windsor Castle and were on the main highway passing the estate.
Coming down a dirt road that crossed the highway was a Rover
station wagon driven by a young lady wearing a *babushka.* Our

driver said, "My God, it's the *Queen*." There was no doubt about
it—it was the Queen driving alone. She naturally had to stop for
the highway as we drove by. We were thrilled, and Randy said,
"Tell me, Father"—she uses that word on formal occasions—
"how in heaven's name did the Queen know exactly when *you*
would be passing?"

We would often have dinner with the Robert Kennedys, and
one time it was at the swanky Colony Restaurant. Randy was
with us, and her mother cautioned her to address them as Mr. or
Mrs. Kennedy. She was shocked to have to be told such a simple
thing. Randy was very quiet, and near the end of the first course,
I heard my daughter say, "Mr. Attorney General, I have three
shrimp left, would you like them?" (Of course, he took them. His
mother taught him manners.)

On one of our trips to Spain, we met Sam Bronston, the
producer, who was then making a film, *King of Kings*, at a studio
outside of Madrid. He asked Randy if she wanted to play a small
part in the picture. She thought that would be a ginger, creamy,
peachy idea and can still be seen in a small scene on television
reruns. In the film, Randy is accompanying Jesus, played by
Jeffrey Hunter, on a donkey into Jerusalem. The experience for
her was so moving that she has never cashed her pay check. She
was, however, very disturbed when between scenes Jesus sat in the
shade with sunglasses drinking Coca-Cola.

Randy slept through her father's success on the "Tonight" program and had little interest or understanding of what went on
after ten o'clock, but because of my controversial personality she
began to be affected by the other children at her school, who
would hear their parents discussing me. It became very difficult
for her, so we took Randy out of the Bronxville public school
and sent her to a wonderful academic institution: Miss Masters
School, in Dobbs Ferry, New York. Most of the students "lived-
in" at Masters and were of a mixed bag of ethnic and geographic
origins, and her identity was never a problem. However, she lived
at home, and we joined a car pool of similar girls who lived
nearby. Often I would drive the car from Bronxville to Dobbs
Ferry.

I enjoyed this as I could listen to the four youngsters talk as I drove, and I picked up a great deal of material for the program. On such a trip, I listened as they were talking about the day's activities. It seemed that a Mr. Jovanovich, whose daughter was in Randy's class, had addressed the honor students that afternoon. Mr. Jovanovich, the publisher, had spoken of a new guru, an author-client of his named Marshal McLuhan, and had said that he was an important new voice to be listened to. McLuhan was the most prescient philosopher of the future, and the students should read and study him.

I was asked, "Mr. Paar, what do you know of Marshal McLuhan?"

I, at that time, had never heard of him, and Randy was crushed since she believed that her father knew everyone and many things. Then, one of the kids asked, "Mr. Paar, why don't you talk to the student body about . . . whatever it is that you do?"

I feared answering because I never felt that I had much to say to young people, having only gone to the tenth grade. These kids spoke French and worked out math problems for kicks in the car. Randy was embarrassed when I admitted that I was an authority only on minor, exotic, historical characters like Zsa Zsa Gabor. However, I made a mental note to check up on this subversive, mysterious McLuhan. I was determined to read whatever this phony had written and would dazzle the kids on my next chance to drive them.

The next day, I went to the book store and asked for anything written by a Marshal McLuhan. I was told that there was just one publication available entitled *Understanding Media*. I bought it and on the way home opened the book that turned out to be one of the most important written in the past ten years. You can easily check up on this, but let me tell you that the first words of the book, not the fifth or the sixth but the first words, were: "Jack Paar once said—."

There were many references to me and my contribution to television later in the book, but again the first words were: "Jack Paar once said—."

Well, on my next turn as driver of the car pool, I waited to introduce the subject again and was stopped with a request from one of the girls. "Mr. Paar, tell us about Zsa Zsa!"

I kid you not!

In passing later Marshal McLuhan moved to Bronxville and wrote me a note asking if we could meet. We had dinner together many times, and although he was, without question, a real genius along with other modern thinkers such as Buckminster Fuller and Alvin Toffler, he was the most egocentric person I had ever met. (His wife was another saint.) The egos of actors are nothing compared to those of academia.

He told me a story that has haunted me for many years. Marshal had had a brain tumor the size of a lemon, and the operation to remove it took something like twenty-two hours. "So long, in fact," he said, "that the surgeons performing the delicate operation could not leave. And *had to be fed intravenously!*"

Randy was very happy at Dobbs Ferry and upon graduation had chosen the discipline of law for her future career. I had wished it had been some form of journalism because she had a very inquisitive mind and even as a young lady was a dangerous debater. An example:

"Randy, don't you realize that there are millions of people starving in India!"

"Name two," my daughter would reply.

Well, so be it! I knew the dean of Stanford Law School, and off we went—Miriam, Randy, and I—for the appointment. I was on my very best behavior in the interview with the faculty, in California, but my daughter, while unfailingly polite, was not enthusiastic. They must have sensed it because they asked to interview Randy alone. Months later, when she received the notice that she was not chosen, she was delighted. We were crushed!

What kind of daughter did we have? All those previous academic accolades, and she was turned down. How could I ever face Zsa Zsa or Buddy Hackett again? Surely, she would end up working at MacDonald's and would look silly in those funny hats! I was ready to give up, but then a notice came "that Randy Paar was accepted at Harvard (Radcliffe)." On her own she had applied to one of the most prestigious schools in the country and was chosen! We never discussed it, but I feel that in that private interview with the Stanford faculty she told them of her real wish to go to Cambridge.

Since we are a very close family, it was the saddest day of my life when she left on her own to go up to Harvard. The house, while considerably neater, was very lonely. Our daughter, perhaps like yours, was not known for picking up things. You could always track Randy, like following the tracks of spoor in Africa—a stocking here, a pair of pants there, one shoe, a brassiere—you knew Randy was home! I run a tight ship hygienically, and my daughter's room was environmentally a disaster area. When times were good, we always had a housekeeper to keep the bubonic plague from breaking out on her floor. I tell you this because during a break in her studies, she informed us that she had joined a task force from school and was going down to Alabama to teach illiterate black mothers how to diaper their babies!

The sixties were worrisome days for parents, with all the crazies and protest marches. Her best friend was Mary McCarthy, Senator Eugene McCarthy's daughter, and she joined his campaign. When I found that they were spending their weekends living in basements in New Hampshire and going from door to door in the snow asking for support, I offered to help. Miriam and I, when last we voted, were registered Republicans. (I had never voted all the time I was on television to prove to myself at least that I was nonpartisan.) We said we would join the senator. I gave a considerable amount of money to his cause, as I am very fond of him as a man. My views about the Viet Nam War were ambivalent, but I did what I could to help end what was becoming an unpopular cause.

We had been very close to Robert Kennedy, and when he entered the Presidential race, somehow and I forget how, we all offered to help. Randy spent the summer working in Washington at Bobby's office, and I ended up being appointed "co-chairman (with Burke Marshall) of the Westchester Democrats for Kennedy." I was still a registered Republican, but no one ever asked me. So if you are confused about my politics, think how I feel. I don't even know what the hell I am, or were, or was!

One time, Miriam and I returned from Africa on a filming safari. It was a Sunday morning, and when we arrived at our home by taxi, we noticed that Miriam's Cadillac was missing from the garage. However, in the driveway was a broken-down Volkswagen.

There was a note in the kitchen: "Dear Mom and Pop—We drove down from Boston yesterday in that Volkswagen and have borrowed Mom's car to drive to Washington to protest. We hope to return to have dinner with you on Sunday night. Love, Randela." (This, I assumed, was Yiddish for Randy.)

Well, we were tired from our long air journey from Nairobi but did the best we could on a Sunday to get food in the house for the return of the mighty gladiators. Miriam put candles on the table, I got out the best wine and silverware, and we went to the freezer and got out a fancy frozen French meal. And waited!

That evening our daughter arrived with three of the strangest looking boys I had ever seen: long hair, of course, attempts at beards, but get this—not even T-shirts, but what are called tank shirts, which expose the armpits, naked and hairy. There Miriam and I are dressed, with candles glowing and chilled wine.

The boys—Leo, Herman, and Harry—were very articulate and personable, but what about those hairy armpits with Mâcon Blanc Pinot-Chardonnay '68? With all those candles going, I was afraid that if the boys reached for anything, they would start a fuzz fire!

We were in shock! The conversation, though somewhat strained, was interesting. Whenever I offered an opinion on anything, I was hit with a chorus of "Name two." So you see, it wasn't easy being a television star, a Republican-Democrat, conservative-radical, father, best friend, and pal of the oppressed.

The next morning the Freedom Fighters all left to return to Harvard. Randy, sensing that perhaps we were underwhelmed by her friends, thanked us and hoped we didn't mind. I whispered to her, "This is your home, but next time try not to bring anyone in who frightens the dogs!"

At about this time, Randy had formed some very close relationships at Harvard, both boys and girls, who to this date are her closest friends. There was one who intrigued me; her name was Margaret, and she is the daughter of a very prominent person. I was drawn to this young lady because she almost never spoke. She sat around with a most beautiful, Madonnalike smile on her face but simply did not speak. She graduated with a bachelor of arts degree, so understand there was no phrenic problem; Margaret was a mysterious observer of everything around her but not a commentator. Whenever Randy would call home from school, I would say, "Did Margaret say anything yet?"

The answer was always no, until one day on the phone Randy reported, "Margaret spoke last night."

"Yes," I asked with great interest, "tell me exactly what she said?"

Now here is the greatest non sequitur I have ever heard: "Margaret is having a problem," Randy continued, "and finally asked for our advice. She wanted to know if she should go to medical school or buy an *ironing board!*"

One of the most embarrassing stories of my life happened about this time. I was in the attic of our home and came across a mysterious, burlap-wrapped pole. I had never seen it before and took it downstairs and unwrapped it. I unfurled it, and my heart went into a small cardiac arrest. It was a flag, red with a white star. My God, I thought, my daughter has hidden a Viet Cong flag. Nothing could be worse. It's one thing to protest the war, but this kind of craziness I would not tolerate. That damn Harvard, I thought, their permissiveness would be the ruin of all the things and love of country that I have always felt.

Miriam, sensing my rage, cautioned, "Are you sure it's a flag of the Viet Cong?"

I explained that I, her husband, was no fool and that, sure as hell, I knew a Viet Cong flag when I saw it, but that I would call NBC and confirm it. I phoned the news department and sheepishly inquired about the description of the VC flag. They wanted to know why my interest, and I said, "You see, one of my neighbors' children has a hidden flag, and they are in a trauma. I have offered to help them."

However, NBC, one of the world's great news-gathering services, could not with any precision describe the Communist VC flag. Well, they didn't have to. I knew one when I saw one. So what was I to do? I took the flag outside and first sawed up the pole; then I poured lighter fluid over the folded flag and lit it. Not wanting to have the garbage man become suspicious and find traces in the can, I dug a hole and buried the ashes. Let old J. Edgar try and get something on me! I didn't, as they say, "get off the turnip truck last week."

That was the end of the story, I thought. Some months later Randy said, "Pop, did you see a burlap-wrapped pole in the attic?"

I slipped and said, "What flag?"

She replied, "Oh, good, then you did see it. Let's go up to the attic and find it. You see, at school the Turkish Ambassador's daughter is one of my best friends, and she asked me to keep their sacred flag for the summer!"

Near the end of her term at Harvard, all the students begin to study night and day for the finals. This is when they live on doughnuts, and gain weight, and break out in bumps, and cry a lot. I could never understand this because when I graduated from the tenth grade, I was simply asked, "Did you ever hear of Napoleon?"

I was always very quick and would write, "But of course, he was French, I believe, and quite short!"

No sweat!

One day I overheard this bit of conversation. Randy was talking with her favorite cousin, Jimmy Shroll, who was in medical school at the University of Pennsylvania. They were telling each other of the pressures of "finals" and how unfair some of the tests were. The students without ethical values would, instead of simply going to the library, use a razor blade and cut the passage out. (There were perhaps ten books for one hundred students in the library, containing information for the tests.) This left the rest with no reference book and no way to obtain it. And no excuse.

The young doctor-to-be said, "It's worse at medical school, because in the finals you have to dissect a frog. There are only two frogs to a student, and if you mess up the dissection you fail. But some kids steal your extra frog and hide them in their room. They then have three frogs. I had to pass on only *one frog!*"

When Randy graduated from Harvard with honors (*magna cum laude*), she entered law school at New York University. She got her own apartment, or rather we bought her a small apartment in what I felt was the safest part of Manhattan. It really was the most protected place in the city. It was surrounded by police night and day. We felt relieved because there were policemen even on the rooftops summer and winter. It was on Sixty-seventh Street, right next door to the Russian Mission Building.

In the last year of law school there is a tradition called the Moot Trial. This is a mock trial before real judges on a complex legal issue. The students who are picked to participate in the event (the varsity of legal debate), are given a situation of law and are required to prepare both the defense and prosecution of the case in a real court setting. After weeks of study, you can only really prepare for one side or the other, but you must be able to take "either side" on the flip of a coin before the courtroom trial.

Randy's team won the class, the University, the city, and the state competitions; and they came in third in the National Moot Trial of her year.

She graduated from law school with honors, and that's all I have to say on the subject. Forgive me if I have made too much of my daughter's scholastic career. I am certain that many of you are saying, "Why so much typing over one student? There are hundreds of young lawyers brighter than she."

I simply and modestly reply, "You may be right, but *name two!*"

16

Don't Leave Home Without It

The Paars are never happier or more excited than when boarding a morning flight for anywhere. I recommend a morning flight if you are going to Europe because of the time change, usually six hours forward, arriving in England or Europe later in their evening. The night flights are not as convenient because you arrive without a night's sleep early in their morning. With the excitement of arrival, you try to do things and find you are a basket case by noon, their time. With my plan you hit London and, after unpacking, hit the sack, get a good night's rest, and start off fresh in the morning.

I am sure that Karl Malden is right about not leaving home without it, meaning a credit card, but if you watch the commercials on television they suggest that you usually lose your credit card in some dinky country and always when it's raining. Never, but never, leave anything valuable in your room, especially in Italy. We have had bad luck there in Rome's finest hotel, The Grand.

This is not to be a travel guide but is meant to provide some observations, stories, and experiences that happened to us, which

Amani at seven weeks.

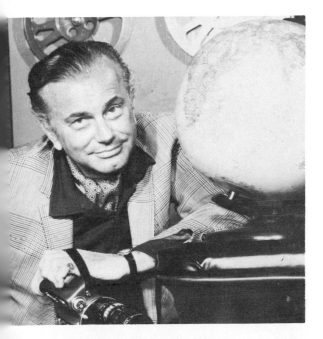

RIGHT, in London. (*Credit: Portman Press Bureau Ltd.*) BELOW, Richard Burton in a rare comic moment.

With Dr. Albert Schweitzer in Lambaréné, East Africa.

UPPER LEFT, Jane Goodall in Tanzania; UPPER RIGHT, Mary Martin in Brazil; BOTTOM, Ethel Kennedy in Hyannis Port.

A quiet Sunday with the Paars.

A surprise anniversary party given for us by Merv Griffin in Monte Carlo. The late Princess Grace is on the left.

Miriam and Randy. (*Credit: Stephen Wells*)

you might enjoy reading about since they didn't happen to you. "Paar's Law" states that if it's funny, it happened to us!

The first thing to be prepared for in most European countries is that even if you travel by train first class on an overnight sleeper and if there are three of you, one of you is going to sleep in a compartment with a stranger. That is always a shock. Since, naturally, if our daughter is with us, her mother and she take the compartment for two, and I am left with some Romanian who already has the lower bunk when I get there and is eating pickles most of the night.

After an overnight sleeper from Vienna to Venice, we arrived in the morning all excited. The first shock is that your bags are thrown out of the window to the station platform, and you have to go through a few minutes of Italian baby talk to get them back and be on your way. The gondola bit is very quaint, but by noon you wish they had other means of transportation. If God had meant for people to move around on the water all day, he would have given us webbed toes.

It was warmer in the fall than we expected, and Miriam decided that she wanted to get a summer dress for our stay in Venice. She shopped around and couldn't find much of a selection as it was then off-season. Finally, she found a shop with hundreds of dresses and went in. I watched from outside, and as she would take a dress off the hanger and attempt to hold it up, it would be rudely grabbed by the owner and placed back on the rack. Miriam would try again only to anger the owner more. Seeing this through the window I rushed in to find out what the problem was and heard the manager say, "Modom, zis is a *dry-cleaning* chop!"

If one gets tired of gondola trips, he can fly to Rome and see a stranger sight—nuns and monks on Vespa motor scooters racing past ancient ruins like the Coliseum and the Baths of Caracalla. The scooter riders almost all wear sunglasses and have wide smiles as they dart recklessly about. Rome is the only city I know where you can find people with bugs on their teeth.

Another idiosyncrasy of the Italians is their hotel bookkeeping system. We might be told, for instance, that the daily rate of our hotel suite was the *lira* equivalent of seventy-five dollars a day.

Yet, when I'd get the bill, it would be roughly double that. The answer lies in a little booby trap called extras.

They make a formidable list. Every Italian bill has a service charge of from fifteen to twenty percent of the total. Then there's a charge of around a dollar a day for central heating. I must say I didn't particularly notice the heat, but there it was on the bill. At some hotels there is even a visitor's tax. In addition, there is another little surcharge known as the general revenue tax, amounting to two percent of the bill.

If you order food in your room, there's a ten percent tax on that. If you order food or drink at the bar, the tax is six to eight percent. Finally, when you pay the grand total, the cashier affixes to the receipt a small and very official-looking government stamp, which is rather like a postage stamp.

This is your official notice that your bill is paid. Then, as a final gesture, they charge you for the stamp! No doubt about it, the Italians don't do things the way other people do. Therein, I imagine, lies much of their special charm. Since the Italians are famous for not paying their taxes, the tourists subsidize the government.

Another observation on the Italians, particularly in Rome, is their sexual attraction to the automobile. To see an Italian businessman or shopkeeper put on leather racing gloves simply to go a few miles home for lunch is amusing. Their fascination with the automobile is awesome. To pass an Italian on the road is an affront to his manhood. The reverence for the Fiat or Alfa Romeo is a sign of his virility. The American pulls into a service station for gasoline, the English for petrol, the German for benzine, the French for essence, but the Italian stops only for an artificial insemination.

The actress Peggy Cass—Peggy with the light brown voice, although she sounds much better since she had a throat lift—would often travel with us. She is Catholic, an old family friend, and a very witty lady. It was arranged that she would have an audience with the Pope while I was still looking for a Masonic Temple. Vatican etiquette requires that women received by the pontiff wear conservative black dresses with high necklines and long sleeves, and Peg was in a swivet about whether the dress she had would be proper for the occasion.

After days of fretting about what she would wear for the audience, Peggy finally sighed, "Maybe it would be better if they just blindfolded the Pope!"

Italian males, be forewarned, think nothing of pinching the derriere of a strange woman on the street and even consider it a mark of admiration to bestow such a playful tweak. Peggy got pinched and complained to a policeman. He, the cop, asked her to point out the man. She did, and the policeman shrugged, "Eetsah hokay. I know heem. He's alright."

With Miriam and Randy along, there was no opportunity for me to participate in Rome's favorite outdoor sport. We spent our time sedately visiting the Coliseum, the Forum, and other historical sights in the Eternal City, as well as watching the everchanging scene on the Spanish Steps below the Hassler Hotel, where we stayed.

We also visited the Catacombs, the underground burial grounds of the early Christians. There are many of these under the streets of Rome, and while they are of great historical interest, the cramped, dark tunnels are no place for anyone with claustrophobia.

Knowing that I'm allergic to close quarters (I even become panicky while driving through Rhode Island), Miriam looked doubtfully at the forbidding-looking entrance to the old burial chambers and asked our guide solicitously, "Do you have any *short* catacombs?"

So have a good time and keep your back to the wall—you men, too. There are a lot of tenors in Italy.

On your first visit to France, it's possible that you will share my early opinion that while you love France—the food and the scenery—you are not wild about French people. You never really get over that feeling, but on later trips you learn to enjoy France and almost ignore the local people, which is easy to do because they have already established that relationship. I always remember what a Latin professor who is an authority on the French, the Spanish, and the Italian once said when I asked how to simply explain the difference between the three countries. He said, "The Italian, for the *family*; the Spanish, for the *country*; the French, for the *self*."

From a show business standpoint—and after all that is all we know of the French, their entertainers—they are all remarkable for their personalities and smiles. For instance, Maurice Chevalier, Jean-Pierre Aumont, and my own Genevieve are almost unreal in their personalities; and that is what they are, "unreal." I have never met anyone in France who smiled or showed any concern for us at all. When I was constantly traveling and filming for my programs, I would stop and enjoy France, but I can't recall of wishing to film a single story there. I had dinner recently with Louis Jourdan, one of the most handsome men I have ever met, and asked him who his friends were in this country. Handsome Lou said, "I don't believe in friendship. I practice it but do not believe in it." The French, they are a funny race . . . !

We used to go to the South of France several times a year, mainly because Genevieve had a small farm at St.-Paul-de-Vence, a few hundred yards from the famous restaurant Le Colombe d'Or. On the Corniche, the road to Monaco, at the fishing village of Ville-Franche-sur-Mer, there is a road to the right down a very steep incline to the fishing village. It's perhaps half a mile almost straight down to the sea. At the bottom are several great peasant-type seafood restaurants. We went down that hill at dusk one evening and sat on the terrace, facing the road that we had just descended. It was a beautiful scene, but what I remember is one of the most unusual sights I had ever seen. On the road that we had just descended, now in darkness, I saw an inexplicable light about five feet off the ground coming down the road. I watched it fascinated. "What could it be?" Surely it was not an automobile with one headlight, too high for a motorcycle. I was mesmerized by this strange electric cyclops coming down the hill. It was like something from a science fiction movie. What could be the explanation for a single light five feet high off the road coming at me?

Well, my dears, it was a young Frenchman on a bicycle with a *flashlight* in his *mouth!*

In Athens we visited with NBC friends who were stationed there. I was amazed to see the kitchen of their modest home. It was a complete room of marble, beautiful marble, which is natural to that part of the world. The wife said to me apologetically, "We couldn't afford *Formica!*"

A few capsule words about Spain: I was so turned off by seeing a bullfight that, as an animal lover, I get livid just thinking about it. What I had not expected, nor would you if you have not been told about it, was the *cry* of the bull as the bastards stick him with *banderillas*. Hemingway is full of crap! Civilized people should not pay to see such brutality. *"Ole,"* my ass!

I know it's supposed to be a fair contest between man and bull, but as Bob Considine once remarked, you see more old bullfighters around than you do old bulls. I never like to see anything fixed, including parking tickets, and the spectacle is even less inviting if the victim is a brave bull. If the Spanish want to have fights where the victim is doomed from the start, it seems to me that they should use something like Volkswagens, not strong and noble animals.

Later that weekend I was most encouraged to learn that soccer seems to be taking over. I was watching my first soccer match with sixty thousand people in the stands, and the bullring down the street was quite empty. Again, *"Ole!"*

Perhaps you already know that Madrid is a very formal city with most unusual eating habits. I was always surprised and tried to get out of invitations to have cocktails beginning at ten o'clock and dinner often at midnight.

One of the finest hotels in Europe is the Ritz in Madrid, and I had lunch there. It is the only hotel I know of that will not accept as guests actors or people known to be in show business. The only theatrical people I know who ever got into the Ritz were Jimmy and Gloria Stewart. But old Jimmy registered by his official title, General James Stewart. *"Ole!"*

There are many fine restaurants in Madrid, but my favorite is Hortcher. I almost didn't make it the first time, since I wanted to eat at eight o'clock. That was too early, so Miriam and I arrived at ten. Still, we were in trouble because I was wearing a *gray* suit. They frown on gray suits in the evening.

Peter Ustinov had a strange experience there one night. He was dining when the waiter spilled soup all over his tie. The waiter asked Peter to remove his tie and said he would immediately have it cleaned in the kitchen. Peter took off his tie, but when the manager came by, he asked him either to leave or put on another tie.

Spain was very interesting a few years ago because many movies were being made there, and I would see my old friends, Charlton Heston, James Mason, and David Niven. The reason there were so many pictures being made in Spain is that the motion picture industry could hire thousands of extras for crowd battle scenes at considerably less than in Hollywood. They could actually hire a good part of the Spanish Army and put them in any costumes they wished. The extras were happy because they made more money in American movies than they made in the Army. This might be an answer to world peace. If people could get decent wages for playing soldiers in movies, they would never wish to fight a real war for *scale.*

While we were in Spain, the American producer Sam Bronston was making the religious movie *King of Kings.* As mentioned earlier, our daughter, Randy, was given a small part. We were on hand the day they filmed the Sermon on the Mount, with the late Jeffrey Hunter playing the part of Jesus Christ. There were nearly seven thousand Spanish extras assembled on the hillside.

The director, Nick Ray, told us that it would be the first time that the Spanish extras for the crowd scenes would see the actor playing the part of Jesus. The Spaniards are very religious and were deeply moved.

Five cameras were running when the handsome actor, dressed in white, came forward to the edge of the Mount. As he did, most of the thousands of extras dropped spontaneously to their knees and crossed themselves. It was an awe-inspiring moment, one of the most touching scenes I have ever watched.

Later, however, Ray and Bronston learned that the practice of making the sign of the cross didn't come into existence until some years after Christ died, so the whole vast, gripping scene had to be filmed again.

While the movie was being made, the picture's press agent sent out a story saying that Bronston was keeping the plot a secret.

A newspaperman called the press agent and asked what the release meant. "Mr. Bronston doesn't want the plot revealed," the press agent said.

"Well, I know a book that has the plot in it," the newspaperman declared. "It's called the New Testament."

"For gosh sake," the press agent implored, "don't tell the producer!"

With show business so much a part of religion today, I wonder whether Jesus could get into the Ritz? He would never get into Hortcher unless he was wearing a dark suit and tie.

I have not spent much time in Portugal but have this funny story. Americans, the world's greatest shoppers, are constantly looking for bargains. One tourist dickered with a youngster for whatever he had and got a bargain. She bought his *homework!*

I have traveled through a great part of North Africa and the Mideast, from Morocco to Beirut. The hospitality of the Arabs is overwhelming, but I did not especially like the constant stopping to have another small cup of coffee laden with teaspoons full of sugar much too sweet for my taste. The Arabs' coffee is so sweet that upon one sip every orifice of your body instantly snaps closed.

It was arranged in Jordan for us to have the use of an army helicopter to film the portion of the Holy Land that was then in Jordanian territory. This was before the six-day war in 1967, which Israel won and, in so doing, absorbed that portion of the land. As we flew over the desert, with the sun above the plane, there was the most wonderful shadow on the sand as we moved above it. It was quite a sight! The Bedouin tribesmen living in tents with their camels outside would fall on their knees in a *salaam*. We didn't realize until later that our low-flying helicopter had the markings of King Hussein's private plane.

One of the biggest thrills was landing for a brief time at the remote Qumram, where the Dead Sea Scrolls were found. All of that area is deeply moving to me and is, above any other place on earth not to be missed, regardless of your faith or even lack of it.

In those early days of travel, if you were going on to Israel, you had to have a special piece of paper that you kept apart from your passport. You had to fly first to the Arab nations and then enter the Jewish state; you could not return to any Arab country if the Israeli entry stamp was on your passport.

You would leave the old city of Jerusalem in Jordan and go through the Mandelbaum Gate into the new country of Israel. It was a strange experience since you had to walk along a narrow corridor of cobbled street with the help of young Jordanian kids, who carried your suitcases. You walked between machine-gun emplacements and armed sentries, across the no-man's-land separating the two countries. The Arab kids then would put your bags down in the exact middle of the road; then an Israeli youngster would come exactly to that spot and help you carry your bags the rest of the way.

Even then, Israel had the tightest security I have ever experienced. It's the only place I have ever been that, when you were flying internally in the country, many times during the flight, you would be told to pull your window blinds down.

We spent Easter in Israel one year, and I can still remember walking in for breakfast into the new hotel in Tel Aviv, and everyone there in the big dining room stood and applauded. It was never explained. Was it arranged? Were the people there American Jews who recognized me and were honored that four Christians wanted to spend our Easter with them in their homeland? I have had only a few real standing ovations. That was the best!

Among the handsome new buildings recently built in Tel Aviv was the Mann Auditorium. I assumed it was in honor of Thomas Mann, the famous author and a German Jew. The building was not named after the German author but a Philadelphia man named Frederick Mann. I asked, "What did he write?"

"A check," was the reply.

I heard Miriam calling the airline to straighten out our next flight to Athens. She was having trouble making herself understood with the Israeli operator at the airport. Several times I heard my wife repeat the word *confirm*. "I want to," she said, "confirm our tickets. No . . . *confirm*, do you understand?"

I finally solved the whole thing by yelling, "Ask her to *Bar-Mitzvah* the tickets." It worked.

It's been twenty years since we were in Israel on our first trip.

In those days people were very confused about the various terms to describe the area or its inhabitants, words like the *Holy Land, Israel, Zion, Jerusalem, Jew, Hebrew, West Bank,* or *Israeli*—there was a general misunderstanding. About that time there was an earthquake in Greece, and the British sent in a ship with supplies. Israel also sent a ship with emergency aid for the victims one night. In the Greek harbor, a British ship saw the little Israeli vessel dimly through the darkness.

"Ahoy, who are you?" the British captain hailed.

"Israeli," replied the Jewish ship.

"Who?" shouted the British captain through the darkness.

"Israeli," was the reply. "You may remember us as *Palestine!*"

"Oh, yes," was the British answer. "I say . . . are you still having trouble with the Jews?"

A similar bewilderment often occurs with Americans in relation to the British. Nothing to me is more jarring than the redundant "I'm going to London . . . you know, England."

Well, about fifteen years ago it was very chic for New York offices to hire English girls to answer their telephones. Americans, or at least some of them, get confused about these nouns: Britain, England, Brits, the Empire, the Colonies, the Commonwealth, Dominion, the U.K.—anyhow, a friend of mine, not too well traveled, called an office one day and got an English girl on the phone. He asked, "Mr. Dann, please."

The operator in her lovely voice said, "Oh, *I am* sorry. Haven't you heard, Mr. Dann has gone to the *United Kingdom.*"

My dumb friend said, "I didn't know. Is it too late to send flowers?"

For many years I have been carrying on an affair with England, an unrequited affair to be sure, as they don't really like us as much as we like them. I have pointed this out in another chapter, but unlike the French, however the British really may feel about us, it's their secret. Manners and courtesy are a way of life that I greatly admire and imitate. *Noblesse oblige;* I am usually unfailingly polite and courteous, but I admit I practice this mainly because it makes me feel so good, so superior. I guess it's a form of conceit.

The thing that I admire about the British is their remarkable spirit, and it is displayed in various small but significant ways whenever I visit there. I was talking with one Englishman and said that with our new American jets you could fly from London to New York in five hours.

The Englishman cocked an eye at me and asked, *"But why?"*

The British are the most insular of people: anything east of the Channel is the Orient. And there is that wonderful weather report that simply stated: HEAVY FOG. CONTINENT ISOLATED.

Everyone in London seems to carry umbrellas, but when it rains, only the Americans open them. The British go so far as to put them inside their raincoats so they won't get wet.

I bought a bowler (a derby) and an umbrella for strolling in London, but somehow they don't feel right on an American, and the British don't take kindly to our using them. I made the mistake once of posing for some pictures for the London press and wore one in bed reading the papers at breakfast. It was my attempt at a small fun picture, but the letters to the editor were quite angry the next day.

"An American wearing a bowler in London," one writer complained, "is like an Englishman turning up in America with a scalp on his belt."

The British are more tolerant of their eccentrics, and while openly kidding about homosexuals, they seem to show an amusing acceptance. The gays are very visible and flounce about more than their American types. I remember Alex King saying that when a British gay says "No!" he practically throws his back out of joint.

About the swankiest club I have ever been in is Annabell's in London. They not only have a glass fender at the bottom of the urinals in the men's room so as not to sprinkle their shoes, but between the porcelain receptacles there is a ticker machine with the world's news being printed. That's class! A man should never pee there unless he's wearing glasses.

What we call rest rooms in America are referred to as water closets in England; and on the Continent, they are called the loo.

London is easily my favorite city. Life there is so civilized. For instance, a taxi driver there can be arrested for having dirty windows or an unclean cab. Taxi drivers in London must first spend at least fourteen months on motorcycles or bicycles and know every street, alley, or mews within a radius of six miles of Charing Cross station. They must be shaven and neatly dressed. I am frequently ashamed when taking a European friend into one of our American taxis, where all the drivers dress like Emmett Kelly.

The reason that I know so much more about London than other cities of the world is that it has been a stopping-off place going and returning from Africa or the Soviet Union.

"It looks just like Connecticut" was my first surprised observation flying over the vast area known as the Soviet Union. The immensity of Russia is almost overwhelming. The huge land is more than twice the size of the continental United States and larger than all of South America. Eleven of the world's twenty-four time zones are included in Russia, and when it's midnight at one end of the U.S.S.R., it is almost noon at the other. But looking down on this portion there were these flat forests of birch and pine, just like the land we now live on in Connecticut.

When we landed, the second surprise was that the sign on the airport more or less spelled москва—not Moscow. The next week was filled with surprises such as learning that part of the dreaded Siberia was, for a portion of the year, a much-desired *summer resort* for the Russians.

We think of this land as *Red* Russia, when actually *gray* is a better color adjective for the U.S.S.R. It is a gloomy, melancholy place. Incidentally, the word *red* in Russian means *beautiful*.

We had a guide assigned to us during our stay who was with us all day, but at night we were on our own. However, since we had to use Intourist vouchers, we could spend them in designated places only, so "going anywhere" was limited.

Our guide was a short, rather dumpy-figured girl, named Marina. At first she was very distant and correct, but later she became friendly and particularly fond of our daughter.

"You speak very good English," I told her.

"It's not my best language," she said. "Malay is. I also speak French and Italian and can read German." She also told us that five million Russians speak English.

We became very fond of Marina as the days went on, and she would ask nearly as many questions as we. Whenever we used a word she didn't know, she would ask the meaning and write it down in her little book. She was very conscious of her clothes. Mind you, this was some years ago; I am sure things are better now. A sad thing happened with her that I found very touching.

I always had a 200-foot newsreel camera with me and would always first ask her permission before shooting a scene. When a camera reel gets down to ten or twenty feet left, it is the custom of all cameramen to point the lens toward the pavement or the floor and run off the remaining footage. The reason for this is to tell the editor that the reel is finished, and what's left of the street or floor when developed is to be discarded. You then take out the full rewind reel and place a new one in. Well, I came near to the end of the reel and put the camera lens toward the street pavement and ran off the unwanted film.

Marina looked hurt and displeased with me. She said, "You disappoint me. I trusted you."

I really felt terrible but had no idea what had troubled her, so I asked her to explain what I had done. She said, "You were trying to *photograph* my *shoes*."

You know, I am a pretty good talker, and words come easily to me, but I just could not find a reasonable way to explain the action of photographing the street. I said, "Marina, it's much too complicated, but will you believe me, that was not and never will be my intention. It's important to me that you like and trust us."

There was a cool fifteen minutes or so, and then we became friends again. Randy taught her to sing "Jingle Bells," and we all became "comrades."

She would sometimes ask me why I wanted to photograph a subject, and I would dissemble slightly. For instance, I wanted to photograph some automobiles, and I would particularly focus on a closeup of their windshields. The reason, and I was the first to discover this story, was that the Russians take off their windshield wipers and place them in the trunk of their cars and lock them up. When it rains, they stop the car, go around to the trunk, get out the wipers, and place them on the windshield. The reason is that they are afraid they will be stolen.

I was always shocked to see old women bending over on the street sweeping with short little brooms. The Russians may have discovered brooms, but they had not yet discovered handles. Their streets are immaculate, and as you know, their subways are not only clean but ornate and beautiful.

Many of the buildings have a wire net halfway down the front to keep bricks, tile, and masonry from falling to the street below. The buildings are going up very quickly and are not well constructed.

We were placed in the old National Hotel, an old rococo building in Red Square. Our quarters, two rooms with high ceilings, were very clean but like, I imagine, those in an American hotel of fifty years ago.

Our suite, Marina proudly told us, had been occupied by Lenin for several months just after the 1917 Revolution. I was flattered —until some American friends later told me that the Lenin suite is bugged and is always given to guests whom the Russians think might have something to say worth tuning in on.

The decor of our suite was early Charles Addams: red plush and white lace curtains, knitted doilies on the furniture, and big old paintings of landscapes on green walls. There were several curious touches about our rooms. There was a telephone but no phone book; apparently the whole country is unlisted. The towels were as thin as tissue paper, but the toilet paper seemed as thick as towels. The plumbing worked, but there were no stoppers in the basin or tub. We used toilet tissue as makeshift stoppers. With surroundings like that, I could understand how Lenin turned on capitalism.

I had a suit I wanted to get pressed. I began a sign-language parley with the burly floor matron who presided over our floor. I held up the suit and made motions as if I were ironing it. She broke into a knowing smile and summoned another husky woman with an iron. She spread out a sheet on the floor, put the suit on the sheet, and began to iron it vigorously. Her technique was different, but I must say it worked. Not only was my suit neatly pressed when she got through, but the rug looked a lot better too.

Randy had a separate room on another floor, but we didn't feel at ease about the arrangement, so she moved in with us. Miriam and I pushed our beds together, and the three of us slept in our makeshift king-size bed. While we were unpacking, Randy sud-

denly asked, "Where are the mikes?" A quick search failed to dis-
close any hidden microphones, although there did seem to be a lot
of extra wires around. Bugging hotel rooms, we discovered, is
practically the national pastime in Russia.

Paul Keyes, an associate of mine of many years, and his wife
were with us on the trip. It was an exciting, adventurous experience for us, and all we wanted was some good film for the program. Now in almost any country, the tourist bureau, regardless
of the political complexion of the country, is personable and anxious to please. This is not true of the Russians; they simply don't
care. And if your wife is the complaining type—fussy about con-
veniences or courtesy—leave her at home! The hotel, the restaurants, the drivers are not concerned with public relations.

And all this, I believe, explains how the Soviet system works.
They really are not at all concerned whether you like them or
not. Nothing is made easy or comfortable for tourists because of
the lack of opportunity for Soviet workers. They appear to have
no ambition for promotion, so being a *good* waiter is of no concern. Tipping is not permitted. At the lower level, with which we
dealt, advancement is fixed, so ability or initiative to rise to a better position is not encouraged. Don't complain to a Russian; it
means nothing.

This is not true at the artistic or scientific level of their society;
artists and scientists are the elite. Russians are really more class-
conscious than we. However, all the Russians we met are very
worried about peace.

The few Russians on a higher social level that we did meet
were quite defensive about these shortcomings and would say that
they are the result of their country's concentration of efforts on
their space program. We were told of the Western diplomat who
said to a Soviet woman official, "You can make spacecraft,
madam, but how is it you can't make nylon panties?"

"It's true," the Russian woman said, "but I think it is going to
be easier to go from space to nylon panties than it will be to go
from nylon panties to space."

We actually saw the bodies of Lenin and Stalin; since then
Stalin's body has been removed from his glass case and buried in
the ground. There were thousands of Soviet citizens standing in

line outside the mausoleum, and they shuffled along with no noise or conversation. Without a sound, thousands waited in line for hours.

With his slight figure, pointed beard, and waxen face, Lenin looked as undistinguished as a jeweler from Toledo, Ohio. It was curious to think that this little man, who had lived and worked in the very same rooms that we were presently occupying, had so greatly influenced the world we live in. I noticed that both men, Lenin and Stalin, were short, as were most of the Russians that I saw.

We, of course, could not film inside the mausoleum, but in the days that followed, we got really interesting film in their department stores and food shops. Politics, *per se*, is not my thing; but wherever I have been, to really know about a country, it is necessary to see their middle-class life. I understand that, and so does our television audience.

Although the Russians are ordinarily disciplined and courteous, the crowded department store brought out the worst in them, and they were elbowing one another as enthusiastically as the ladies on a bargain day at an American discount house. One reason for this is probably the Russian retail-selling system, which must have been devised by some enemy of the state. This is how it works. Say you want to buy a cabbage. First you find out if they have any cabbage. Then you stand in line a half hour to pick out the cabbage you want. You are then given a check for the cabbage you chose. You then head for the cashier and stand in line for another fifteen minutes to pay for your cabbage. Then you go back and stand in another line with your check to show you paid for your cabbage. Then you get your cabbage—which, by that time, is wilted. It's all very simple. In fact the Russians have a joke about it. "What," they ask, "is fifty yards long and lives on cabbage?" The answer is "The line in front of a meat counter."

We even filmed a story at a Soviet fashion show. The models are plumper than our cadaverous American models, and when they first came out, I thought the commentator was introducing the Green Bay Packers. At any rate, the ample curves of the Russian women are *one* thing that is not controlled by the Kremlin.

The clothes modeled at the fashion show were not unstylish,

but there is a catch. The dresses worn by the models are not for sale. If a Russian girl sees a dress she likes, she can buy only the *pattern*. First, she gets in line . . .

We attended a performance of Moscow's famous Puppet Theater, featuring Sergei Obratsov, who later had a successful run on Broadway. Although the puppets were the greatest I have ever seen, the crowd was curiously silent and laughed very little. We also went to a concert (as they call a variety show) where the master of ceremonies was an attractive young Russian man. He was well dressed and wore a white handkerchief in his breast pocket, which we hadn't seen any other Russian doing. I nudged Miriam and called her attention to it by pointing to my own pocket. When the young man came out to introduce the next act, the handkerchief was missing. I never did understand that. Perhaps he was offended at my noticing his handkerchief. Or maybe he just had to blow his nose.

As an important American television entertainer and his party, we were constantly watched—thus my reaction caused the removal of the handkerchief. The next day our guide, Marina, asked if we enjoyed the concert. I went overboard and said we were thrilled by it. Marina, who was not with us in the evenings, said, "Then why did you not stay after the intermission?"

The spookiest thing that happened was something I now know was prearranged and plotted. I have since learned—but did not realize it at the time—that a man, who turned out to be Victor Louis, a famous Russian agent and go-between, was waiting for us at the concert. He gave us no alternative but to follow him and do as he suggested. I was not anxious to be practically ordered, if however so politely, to get in a complete stranger's automobile late at night in Moscow and bring my wife, daughter, and friends, Without making a scene, I did as he told me to, although I was somewhat frightened.

This is what happened: During intermission, while we stood around munching salami sandwiches, an English-speaking Russian struck up a conversation with us. He was a slim, dark-haired, outgoing man and proceeded to invite us to his home for dinner. We had been told that Russians almost never invite foreigners to their homes, and we certainly didn't want to go to the home of a total stranger we had just met, but he wouldn't take *nyet* for an answer. "I want you to come for a proper meal," he insisted. "But there are six of us," I objected. "Good," he said. "My car holds six."

Our host, whose name was Victor, drove us to his apartment, where we met his attractive English wife and a group of their Russian friends, including the puppeteer Sergei Obratsov. Although Victor lived in one of the new apartment houses, his four-room apartment was already rather rundown. He said the apartment cost one hundred dollars a month (very high for Moscow) but there were cracks in the masonry, the doors didn't fit properly, and the bathroom ceiling sagged. It had transparent plastic pipes, so if you had nothing better to do, you could spend an evening watching the plumbing. However, he had fine furniture, expensive modern paintings, and two cars. He also offered us scotch, bourbon, and even American beer—all extremely rare in Russia.

Victor asked me what I did, and I confessed that I was a television entertainer. Then, like so many Russians, his next question was "How much do you make?" For probably the first time in history, an actor understated his salary. I didn't want Victor to know how much a tool of decadent capitalism makes. Victor told us he was a translator as a cover, I think. He had just translated *My Fair Lady* into Russian, he said, where it came out as *Maya Prekrasnaya Lady*. There were a few other little changes, Victor said. For instance, "The Rain in Spain Stays Mainly in the Plain" emerged as "Carl Stole Corals from Cora." I asked if Russia would pay royalties for the use of the musical in the Soviet Union. I just wish I could have gotten laughs with my monologue like I did with that question. We discussed Russian and American writers, artists, and composers, and he inquired about Jackson Pollock, the American painter, who had been killed in an automobile crash on Long Island. "Pollock was killed recently, you know," I told him. He puffed reflectively on his long Russian cigarette. "Who did it to him?" he asked.

At one point in the evening, the inevitable Russian toasts began. Victor poured vodka and asked that I propose a toast. "Peace," I said, raising my glass. Obratsov got up and went to Randy. "Not peace to us," he said, "but peace to this child."

All during the evening Victor kept the volume of the hi-fi, on which he was playing Louis Armstrong and Noël Coward records, turned up to a deafening pitch, presumably so our conversation could not be bugged. It was so loud that I was finally willing to send in a signed confession rather than hear any more Louis Armstrong at such an ear-splitting pitch. A couple of times I casually turned the volume down myself, but each time our host turned it back up full blast.

Here's what was really going on with the record player. You and I would naturally assume that the music was being used to drown out the conversation in Victor's apartment, and that's what I thought for some years. Not at all. I learned that it is not to obscure what is being said but that the background music keeps anyone from *editing* what has been said.

For instance, if Comrade Victor Louis is talking, and Armstrong on the record player is singing "Mack the Knife," there is no way to edit or jump the conversation ahead without noticing something missing in the song. This is a system, I later learned from friends in the U.S. government, that is used by our people also for the same purpose—to protect themselves from their own spies.

My daughter, Randy, spent some time in Washington during the Watergate trials in the offices of government attorneys who, during their phone conversations, would always have a radio playing, or some would have a metronome ticking. One lawyer would rock his chair back and forth with a constant squeak in perfect rhythm so as not to be edited.

As the years have gone by, I have read many stories about Victor Louis. Much has been written about him, and our government experts on Russia describe him as one of the most mysterious characters in the Soviet Union. I often wonder if I would have gotten a better story if I had known all that before I was taken to his apartment. To this day, I do not know why he did it or what the purpose was. It was a hell of a night.

I look back on our trip to Moscow (at that time it was the only city that we were allowed to travel in), and it was the most interesting worldly experience we have had. I really would like to return and check up on old Victor. I remember him still with his long Russian cigarette asking me questions. For reasons I don't understand, the Russians allowed him his contacts with the West —he was a one-man Hong Kong.

Oh, by the way, do you know about Russian cigarettes? They are longer than ours by two inches, and at the end there is only one inch of tobacco, but at least three inches of the cigarette is a cardboard tube. This is not because it acts as a filter or that they are stingy with tobacco, but rather because they are made to be smoked by someone wearing thick gloves.

More recently I have talked with Ambassador Averell Harriman and my British journalist friend, Malcolm Muggeridge, both experts on the Soviet Union, and they told me that Victor Louis is a most mysterious figure and that it was quite a coup to have spent an evening with him. A few years ago, when the autobiography of Khrushchev was published in the United States, it was Victor Louis who was the go-between and made the deal and got the money. Later there was a strong suspicion that the autobiography was a fake. More than with anyone else I have ever met, I would like to know more about him and what his function is. As I left him that night, he took me aside and asked me not to mention his name on television or talk about the evening. I have kept my word, but I didn't promise not to *write* about it.

When we asked about religion in Russia, we were told, "That's for the old people." This does seem true, and most of the churchgoers we saw were older women. Although the press rails constantly against religion, and the famous St. Basil's is now an antireligious museum, many older people, particularly women, stubbornly continue going to church. The government grudgingly permits churchgoing, even while scoffing at it. Paul and Miriam Keyes, who are Catholic, were able to attend mass on Sunday in the small apartment of a priest in an ordinary apartment house. There were six other worshippers, and the Keyeses went to confession in the priest's tiny kitchen. Oddly enough, despite the state campaign to abolish religion, and the fact that no one can become a Communist unless he is an avowed atheist, crosses still topped some of the Kremlin towers, and we saw some of the most beautiful icons and religious art in the world inside the Kremlin. Sunday is still a special day, but the Russians observe it not by praying but by shopping. They get all dressed up in their Sunday best and head for GUMS Department Store.

The campaign against religion has taken most of the romantic atmosphere out of marriage. We visited the Palace of Weddings, which is where Russians are married rather than in a church. A commissar of weddings in a business suit stands at a desk and marries a couple in a brief, one-paragraph statement. Divorce was formerly similarly cut and dried, we were told, although lately it has become more difficult to get one. Previously a Russian who had grown tired of the little woman simply wrote the government a letter saying "I've had it with Natasha." A few days later Natasha got a letter telling her that she was at liberty.

The night before we were to leave, a scary thing happened. At about two o'clock in the morning, our phone in the Moscow hotel rang. I jumped out of the bed that also contained Miriam and Randy and answered it. It was a call from New York—a Mr. Sid Eiges, who was a vice-president of NBC. I could barely hear his voice. In this cavernous room, to speak up on a long-distance call would shake the curtains, so I tried to whisper and shout at the same time. No way. You had to scream. "SID, WHAT IS IT?" He spoke very slowly and distinctly, almost casually. But it was so unnatural for him that I knew something was wrong. Sid said, "When are you planning to leave Moscow?"

I told him I planned to leave in the morning and asked if there was any reason for the call. I was worried about this because NBC knew my complete schedule. Why the phone call at two o'clock in the morning? Not only had Sid awakened us, but by now I am sure the poor guy who was bugging the room was alerted.

"I want you to leave as quickly as you can," Eiges said. "Dag Hammarskjold has just been killed."

Then our connection was broken off. I didn't know whether he had hung up or we had been cut off. All sorts of wild thoughts raced through my mind. I envisioned Hammarskjold being shot at the United Nations—and by a Russian. Miriam and Randy had been awakened by the call, and since we were all too keyed up to go back to sleep, we got up and began packing.

We were relieved when we got to the airport and went through customs without incident, and began to feel still easier when we settled back in our Aeroflot jet for the flight to Prague and Zurich. The plane was about to take off when I was called and an official asked to see our passports. Since I had just shown our passports, I got the panicky feeling that some problem had arisen to prevent our going. I showed the official my passport and Miriam's, on which the photo of Randy had been canceled out with an X on a trip to Japan.

"This, this," he said, pointing angrily to the defaced photo.

I explained that it was crossed out in Japan because Randy now had her own passport. He frowned at the photo with the X stamped across Randy's face. "It's inhuman," he snorted, handing back the passport. "You may go."

Our collective sighs of relief generated as much thrust as the jet engines as our TU-104 raced down the runway and took off for Prague. Even when we were airborne, though, we still didn't have a sense of being completely at ease. I did not know until much later that day, in Zurich, that Dag Hammarskjold had been killed in the Congo. It was just that NBC wanted me out of the Soviet Union in case his death was linked to the Russians. It was the first time in my life that there was a big event happening and no way to get any news. Nothing was said in Moscow, nothing on the radio, nothing in the press. I was one of a few people who knew of the death in a country of three hundred million.

It was wonderful to arrive in Switzerland. Paul Keyes and I checked our luggage to see what, if anything, was missing. All we lost were two rolls of film and three pairs of Jockey shorts. Not a bad week's work. My stories and film were a big success back in the United States.

I seem to have stirred up more than my share of uproars in my day. However, it wasn't until I took our show to Berlin that I managed to create an international incident. In international blow-ups, as in the domestic variety, I discovered that the fallout often far exceeds the explosion.

My instant incident erupted in September of 1961, when I went to Berlin to telecast our program from that troubled city, just after the Soviet-sponsored East German government had slammed shut the border that divides East and West Berlin. We filmed one hour of the program at the border of the American sector on the Friedrichstrasse, showing the newly erected wall and other points of interest on both sides of the border. We also interviewed a few United States soldiers.

Overnight the appearance of American soldiers on the show set off a chain-reaction flap that reached all the way to Washington.

Members of Congress called the incident *shocking* and *intolerable*. The White House was reportedly disturbed. The State Department was upset. The Army took disciplinary action against the two officers who had assisted us. Lt. Col. Dallas Hoadley, the information officer in Berlin, was relieved for "improper performance of duties," and Col. John Deane, Jr., was admonished for showing "poor judgment." The Hearst papers denounced "*massed troops and armor*" at the border, and the Communist East German *Neues Deutschland* said darkly that we had "*staged war games*" and "*provocations.*"

All this was before anyone had seen the program in question!

What touched off the international uproar? What really happened to create such a far-reaching clamor? The truth is that the whole story was blown up out of all proportion and was the biggest exaggeration to come out of Germany since Baron Münchhausen was operating there. As is often the case, the whole crazy chain of events was started by one distorted newspaper story.

It began: "Fifty American soldiers yesterday moved rapidly down the rain-spattered street and took possession of buildings overlooking the East-West Berlin border.

"A jeep mounting a 106-mm., recoilless antitank gun and others mounting machine guns went into position at the Friedrichstrasse crossing.

"One jeep with a machine gun had a front wheel planted on the white stripe that indicates the border.

"Two colonels arrived.

"The situation looked grim.

"It was the biggest turnout the American Army had yet made along the wall that divides Communist from Free Berlin—and it was all for Jack Paar."

That story—written by one anonymous reporter and relayed

back to the United States by United Press International—touched off an explosion in the capital, and no wonder! Without bothering to check the facts, Washington officials began to raise the capitol roof.

Assistant Secretary of Defense Arthur Sylvester called the incident "disgraceful." Senate Majority Leader Mike Mansfield said the Berlin situation "was not a television spectacular to be made into some kind of game for the personal profit of personalities in the entertainment world," and Senator Leveritt Saltonstall claimed it "might have led to a shooting scene." It took eleven columns in the *Congressional Record* to chronicle the senatorial fulminations over the imaginary "incident." And all this was based on one inaccurate newspaper story.

The newspapers and magazines added to the general hubbub by taking the highly exaggerated original story and further distorting the distortions. While the original UPI story mentioned fifty soldiers and two jeeps with me at the border, *Newsweek* managed to boost it to eighty soldiers and seven jeeps.

For the record, here are the true facts behind the phantom Berlin "incident." Because of the tremendous interest sparked by the crisis there, I decided to take the show over and give our viewers a picture of what was happening. Whereas news and commentary programs were already exploring the military and political aspects of developments, I hoped, through a more informal approach, to show the human side of what was taking place.

The Army offered us their co-operation, just as they did for other American TV shows in Berlin. As a matter of fact, two other programs—NBC's "Here and Now" and CBS's "Eyewitness to History"—were both filming at the Friedrichstrasse border at the very time of the alleged "incident."

This kind of co-operation by the military is commonplace. At the same time that I was filming a handful of GI's for an hour, sixteen hundred marines and twenty-two ships of the U.S. Sixth Fleet were performing for Darryl Zanuck, who was shooting a movie about D-Day! Also the Army ordered seven hundred soldiers from Germany to France to support rock-and-roll singers Fabian, Paul Anka, and other Hollywood heroes in the same picture.

Our request in Berlin was very simple. I wanted to interview Col. John Deane, Jr., a much-decorated officer, and I asked him to bring along one or two other soldiers so that Peggy Cass and I could talk with them.

As it turned out, he brought a squad of twelve men, explaining that he didn't want to single out some and leave others behind. I also asked for a jeep to have something to sit on during the interview. That was the extent of it.

There happened to be an operational changeover of units while we were preparing to shoot, which accounted for more military personnel being at the border than normally. Also, a few off-duty officers had drifted up out of curiosity to watch the goings-on. The blown-up UPI story made it sound as if the Army had restaged Pickett's Charge for my benefit.

This hour-long ad-lib documentary at the Berlin Wall was taped on a Thursday afternoon and was to be seen on the "Tonight" program the following Tuesday evening. But you cannot believe the furor it caused in the American press for the next five days! And no one had actually *seen* it! There were front-page stories even in the New York *Times*. And when the show was finally seen, what they saw were three people sitting on the curb in the rain. And who were the three people? Peggy Cass, me, and my teenage daughter, Randy. Does it seem likely that a man was creating an *incident* with his young daughter sitting on a curb in the rain?

Our interviews with a handful of soldiers consisted mostly of talk about their wives and babies. The conversation was about as provocative as the small talk at a PTA meeting. There was no tension evident. In fact, while we were shooting, busloads of American GI's were crossing into East Berlin on sightseeing tours.

Across the border were a few bored, unarmed Vopos (People's Police) and a half dozen curious East German cameramen taking pictures of us taking pictures of them. The show ended with Peggy and me sitting alone on a curb in the rain. It was all decidedly unwarlike.

When I pointed out a water cannon across the border and told

Peggy it could knock a person down at fifty yards, she said, "I hope they won't use that. I just had my hair done."

That was the extent of the "incident" that U.S. papers called "provocative." When the program was finally televised, showing on film exactly what had really taken place, it was generally admitted that the whole thing was a tempest in a TV pot. The Senate Communications Subcommittee's watchdog said he could find nothing wrong with the show. Subcommittee staff director Nick Zaple added that he saw no question raised involving broadcast regulation.

The morning after the program had been shown, the consensus of opinion was, "What was all the hullabaloo about?" There was an embarrassed silence from the most caustic critics but apologies from the more fair-minded papers and columnists.

"Anyone who saw the program," wrote the distinguished Washington columnist David Lawrence, "must have wondered why members of Congress who hadn't seen it, but had read newspaper accounts of the filming episode, went off the deep end in their criticism. In presenting worthwhile information, 'The Jack Paar Show' was an effective piece of work. He deserves not brickbats but applause for his revelation of the human story behind the Berlin crisis."

Columnist Paul Molloy of the Chicago *Sun-Times* felt that the programs were a restrained, low-key look at both sides of the wall. "The episodes showing actual escapes across the wall," he wrote, "and interviews with the escapees were among the most dramatic I have ever seen on television."

The Chattanooga *Times* was also among the papers conceding there was no wrongdoing on my part or the Army's. "Mr. Paar's actions at the border were above reproach," it editorialized. "So were the actions of the officers and men. The mild co-operation given to Mr. Paar appeared to be no different from that usually given the newsmen and others who are trying to present an accurate picture of the situation to the people back home."

The most gratifying aspect of the final outcome of the Berlin episode, as far as I was concerned, was not my personal vindication but the withdrawal of disciplinary action against Lieutenant

Colonel Hoadley and Colonel Deane. The Army reinstated the two officers who had co-operated with us with the explanation that reinvestigation showed that they had done nothing wrong. General Bruce C. Clarke, commander of the U.S. Army in Europe, said the reinstatement was made to "right an injustice."

The army officers, however, still had the "incident" in their personal files, which was a negative mark in their army careers for promotion. Only a few years ago, I learned that two congressmen became interested in the injustice and had the information removed from the officers' files. The two congressmen were Gerry Ford and Hugh Carey. They are both my friends.

Oh, yes, if I were really trying to provoke a war with the Communist world, would I have left four days later for Moscow?

This experience was very painful, though it seems absurd now. But it has made me question everything I have since read in newspapers and magazines. I had a good parting shot. As we were leaving for Moscow, at the airport I was again interviewed and asked, "Why are you going to Russia?"

My reply was, "I just want to see if the Soviet press is as fair and accurate as the papers in the United States."

17

Dr. Schweitzer, I Presume

Of course I never used that African cliché when first I saw Dr. Albert Schweitzer, one of the most celebrated men of the century. My first impression was the same as my last impression of the famous doctor; both views of him I saw from a *pirogue*, a kind of dugout canoe that is hollowed out from a tree, as we approached and later left the island of Lambaréné on the Ogooué River, a muddy but powerful stream of water full of hippos and crocodiles in the former French colony of Gabon, Equatorial Africa.

Dr. Albert Schweitzer, a Nobel Prize–winner, was called one of the most talented men in the world; he looked like a young actor in old makeup. He could have been Gregory Peck if his imaginary Max Factor disguise was removed. He was thin, tall, and straight, wearing white pants and shirt, a black bow tie and a pith helmet. He was then in his eighty-ninth year, having spent fifty of those years at this native hospital in one of the most primitive places on earth. In fact, Dr. Schweitzer was better known than the country he lived in.

Schweitzer: a philosopher and proponent of the theory of "reverence for life"; a medical doctor and surgeon; a musician (an organist) and leading authority on Bach and Wagner; a botanist; an architect; and a builder. His work as an author and theologian on the life of the historical Jesus is considered as definitive throughout the world.

My crazy career in television has allowed me to fulfill all my boyhood fantasies; there isn't anything that I ever wanted to do that I finally did not do, and spending a week in Lambaréné was the highlight of my younger dreams.

It's a tough flight—twenty-two straight hours of flying to what was then called the Congo. And like so many out of the way places, you must overfly to make connections with smaller aircraft to reach the country of Gabon. The capital city is Libreville, and the President had the interesting name of Omar Bongo. (The most colorful name in Africa now is Canaan Banana, the President of Zimbabwe. I imagine that our State Department must be careful in "carrying out *fruitful* negotiations" with him.) The leading tribe in Gabon is the *Fangs*. As you can gather, it's a pretty colorful place.

My companions on this adventure were John Reddy, of *Reader's Digest*, and Tom Cochran, a long-time associate from all my television programs. Also joining us was Louis Hepp, one of NBC's top-ranking cameramen, who flew in from his station in Nairobi. I had risked about ten thousand dollars on this adventure, because we could not get an answer on our acceptance from New York. Although Dr. Schweitzer was voted year after year as one of the world's most honored men, he had no public relations representative. Only a very small number of Americans had ever attempted the 15,000-mile journey.

When we arrived in the city of Libreville, we first tried to make arrangements on a small native aircraft to get to the doctor's remote island.

We finally got on Trans-Gabon's popular white-knuckle flight to the jungle hospital. It was a very small aircraft seating about fifteen people. Hanging from the roof of the cabin were dead animals that had just been slain at the airport because there was no refrigeration; they were taken to the interior as quickly as possible. There was also a small piano tied to the sides of the cabin that began to shift about as we flew.

"Getting there is half the fun," I kept telling myself as our Trans-Gabon DC-3 hit another air pocket. The cabin, into which we were crammed with some Africans and a jumble of cargo, was stifling hot, and there was not a breath of air. Everyone was holding his breath, waiting for the next bump. Even if there had been any air in the cabin, I don't think any of the passengers would have inhaled. The air was too turbulent even to *breathe*.

The Africans, however, seemed not in the least perturbed by the rough flying conditions. Several of the Gabonese women around me were calmly nursing their babies, and I had a terrible vision of what might happen if they were still nursing them when we landed and the plane came down with a jolt! In fact, everywhere we flew in Africa, some of the passengers were nursing mothers. I always half expected the captain to announce, "We are now about to land. Please fasten your brassieres and observe the no-nursing sign."

Apart from the discomfort and turbulence, our flight from Libreville to Lambaréné was uneventful. The plane landed smoothly, and none of the nursing mothers got anything nipped off. However, the wait at the little, dinky, thatch-covered airport took nearly as long as the flight. The Africans have picked up the white man's burden—red tape—and the Gabonese lassoed us in yards of it. We spent an interminable time in the sweltering heat of the airport shack filling out lengthy forms. Why, I will never know, as we were flying internally within the country of Gabon. I gather they have picked all this up from seeing movies of the Western world. What infuriated me, and I have a short fuse for nonsense, is that they usually read our passports *upside down!*

We finally were permitted to go to a small hotel three miles upstream from the famous hospital; the rest of the journey would be by *pirogue*.

We left all our baggage and film equipment at the hotel and took the trip downstream. This was the smartest thing we did because when we arrived and talked with Dr. Schweitzer's daughter, Rhena Eckert, she informed us that her father was quite ill and didn't wish to be on television. Later, when she asked where our equipment was and we told her it was back at the hotel, this impressed her and later the doctor. The fact that we did not barge in uninvited with cameras gave us points for courtesy. After all we did not have permission.

Rhena, the doctor's daughter, whom I had known slightly in New York, said she would do what she could with her father, and we should wait at the hotel for a message by canoe.

We returned to the jungle hotel to sit and brood—something I do rather frequently. "Do you suppose," I wondered, "that we've come fifteen thousand miles for nothing?" I knew that Dr. Schweitzer had been ill, and his daughter had been very noncommittal in talking with us. A note delivered to the hotel in the morning would be a graceful way of refusing us. Between my foreboding and the intense humidity, it was a restless night.

In the morning there was nothing to do but wait for the note from the hospital. Tom Cochran, a devout Catholic, announced that he was going to church in the village, and I decided to go along. Cochran is one of five handsome Erie, Pennsylvania, brothers, another of whom was a World War II flying hero, the late Colonel Phil Cochran, who was portrayed in the comic strips as Flip Corkin. Tommy has been with me through thick and thin —mostly thick—and is one of the finest men I know. As I mentioned earlier, he is so devout that he sometimes goes to several masses on Sunday. Although he has no vices that I know of, he goes to confession regularly. I suspect he's trying to get a reputation. It was characteristic that we no sooner arrive in Lambaréné than Tommy wanted to go to mass. Since it looked as though our hopes of seeing Dr. Schweitzer could stand a little prayer, I went along. To get to the church, we had to take a *pirogue* down the Ogooué. A *pirogue* is a very frail craft, and the Ogooué is full of hippos and crocodiles, so I suddenly found myself wondering what I was doing in a tippy canoe with a Catholic. A Baptist would make sense, since they believe in total immersion. But Tommy doesn't smoke, drink—or *swim!*

The church was a little bamboo hut with open windows near the river's edge. The congregation was entirely Gabonese, except for Cochran and a couple of French people. Since I am not a Catholic, I waited outside during the mass, which I could hear through the open windows. The mass was in Latin, of course, but the priest preached the sermon in French. There were several little

Gabonese boys playing near me outside the church, and their chatter and laughter began to intrude on the sermon. Even with my fragmentary knowledge of French and the chatter of the boys, I could gather that the sermon dealt with brotherly love. Finally the talk and the laughter began to distract the priest. *"Et Jesus dit* [and Jesus said] . . ." he said. A burst of laughter came through the window. *"Et Jesus dit* . . ." he repeated. More squeals from outside the window. The priest walked suddenly to the open window, made a fist, and rapped the offending youngsters smartly on their heads. They scattered in a final burst of glee. The priest adjusted his vestments, walked back to the front of the church, and resumed, *"Et Jesus dit* . . ."

We spent the rest of that Sunday rounding up some American Peace Corps kids and taking them to the best dinner that they had had in months. They were wonderful young people, and while some seemed to have problems of their own, helping others —sincerely, I am sure—would contribute to their own lives. Later, when I met some nurses with Dr. Schweitzer from the Western world, I found there was a pattern of troubled but good souls who had personal problems that had brought them to this remote place. It was a humanitarian Foreign Legion. Trouble and problems were not unknown to me—these were my kind of people!

Cochran's prayers must have worked. When we arrived back at the hotel, there was a note from Dr. Schweitzer's daughter. The doctor would be happy to see us, it said, and would like to have us as his guests for lunch.

Within minutes we had piled our camera equipment in *pirogues* and were being paddled downriver to the hospital. The jungle on either side was lushly green, and the humid air was like steam rising out of a green mist. The native paddlers increased the tempo of their rhythmic strokes as we neared our destination. Then the hospital came into view—a sprawling cluster of tin-roofed wooden buildings straggling down a green slope to the water's edge. Small cooking fires winked through the haze. Our *pirogues* slid up on a sandy beach, and I jumped ashore. Looking up, I saw the familiar figure of Dr. Schweitzer coming down the winding path to greet us. He wore a white pith helmet, thin white shirt and black bow tie, and baggy white pants. A smile lighted his craggy features as he greeted us in French and invited us to join him in a cup of tea.

I had arrived at a troubled time in the life of Dr. Schweitzer. He was in his eighty-ninth year and his fiftieth year at his jungle hospital. For years he had been hailed as one of the great men of our times. He had given up notable careers in philosophy, music, and theology to go to Africa to minister to the natives. His philosophy of reverence for life was known around the world. He had been awarded the Nobel Peace Prize. Yet now he had suddenly become a controversial figure, caught in the winds of change sweeping across an emerging Africa. There were cries of "Colonialist" and "Jungle doctor go home" hurled by newly independent Africans. There were charges that his hospital was dirty and antiquated and that time had passed him by.

Despite his recent illness and the controversy raging around him, he looked well. His piercing eyes, drooping mustache, and strong, aquiline nose gave him the appearance of a pioneer of the American Old West. His hands, which had so beautifully interpreted the music of Bach and Wagner, looked strong but worn from wielding shovel and saw. Over a cup of tea, he told us of his work at the hospital that he had literally built with his own hands. He had given up operating at seventy-five, he said, but still supervised the hospital and the new construction. With obvious pride, he said he had worked eight hours the previous day pouring cement for a new building. He told us something of the special problems of his jungle hospital. "We get many cases of hernia, malaria, and sleeping sickness," he said, "but cancer and appendicitis are almost unknown here." Natives are occasionally brought in who have been injured by gorillas, and one man had been treated for being "hit by an elephant." "This is how to act if you come face to face with a gorilla in the jungle," he said. Smiling, he walked slowly backward and grabbed his throat. In other words, if I met a gorilla, I was to choke him. My leg was being pulled, because I, as an animal lover, would never try to *strangle* a *gorilla!*

After finishing our tea, we set out on a tour of the hospital. "Do you mind if we film as we go?" I asked. A smile creased his grizzled face. "I'll do anything with you but box," he said.

Dr. Schweitzer's jungle hospital was not a hospital in the sense that we envision one; it was more like an African village. There were some fifty ramshackle buildings, mostly little more than shacks and huts. There was no electricity, and the only water came from one hand-pumped well. The only sanitary facility was an old-fashioned privy for the staff. The rest room, loo, or water closet was a long, high dock out over the water with many booths. It was like going to the bathroom on the *Bridge on the River Kwai!* With the building skill of Schweitzer and gravity, this was one place where they would never need Drano! And to the fish far below, it must have been a funny sight.

The Schweitzer mission was not a sterile, antiseptic hospital, but a native village of huts built so that the African patients would feel at home. You see, when a native in this part of the steaming world was sick or injured, he did not come by ambulance but by canoe. His family, maybe four or five people, would come with him. There would never be enough space for all the family in a hospital room.

While the mother was being treated for a tumor or to give birth, or while the father was being operated on for a hernia, the rest of the family had to be housed and fed. The family would then have to cook and prepare the meals for each member. There could not be one communal dining room or kitchen facility for all, because the tribes—the Fangs and the Galloa tribes—did not trust each other and were in fear of being poisoned.

Schweitzer had been responsible for feeding five hundred people a day for fifty years. He was tough and firm with the Africans and expected the able members of the family to work and help grow the food while the sick relative was recovering. He expected the male members to help crack the stones, to make the cement, and to build the huts and roads of the hospital.

It had been written that he occasionally kicked a native's behind to get him to work and help him. He had been even tougher with some men, but you have to understand the African male. If a mother had been operated on and was lying on her cot in the cabin, the father might very well have pushed her to the ground and lain on the bed himself. So I am in favor of the "kick-

in-the-ass" method of cultural advancement. It gets their attention!

There was something magnificent yet sad at the sight of the
crusty, stubborn old man going his way as he had for half a century while the world around him changed, even in the African
jungle. Dr. Schweitzer clung fiercely to his ideas, despite criticism
or change. "I know what is best for these people," he said. "The
natives still come here because they know they will be cured."

After spending many days with Dr. Schweitzer and seeing the
good he had done by comforting and healing the sick and
wounded, and giving the lepers care and housing, however primitive, you wouldn't think it would be necessary to present a defense on his behalf. But at the time I was there, he was under
strong criticism from uninformed liberals who were against his pa-
ternalistic, colonial-style care of the African.

Let me now in his memory offer up what I saw and understood
about his work. Dr. Schweitzer was born in Gunsbach in Alsace, a
part of France. Gabon is now a free, independent country. His
staff, both men and women, were volunteers and came from Switzerland, Holland, Germany, England, the United States, Japan,
and (wouldn't you know) there was a psychiatrist from Israel!
Dr. Schweitzer told me that he was not at all interested in politics and that his main worldly concern was in banning atomic-
bomb testing. The government of Gabon did not help him at all
in running the hospital, and some were in favor of burning it
down.

It is true that in half a century he had not trained any Africans
to be doctors. It's absurd to think that he could. He told me,
"We don't have the facilities to train them here. The local native
people could not begin the study of medicine without at least a
primary education, and that was the responsibility of the government. The few who were educated and sent to medical schools in
Europe stayed there."

I later learned that at that time in the history of Gabon, only
two trained African physicians had ever returned to their native
country after being educated in France. Then he said, "Africa is
so vast that if one feels he can do good in this continent, why not
go and do it? Why climb on this old man's back?"

The doctor told me that one of the problems in treating the local people was that sometimes late at night, witch doctors would creep in and treat the patients in the old jungle ways. Schweitzer allowed this, so long as it did not interfere with medical practices for recovery. As a realist and the most experienced person in the area, he believed that any native custom of their own African culture was helpful. And what is wrong with that?

There were some amusing changes that I observed. The local people, who had for hundreds of years performed their tribal dances around a wood fire, were now dancing with a Coleman lantern in the center. Is that progress?

Schweitzer's rather poetic philosophy is a reverence for all life. That meant a respect for all humankind and animals and trees and flowers. Nothing was to be destroyed or killed. He was a vegetarian and would allow no one to touch any of the animals that roamed the hospital. When a dog chased a chicken, I heard Dr. Schweitzer yell in French, "No! No! Remember we have won the Nobel Peace Prize."

My three guys and his staff would eat all meals together in a screened-in jungle dining room. There was one very long table with the doctor in the center. I was always placed opposite him and later became self-conscious when one of my group pointed out the symbolism of the setting. It was an exact replica of the Leonardo da Vinci painting of *The Last Supper*. And while I was opposite Schweitzer, on his side of the table, lined up by rank, would be the women of his staff.

The other doctors and surgeons would spread out from the center, and I gathered that the seating arrangement had great social significance. It is interesting to point out that the whole Lambaréné compound was a *matriarchy*; women were in charge of everything. Some of the female staff had been with him for twenty years. Everything, but everything, had to go through them. They would kill for Schweitzer!

My seating opposite him was a little unnerving, for here I was the daily guest, opposite a modern *jesus* (with a small *J*). And for those of you who are curious, I can tell you that this *jesus* was not a drinking man.

All of the conversations between us were interpreted by his

daughter or Erica Anderson, either in French or German. He did
not wish to speak English with me, although I knew he understood it. I would make many asides over the days in English, only
to have him laugh long before the interpretation. Dr. Schweitzer
also read Greek and Hebrew.

Many of the women—staff and nurses—had faces that ranged
from Biblically beautiful to troubled. I certainly would like to
have known the story behind each face. What caused them to
join with such passion this humanitarian Foreign Legion? Several
were very attractive, and a girl from Westchester, New York, was
a knockout.

After lunch, when the doctor would take a nap, I would usually
flirt with the nurses and hold court on what was going on in the
outside world. I never had such an attentive audience since most
spoke English; sometimes one would interpret my gossip into
different languages for the rest. The main communication was
carried out in German.

After one lunch, I explained to the nurses that my program was
a commercial operation and that I could well afford to contribute
something to the hospital. I could easily give what I would have
to pay some singer or comedian to fill the same time and who
would not have performed nearly as well. I told them the standard fee at the time on network television was seven thousand
dollars. What could we buy with that amount?

Well, they were like kids in a candy store—they got out medical and surgical booklets, and we began to look through them.
What would they really like? The decision was an *obstetrical
table.* This is a stainless-steel examination table with stirrups for
the women's legs and an adjusting position for the hips. They
really needed one. I then told them of an actress I knew, Cornelia
Otis Skinner, who once told me that whenever she went on such
a table, naked of course, she always insisted on wearing her *hat!*
This story got pretty funny when it was reinterpreted into German.

At first, I was going to buy the table from a surgical firm in
Ohio and have it shipped, but the details got to be horrendous, so
I said, "Here is the check and you let the doctor order it."

Well, my dears, the head of the staff, Ali Silver, a Dutch nurse, was beside herself with delight. She later gave the check to Dr. Schweitzer and *ordered* him to thank me. He said he was too embarrassed. She gave me *orders* to accept his thanks, and I said I was too embarrassed. So it was arranged that we were to meet behind a tree at a certain hour, like a shoot-out at high noon, to give and receive thanks. We were both embarrassed as hell, but with the whole staff watching, we went behind the tree, and he simply said, *"Danke."* I got choked up, and the whole scene became warmly funny.

He never personally asked for funds but raised the money by his writings and contributions. All of the money he got for the Nobel Peace Prize, as he proudly showed me, he had spent on tin for roofs on the huts in the leper village. In a jeep we drove to the leper village, where over a hundred poor souls were hidden away. All I remember is the look of affection they all had when they saw him. They yelled, *"Papa. Papa. Le Grand Doctor!"* Two outstanding and dedicated Japanese doctors were treating the leper patients. Each of the lepers had a few members of their family living with them and all expenses for medicine, care, and food—even laundry—were courtesy of Albert Schweitzer.

This, I believe, was the best tribute to my tall, silver friend. The Gabon government had built a modern hospital several miles upstream from Lambaréné, hoping to get the native people to come to them. But at the time we were there, it was quite empty. For fifty years the natives went to the man who understood them and could heal them.

After awaking from his nap, the doctor invited me to his little room to talk. It was a spare, plain room with a bed, a couple of chairs, a wooden table, and a wash basin. The table where he wrote was littered with books and papers. Both ends of the room were open, with a latticelike construction that Dr. Schweitzer said kept the room cool even in the hottest weather. Of all this man's accomplishments, he seemed most proud of his understanding of tropical winds and how to build a hut with cross-ventilation. He really made a big thing of his knowledge of natural air conditioning. The heat was unbelievable, and I had been told that he would not allow a weather thermometer at Lambaréné because if the staff had known how hot it was, nobody would have stayed.

As we sat talking, the doctor would wind surgical gauze around his wrists. I asked, "Why?" It was explained that he would write into the night, and the gauze would keep the perspiration from running onto his hands.

He was fascinated by fountain pens. I gave him the few I had but made a mental note to send more. This becomes important at the end of this tribute.

Outside the window was buried Mrs. Schweitzer, who died in 1957 at the age of seventy-five. Tools are propped on the porch railing outside his door as a precaution against their being stolen. "The chickens roost on the railing," the doctor said. "They make a good burglar alarm." He instigated his unique burglar alarm system after he discovered that the natives were stealing the hospital's chamber pots and using them as cooking pots in the villages.

In this small, cell-like room, Dr. Schweitzer lived a spartan existence. He shaved with a straight razor, without soap or water. He cut his own hair. Recently a member of his staff appeared with a fresh haircut. The doctor asked him who cut it. "A brother at the Catholic mission cut it for five hundred francs," the man said. "I'd have done it for less," declared the doctor.

He always dressed the same: white pith helmet, white shirt and pants, and a black tie. He had had one hat for forty years and a tie for more than twenty years. He was told that some people had dozens of neckties. "For one neck?"

There was only one gasoline generator on the island, and that was in the operating room for X rays and a strong surgical light. Animals were everywhere, and not one was to be touched by anyone. Once, I was told, a goat got into the operating theater, and Schweitzer was furious because he said, "Don't you realize, that the goat could have eaten one of those rubber gloves and died!" When we were walking in the jungle, he told me to be very careful and look out—not to step on any snakes since it might *harm them!* (This was in jest, like the gorilla bit, I am sure, because if there is one thing I am not, it is a *snake stepper-on'er!*)

After a few days it was certainly my impression that he was not an aggressively evangelical, religious person. I also believe that his politics, as much as they would concern him at all, were rather to the left of center. He made a big thing to me about a brass bell he had just received from the East Germans. This surprised me. He was also against the United Nations sending a force into the Congo and called them "bandits" and "assassins" at the time. This side of him few people knew or have discovered; it was my view that he was quite a leftist Socialist. He had stopped his Sunday religious sermons to the patients, but was very concerned about atomic tests.

We had been in the area for a week and had spent three whole days with the doctor; then it was time to leave. I had never been more thrilled by an experience, and after it there was nothing else I really ever wanted to do. I then decided I would leave live television, at least on a weekly basis. I had accomplished what few men had done in making that trip to Lambaréné. The two others, whom I knew personally, who had made the long journey, were Eddie Albert, the actor, and my pal Pete Kriendler of the famous 21 Club restaurant.

The doctor walked us down the crooked path to the river's bank to say goodbye. It was late afternoon and the palm trees cast long shadows. Cooking fires burned redly in the gathering dusk. Children trailed behind us and dogs and chickens scrambled out of the way. The doctor asked us to come again and I said I'd be honored. "Never use that word with me," he said. "One need not honor another man."

Two *pirogues* were pushed out in the river to take us back to Lambaréné, from which we would begin our long flight home. We climbed into the teetering craft and the native paddlers steered them out into the current. All alone, the old doctor walked out on a little jetty. It was a sight I will never forget. We waved at him and shouted farewells. He removed his worn pith helmet and his long, white hair blew in the breeze. He bowed low, like a great actor acknowledging a tremendous ovation. That was our final sight of him . . . still standing and bowing gravely . . . a frail, fierce figure, seeming to defy time.

A year later, after I had left my weekly night program, I had refocussed my interests on a television and radio station that I bought in Maine. Our transmitter was on top of Mt. Washington, one of the highest peaks in the East, and at a height of over six thousand feet the signal covered a portion of southern Canada, Maine, Massachusetts, Vermont, and New Hampshire. Our studios were in a colorful Victorian hotel and ski lodge in Poland Spring, Maine. It was a great place to get away from my past hectic life and was a good investment.

On the hour, whenever I remembered to, I would rush upstairs from my office to the radio station and read the news. I enjoyed doing that.

One afternoon the bulletins placed before me to read began: "Dr. Albert Schweitzer died this morning in Lambaréné, Equatorial Africa." He was then ninety. I was saddened by the passing of this great man and yet so proud that I had known him.

I went down to my office after the news broadcast and opened the day's mail; there was a letter from Albert Schweitzer, mailed three weeks before from Africa. He thanked me for the box of the new Japanese felt-tipped pens that I had mailed him months before. He also cautioned me again, in French, "to look out for the gorillas and snakes and not to harm them."

I can honestly say that I have kept the faith; I have never teased a gorilla and never will. I keep my word!

18

East African Notebook

Swahili, the *lingua franca* of East Africa, is a most interesting language and is made up of pidgin Arabic, pidgin Bantu, and more recently a great deal of pidgin English. The English which has been added sounds much like the "baby-talk Italian" that I have written about earlier. For instance, in Swahili a bicycle is *baiskeli*, gasoline is *petroli*, a breast is *matiti*, a cookie is a *biskuti*, and a passport is *paspoti*. My two favorite words are: the one for an automobile, which is *motocaca* and sounds like someone just peed on your car; and the one for gonorrhea, which is *kissinono*—say that slowly again, and you will see that it's also a warning! They use the same word, *ndege*, which means both airplane and bird.

The African, now completely in charge of his own continent, is inclined to be very cool but courteous in his relations with the European. (Incidentally and very importantly, one never uses the terms *white* or *black* in Africa.) The words describing racial color are offensive and are to be avoided. One is called either an African or a European. They may refer to you as *mzungu*, their word for white, but forget it. Some of my best friends are *mzungus!*

Since *uhuru* (freedom), when addressing an African male, you now use the term *bwana* for mister, although occasionally I have been called boy, and at my age I was flattered. Swahili can be a language of great hospitality—for instance, they use the same word for guest or stranger: *mugani*.

My favorite country in East Africa is Kenya (pronounced KEN-YAH, not KEEN-YAH, although some British pronounce it that way). Nairobi is a modern city, but walk a few hundred yards outside the city limits, and you are in a culture of a thousand years ago with lion (*simba*), giraffe (*twiga*), and elephant (*tembo*). My best friends there, Jock and Betty Leslie-Melville, who live in a suburb outside Nairobi, can never let their dog out at night because of the leopard (*chui*).

The contrasts will amaze and amuse you. You can leave a fine restaurant after a dinner with French wine, pick up the early edition of the local newspaper, and find two stories on the front page. They read—ITEM: "The American magazine *Playboy* has been barred from the newsstands because the women of Kenya find it offensive. Also mothers find the pictures demoralizing to the young. It will no longer be allowed in this country." ITEM: "Man killed by poison arrow."

Nairobi has a fine drama theater. Miriam, Randy, and I saw the play *Sleuth* with a British cast six months before it appeared on Broadway. A little later the next morning, we were living in a tent at Amboselli, a safari camp, surrounded by elephant.

On the highways, good paved roads go only a few miles; then you are on dirt paths with road signs that say, ELEPHANT HAVE RIGHT OF WAY. Never honk your auto horn at an elephant, or you may find yourself up to your hips in Volkswagen.

You may be driving past a Masai village and see tall, dignified males dressed as warriors living in huts made of cow dung, and the next half hour be playing golf on a fine course with a sign that reads: BALLS MAY BE REMOVED FROM HIPPO FOOTPRINTS.

As you are driving out of Nairobi, you will notice that the telephone poles are three feet *higher* than in the U.S. This is necessary because of the height of the giraffe. No one wants to share a party line with the *twiga*.

Nairobi, a city of four hundred thousand, has all the problems of your community, such as traffic jams, prejudice, crime, and power failures. The power goes off so frequently that the local people refer to their utility as the East Africa Power and *Darkness* Company.

There is greater crime in Kenya now than there was when it was a colonial country. On the coast at a resort city, Malindi, a former slave-trading community north of Mombassa, they were having a serious problem with "pole gangs." These are thieves with long poles who, late at night, stick the poles through your window and take your clothing or purses. They have sharp razor blades on the ends of the poles so that if you were to awaken and grab the pole, you would have your hand slashed. Who wants to sleep wearing barbecue gloves? I never knew why, but there are no window screens in Africa. All windows are open, and if your wife is frightened by large flying bugs, she had better stay in Toledo. Your bed, however, is covered by netting.

Some friends told me that they called the local police in Malindi when someone was trying to get into their home. The African policeman at the desk said, "We'll come right over if you can send a car for us!"

In nine trips to Africa, we never saw an "Afro" hairdo, which was so much the style with our American blacks. Africans wear their hair just like the European male and female.

With the well-to-do African, the most popular motor car is of German make, and a new, amusing word has been coined for the *nouveau riche*. The showy, newly wealthy are called *wahbenzi*—*wah* for people and *benzi* for the Mercedes.

I have had dinner with the Attorney General of Kenya several times; he is a very chic African, Charles Njonjo, and I have never seen him when he was not wearing a carnation in his lapel. The former Vice-President, Joe Murumbi is also a friend; he takes great pride in owning the largest personal library in East Africa.

We would often stay with our friends, the Leslie-Melvilles or Jack and Doria Block. Block is the owner of many of the finest hotels in East Africa. Staying with them, we learned a curious custom. If we would spend the afternoon out on *safari* (which means to travel), we would return to their beautiful home to find five or six servants waiting to serve a formal dinner. But first you shower, put on pajamas and a robe, and then return to the living room for cocktails and dinner. We always ate that way. It is the custom. Fortunately, I have more pajamas than Doris Day does.

The British friends in the past did not have a television set inside their homes, but they would have one outside in a *tree*. Does this mean that television is for the birds? No, it's just the easiest way for the servants to see it sitting around outside. The Europeans did not have television sets in their homes until recently. The programming was pretty awful, but now they all have TV sets because of the video-taped movies that they can rent. It is a big business in the cities. I did see some of the African programming, and would you believe, they have a "Dear Abby"–type program? I still remember one of the questions:

"Whenever I watch American movies," one African writer wrote in, "they say things like, 'Me Tarzan, you Jane.' Do all Americans speak so primitively?"

East Africa will not show any television pictures of a gun or any scenes of shooting. Many American programs have been canceled because of their violence. And yet it is no secret that African tribal feelings are very violent. In parts of Africa, probably this week, hundreds have been slain in wars we never hear of. This is being written in late August of 1982, and this week I received a letter that three thousand were killed in Kenya early in the month in a short revolt.

I made a film documentary on African television for NBC that, I think, had many funny moments—particularly a quiz-show skit in Swahili called "Stop and Go." In editing it and playing it over and over on my Movieola, I was struck with the observation that laughter even from a group of spear-carrying Masai in the audience and from people who were a few hours out of the bush sounded just the same as any laughter heard on any program in America. I am speaking of the *sound* of laughter; turn off the picture, and there is no difference. If that seems rather imperious or pompous, I only offer the thought that it begins to sound different only if heard *with* the picture.

As another example, I once toured Tanzania and Kenya with a group of youngsters who are known as "Up With People," a really wonderful gathering of twenty talented American musicians and singers. I can quickly prove by showing you the film that there is a difference in the Africans' reaction to "rhythm songs" and "melody." We played our show out on the plains in a Masai village. When our music began, the entire group of barefoot, painted Africans would just automatically start to move about and tap their feet on an "up" number. As soon as some of the fine girl singers would sing a ballad, they would begin to move away. There was no reaction or emotion at all. Some of the African women would run away, frightened at the sound of loud, electronic guitars. Mind you, these were people who had never seen a live show.

Oh yes, on their television they also follow the news with a Swahili weather report, complete with a map, a pointer, and a few funny jokes. What is it, why is it that it seems universal that weather people are supposed to be silly?

The commercials in the various tribal tongues seem so very funny because they are imitations of ours but in Swahili, including beer-sipping, saying "AHHHH," and even the look of comfort on their faces after trying Preparation H.

It is said that no one can beat an African playing checkers. A game there lasts from fifty seconds to a minute, and most Africans who are watching know who will win after the first four or five moves. They play with beer-bottle caps, one side up, the other down on homemade cardboard squares. My daughter Randy, who plays fairly well, never had a chance with the many men she played with. They were drivers at a motor pool. A chess game with one of them was always a no-contest.

Africa, the oldest continent, where it is believed that all life began, remains a great mystery. For instance, it is widely believed by social scientists (and at the moment undocumented) that as a predominantly nonliterate people, who can neither read nor write, Africans possess a natural gift for observation that is *superior* to ours. Tests have been conducted in Africa in which large cards of pictures were held up, observed for fifteen seconds, and then taken away. The same tests were then conducted with Europeans. The Africans were able to remember more correctly and with greater detail than more "sophisticated" people. This talent is called *eidetic memory*; in which a picture or image is retained in the memory and recalled and then can be seen again in the "mind's eye." It may have something to do with their amazing skill at checkers.

It is also believed that all human beings once possessed this ability but lost it in modern society. And it is said that this strange talent is lost by an African six months after moving even to a small city. If my ancestors ever had this, I wish I could get it back. At the moment, I am sitting here wondering if I have had lunch yet, but since I am smoking my pipe, I have to assume that I have.

When TWA flew into East Africa, they had to stop first in Uganda. Few people got on or off at Entebbe, their airport, but they were forced to do it for political reasons with that crazy Idi Amin. (Can you picture Amin singing "Mack the Knife"?) On one trip we got off at Entebbe and stayed at the airport motel. Years later it became more exciting to us during the Israeli raid to free the hostages. We knew that area and could imagine the scene of the heroic rescue operation.

Uganda was rather an advanced society by African standards and had one of the best universities in that part of the world. It's a beautiful country with many wild animals and, of course, Lake Victoria. We were not aware that it was such a dangerous place then as we knew little of Amin. We did notice though that the British were planning to get out; the friends we had made escaped before all the murdering began.

I recall a wonderful lesson I learned one day in Uganda. There were four of us in a land rover high on a mountain road in the section known as the Mountains of the Moon, a very high range that looks down on the Congo on the other side. At that time, only seven miles away, the Congo, a former Belgian colony now known as Zaire, was going through a revolution, and there had been killings of Europeans and several Catholic nuns. We stopped our car to have a basket lunch and to observe what we could with binoculars. We were with our friends, Jock and Betty Leslie-Melville. He was British and became a Kenyan citizen, while Betty, an American, became a Kenyan resident. Jock was born in Africa and educated at Eton and Sandhurst; he was a former lieutenant in the Cold Stream Guards and a part of the police force of British Kenya in fighting the Mau Mau. He also spoke many African dialects. Jock loved all of Africa with a passion. I must tell you that Africa is a very clean country. There is no waste, no trash, and the bush country is spotless. When anything dies, it is immediately cleaned by the vultures, and nothing remains but white bones.

In my excitement I casually and carelessly dropped a sandwich wrapping on the ground, a hundred miles from nowhere, but no matter; as I got back in the land rover, I was ashamed to see Jock quietly go back and pick up my wrapper and put it in his pocket. I never did that again, despite the fact that perhaps ten miles away people were killing each other.

The other part of the then-British East Africa was then called Tanganyika; now it is known as Tanzania. The capital is a quaint and attractive city, Dar-es-Salaam. This was a former German colony before the First World War, and the architecture is Germanic. It has become dominated by a strange combination of African and Chinese Communists, and the government of Nyerere no longer wishes tourists to enter. So what was once a combination of Tanzania, Kenya, and Uganda, mutually sharing an airline, a railway, and commerce, is now torn apart by tribal and political strife.

Off the coast of Tanzania and an integral part of that country is the island of Zanzibar. We were told we must go there because it was a great place to send postcards from, as it is one of the most exotic places in the world. We went. That's about all I can say for Zanzibar: you can impress people with your postcards! It has good beaches, and I remember that we had to tippy-toe into the Indian Ocean because the water was so *hot!*

An interesting observation is that Africans are seldom seen swimming. This, I believe, must be because of the disease *bilharzia*—a weakening of the body that is caused by the snails in the slow-moving water of the inner streams and rivers of Africa. This avoidance of swimming has been carried over somehow through the years by many African-Americans who excel in many sports but usually not in swimming.

I have seen soccer played by Africans wearing knee socks with the fronts cut off and actually kicking the ball with their bare toes. Why they wear the socks at all is a mystery. It hurts just to watch.

It is a custom of the Masai tribe for anyone speaking against the chief to stand on one foot supported by a stick. He can speak only so long as he can remain on *one* foot. This is an idea we would welcome if our politicians were forced to use that method. Most of ours would lean against a tree.

I have filmed the way some of the exclusive clubs in Africa have their floors waxed. What I saw was eight men with sheep-skin booties on their feet dancing side-ways to the music of "Tea for Two." As they moved about, the floors were shined beau-tifully. Don't tell me I have made this up. I have film. And be-sides, there are no bags to empty.

I have stood in a line at the bank in Nairobi to find a Masai standing behind me in his bare feet, wearing a pink blanket and carrying a spear. It's all very interesting and casual.

We often rented small aircraft to fly into the interior of Kenya and Uganda. The landing strips are mostly cut out of the bush for small planes to land. There is no airport or ground crew. These airstrips are mainly for the emergency landing of doctors in that area. The interesting thing is that before one lands, he has to buzz the field at a low altitude several times in order to clear the strip of wild animals. We have had many close calls with cape buffalo who didn't wish to move.

John Reddy, my late good friend who accompanied me on many of these trips, has written of some of my adventures for *Reader's Digest* and *TV Guide*. Here is one that my friends par-ticularly like:

> We were in a land rover in Uganda going into the Ituri Forest where Jack wanted to film the Pygmies, a small people who are only found deep in the forest. By some fascinating anthro-pological fact, as you go into the woods the people get smaller and smaller. The first were about five feet tall; then miles deeper, they became close to four and a half feet. Jack insisted that we go all the way. When Paar wants to see a Pygmy, you humor him and push on. Miles later we had to walk in as the car path ended. But before that the little people, anxious to see a Euro-

pean, began to follow the car and sell Jack things. He bought plenty but was becoming impatient.

At one point, the rover slowed down, and a small native, about four and a half feet tall, reached through the window where Jack was sitting and said in Swahili, "Me Pygmy! Me Pygmy!" He was hoping to sell Paar a poison arrow.

"I beg your pardon?" Jack replied, not understanding. The diminutive African repeated, "Me Pygmy!"

And our leader Paar said, "I am sure you are a perfectly nice chap . . . but you are NOT A PYGMY! Now BUZZ OFF!"

And that alone has kept me from being appointed to the State Department.

Many miles from that joke, we came into the area where the little dark Munchkins were. They are most illusive and keep moving about to avoid being attacked by their taller neighbors. They are, despite their size, the most ferocious of hunters. They are less than four feet and will attack an elephant with bow and arrow. They live deep in the forest and only come out to sell the Bantu tribes meat in exchange for salt and flint for fire. They then disappear back into the tall trees and keep changing their location so as not to be enslaved by the tribes who live on the edge of the forest. All races seem to need to have someone to look *down upon,* and when you reach the level of the Pygmy, at least optically, there is no other way to look.

We started off with five people, and as we walked we knew we were being followed by ten, then twenty African adults and children. We could not see them; they would dart in and out of the bush ever so quietly, but as Karen Blixen has written: the African has a *presence;* you know they are there!

They are simply curious. After all you are tall, of a different color, and dressed oddly; you speak strangely and wish to enter a part of their world that has no interest for them. In a sense, you are the best show in town.

When we reached the living place of the little people, I was told by our guide that the foliage was all marijuana, which the local people called *bang,* and it grows wild there. Suddenly we were up to our hips in people who were high on pot and ever so friendly. They were shooting their arrows at a kind of target and wanted us to join them. Well, I have always felt that marijuana and poison arrows don't mix. I am an old-fashioned party pooper. I had some gifts: cigarette lighters and some matches; Miriam had some shorts to give, as well as candy bars and chewing gum— we were a smash!

I wanted to know how they made their poison, and Jock Leslie-Melville explained. A Pygmy makes it from bark and root, and to test its potency he raises his arm upward, makes a cut on his wrist, and as the red blood flows downward on his arm, he touches the poison to the bottom of the stream of blood; as it flows upward on his arm like a white thermometer, he stops it before it reaches the wound. The speed of the poison going upward tells him the strength.

I do not vouch for the following story; it's possibly apocryphal. I was told that a Pygmy chief wanted to be taller and consulted the local witch doctor. The W.D., or witch doctor, succeeded by sneaking in at night and cutting an inch off the chief's cane.

Here are some interesting thoughts on Africa: Did you know that seven out of ten Africans have never seen a lion? Or that lion do not live in the heavy jungle? If they did, God or nature would have made them *green*. Or that one never uses the word *jungle* in Africa, and there is no word for it in an African language? (Lion live on the plains in heavy grass which is the exact color of their bodies.)

Or that nearly all animals will run from you as soon as they hear or get the scent of a human? The great danger is stumbling onto one who is resting. This is why the Pygmy goes through the forest clapping his hands.

That one of the most dangerous animals can be the ostrich? When I was told that an ostrich does not bury its head in the sand, I reasoned that certainly the *female* would not—especially during the *mating* season!

That the author of the Tarzan series, Edgar Rice Burroughs, had never been in Africa? And that Bo Derek and her husband should never have gone there?

That in 1871, when Henry Stanley, a reporter for the New York *Herald*, achieved worldwide fame for going to Africa and "finding" the Scottish missionary and explorer, David Livingstone, Livingstone wasn't lost and refused to be rescued?

That a hunter must be from two hundred to five hundred yards from his motor car before he shoots any animal, depending on the country he is in?

That some of the finest writing on Africa has been by *women*: Elspeth Huxley, Karen Blixen, Jane Goodall, Joy Adamson, and Martha Gellhorn?

That an unwritten hunting law is: "A gentleman never shoots anything after five o'clock"? This is because on the equator after five, there is not enough daylight left to track a wounded animal.

That in nine trips through East and West Africa, I have seldom seen a gun? I have never carried one because it would be considered "corny"; besides, unless it's a rifle and you have a permit, a gun is illegal.

This is interesting: British colonial children, who played and grew up quite naturally out on the plantations with African children, would more often than not be led by the local black boys. At about age twelve the roles reversed, and they went their separate ways, although many friendships remained through adulthood but in a different relationship. In games, in boyish adventures, and in big-brother protection, it was the African boys who were the *leaders*. But then the roles *reversed*.

There are job opportunities for the bright African young man, and his wish might be to become a clerk with the government or work in a bank or office. Although he may be trained and able, he has a problem at both ends of his social life. What I am about to describe is quite true, and one sees it all the time in the offices or on the streets of the larger cities.

Among certain tribes in East Africa, there is the strange custom of putting a hole in the ear lobe and, gradually over the years, stretching it until the hole is about two or three inches wide like a doughnut. This leaves a large loop hanging downward. Out in the bush one can often see women with yellow film canisters that have been discarded by tourists, placed in this opening. When the young man comes to the city and wears a blue suit, he becomes conscious of his hanging-loop lobes and places the bottom of the loop up over the top of his ear. This makes for a slightly disfigured appearance by our standards, but it is not as noticeable as far as he is concerned. However, on weekends, when the young man goes back to his native village and has his ear positioned in the city manner, they have an expression: "Come on, relax, be yourself. Let your *ears down!*"

Here is a scene one morning at the Nairobi post office. I had some Havana cigars sent on to me in Africa from a tobacconist in London. When I presented my notice to the African clerk, he explained after some thought that I would have to pay an import duty on the cigars. I agreed and asked, "How much?" He figured that the duty on tobacco was by the ounce. Well, I suggested that the best way to weigh the cigars was to take them out of the box and put them on the scale. He did. He took out each of the fifty cigars and weighed them individually. Then he had a hell of a problem with addition!

Behind me was a British colonial lady who was in a Greer Garson–type rage because she wanted to claim her box of "shoe trees" sent out from England. The clerk said, "No, if they are 'shoe trees,' you must get a permit from the Department of Agriculture."

These are semantic problems and understandably so. The African uses English in a literal sense. I would never order *toilet water* without checking the label.

The early missionaries had difficulty with the word *adultery*. The Africans had no such word in their language because they didn't practice it, which put the reverent folk in the embarrassing position of having to explain it; without the word *adultery*, they could not teach the Ten Commandments.

Mount Kenya, at seventeen thousand feet, is the second highest peak in Africa and is so beautiful to see. Although located on the equator, where summer occurs year-round, it is snow-capped all year because of the high altitude. Mount Kilimanjaro in Tanzania, at nineteen thousand feet, is *higher*, but who counts? We once climbed by jeep to about five thousand feet on a dirt path with our pals, the Leslie-Melvilles. Coming down the mountain at the base, there is an inn and bar. We stopped and met the most colorful character—the owner, who is a former British Commander named Logan Hook. He was a large man looking much like the motion picture actor Sidney Greenstreet. Wearing a plantation straw hat, he was very aristocratic and superior. I loved his act—he was really far out! In his tavern there was a long bar, and on the bar was a three-foot brass arrow pointing to the center. At the tip of the arrow on the bar was a brass sign which read, "You are at the exact point of the equator."

I am always interested in anything that is "exact"; whether it is where Lincoln was shot, or where Columbus came ashore, or where Arthur Godfrey sat. I am moved by things like that. So I said to Mr. Hook, "Sir, how does one know that this is *exactly* the equator? I mean, is it done by magnetic compass, or astrologically by shooting the stars? How can one *know exactly* where latitude zero is? How can one be certain that I am standing on either the celestial or is it the galactic exact latitude of the ecliptic plane? Things like that are important to me!"

Commander Hook drew himself up to his full six feet four, two hundred fifty pounds, and said in the most marvelous British sarcastic voice, "Dear boy, you have become a pain in the ass. It's all very simple. When one *owns* a bar, one just *knows where* the equator is!"

Mr. Hook was killed a few years later. He was murdered by an African. In his memory, I would like to think that he was only a few inches off.

Mount Kilimanjaro used to be in Kenya; now it is in Tanzania. No, they didn't move the largest mountain in Africa, but Queen Victoria, the Empress of Kenya, gave it to Kaiser Wilhelm, the ruler of what was then Tanganyika, and they redrew the border between the two countries. That's pretty damn cavalier—giving a mountain that you don't own away to your German cousin! I wonder what the Kaiser said—perhaps, "Oh, Vickie dear, you *shouldn't* have!" I suppose for Christmas he tried to send her the Nile.

Lake Naivasha is about fifty miles from Nairobi and is a very interesting colony of somewhat bohemian, bizarre residents. There are some Italians in the area who were captured by the British in Ethiopia during the Second World War and brought to Kenya as prisoners of war to work on the roads. After the war, the Italians wished to stay on, and now they own some very nice farms and plantations, called *ohambas.* Some have married, and in a mixed bag of races many of the women are attractive, chic, and educated.

Joy Adamson, who wrote *Born Free,* had her home at Naivasha and was the local celebrity. Ian Douglas-Hamilton and his wife— he is the leading authority and filmmaker on the elephant—are residents there. Another famous writer, Martha Gellhorn, former wife of Ernest Hemingway, lived nearby. My best friend, Shuki Bisletti, is married to an Italian count, lived in Naivasha, and is a fascinating woman. She is of Dutch descent. Shuki, who was captured by the Japanese at Singapore and held prisoner for three years, speaks five languages. She is also a pretty lady. Her fame, though a quiet one, is as a trainer or "handler" of wild animals for the motion pictures filmed in Africa. It was her lion that portrayed Elsa in *Born Free* and *Living Free,* and the cubs that I brought to America were hers. She had a wonderful way with animals and a great deal of courage. When they were making the motion picture *Hatari,* another female "handler," Diane Hartley, was attacked by a lion and was killed. Shuki threw herself on the lion to try to divert his attention until they could pull Diane out of the way. They had to shoot the lion. Shuki told me, "Damn! Damn! It was unnecessary. Diane should have known better."

This intrigued me . . . "*What* should Diane have known? What did she do wrong?"

It is not my wish to be indelicate, but as a point of information, Shuki replied, "We all know, and Diane knew, that a woman is never to go near a wild animal if she is having her menstrual period!"

Miriam and I brought Shuki to the United States for a television program that I was shooting for NBC. After placing her three fully grown lions that I had brought from Africa in a safari park in West Palm Beach, Florida, the idea was to see if a year later Shuki could walk into a pride of fifteen or twenty lions and be recognized by the lion she had raised.

It was very dangerous, and the owners of the safari park were against it because they didn't have insurance for such craziness. I knew that if we could do it and if we were protected by armed guards, it would be one of the most exciting, unrigged, unrehearsed scenes on television. It was, as some columnists wrote later, "goose-pimple time." Cameramen stayed in their station wagons, and I planned to also, but I was holding a tape recorder with a long cord, and Shuki had the microphone pinned to her shirt; I either had to get out of the car and follow her or blow the exciting bit. I ended up beside her with my usual stuttering and stammering.

With only a small stick in her hand, she walked among the lion speaking in her Swahili, Dutch, Italian, and Japanese baby talk, and by God two lions eventually came to her in a period of three minutes. They knew! They remembered! What a smashing five minutes of film. Shuki got on her knees and hugged them. I admit that I stood there with tears streaming down my cheeks—still laughing at the same time, but still too frightened to move!

If you saw this film, and it has been rerun three times, you may remember that one tough South African armed hunter, who was standing by with a powerful rifle, said, "It's the most unusual scene I have ever witnessed. I still can't believe it!" Of course, a few television critics had the usual comment: "Another of Jack Paar's 'home' movies."

My favorite story of dear Shuki is that after the filming and showering, I took her to the swankiest restaurant on Worth Avenue in Palm Beach, called the Petite Marmite. Over a cool glass of Chardonnay in celebration of her splendid performance and courage, I gave her what she really wanted: a simple Zippo cigarette lighter. This one I had gold-plated with rubies and the inscription: "Love from Mim, Ran, and Jak." She very haughtily asked an American waiter to have it filled with lighter fluid. He went away and returned, saying there was no fluid at the bar. Then Shuki raised one eyebrow and said in the most superior but gentle manner, still that of a great lady, "No lighter fluid? I say, then have them fill it with the best brandy, Bwana—Upesi! Upesi!" (Swahili for "Quick! Quick!")

The waiter looked startled but did as the mem'sab (woman) ordered, and I can tell you that if you are ever hard up and out of lighter fluid, improvise—use brandy, but use a good year!

We all loved Shuki so much that we gave her our greatest honor   we named our next dachshund puppy after her.

Joy Adamson, the author of *Born Free* and *Living Free*, the story of Elsa the Lion, had a very lovely home at Naivasha. Your picture of her, if you only read the books or saw the motion pictures, would be quite far from reality. In the films she was portrayed by Virginia McKenna and later by Susan Hampshire—two very attractive British actresses. They were both glamorous and had soft, gentle personalities. (Indeed, they were classical performers of the English stage.) The real Joy Adamson was something quite different.

First, Joy Adamson was not at all British by birth, manner, or speech. She was born in Austria, and her speech was very difficult to understand. Second, Joy was an extremely intelligent and gifted writer and a worldwide-accepted authority on ecology, but what is not so well known is that she was a most gifted artist. Her paintings of the African tribes are the best I have ever seen. The real Joy Adamson was a driven zealot in her quest on behalf of the Elsa Fund for animal preservation. I can't think of anyone her equal in dedication on behalf of all wildlife.

On a personal and social level, she was a difficult lady. I found her hard to be with; although she was very nice to me, she became tiresome and was quite rude to Miriam and Randy, whom she figured she didn't need. The real Joy Adamson was a cross between Shelley Winters and Otto Preminger.

Interviews with her on the air in New York and later for five days with her at Naivasha were a disaster. I had given several thousand dollars to the Elsa Fund, and there was no question that the money would be used for her cause. She could have been a very wealthy lady from her book sales and the rights to the motion pictures. But to her credit she was not after luxury or self-comfort.

The filmed interview with her in Africa was most difficult. She would not enter into a conversation but did a ten-minute commercial for her fund. I tried many ways to get her to relax and become what she was—a fascinating, driven woman—but she insisted on sounding like a burlesque of a German evangelist. I was criticized, and rightly so, by people who didn't know the facts, by having only a minute or so of her on the final program. My loyalty always was to the TV audience, and if I had shown the entire harangue, it would have done us both harm.

If she had exhibited a little charm or had spent a few moments telling about her relationship with Elsa the lioness, or about her life in Africa, which must have been fascinating, or about her experiences with her estranged husband, George—it would have been so much better for her cause exposed on a national network television program. But, no—she believed in the *hard* sell; using every moment to ask for funds was a turn-off.

Joy was having trouble with her African servants, whom she treated with contempt. Since her Elsa Fund was worldwide, she needed a secretary, but she had difficulty in keeping one for more than a few weeks, and the one I talked to was frightened to death of her and was leaving on the next bus to Nairobi.

In a week with her at Naivasha, I only experienced one natural, human moment from a woman who had written one of the most touching and moving stories of the decade, *Born Free*.

In the making of the second movie, *Living Free*, there was an important scene in her book and later in the movie that I had to assume was from a real experience with her husband George.

Miriam, Randy, and I were there during the filming on location outside Naivasha. We lived with Shuki Bisletti, who was working on the picture as an animal consultant. Shuki and Joy did not get along, and there was some ill feeling because poor Joy was eventually barred by the producer Carl Foreman from even coming near the actors or the director.

The movie company went to considerable expense—I would guess over a hundred thousand dollars for just three minutes of film. It was a scene in an African valley where Joy and her husband had pitched a tent and made a small camp that was washed out by a flood. The scene would take in a quarter mile in the long shot, and then at the end a dam would burst and flood the camp, wiping out their tent and jeep. German engineers were flown from Europe to dam up the small stream that could then be released after three weeks of storing up millions of gallons of water. It had to be absolutely perfect in its release and timing and could only be done once. It was also very dangerous because

Susan Hampshire, playing Joy, had to swim out from under the washed away tent at the peak of the force of the water. The cameraman could be knocked down and had to photograph from behind large boulders or rocks because the waves of onrushing water were three feet high. There were four different cameramen, and in the actual shooting one cameraman was washed away but saved. It had been rehearsed for days without, of course, the dam bursting. My daughter had her own place behind a rock with her movie camera, and I was up on a hill with my camera, and standing beside me was Joy.

The actual countdown was exciting, and then came the thundering rush of water down the valley and into the tented area. The water was so strong that it picked up a jeep and moved it six feet.

The scene was so spectacular that everyone in the crew of about thirty was overjoyed. I was so happy because I had gotten some most unusual film for my television program. It was really a great day. At the time a question crossed my mind: Was this dramatic license? Did all of this actually happen to Joy and her husband in real life?

I looked around and couldn't find Joy. A few moments later I saw her behind a rock sobbing uncontrollably. I went over and held her for a moment—her head on my shoulder, she said, "It *was* like that." There was no question then in my mind that it was real.

One amusing thing took place just before the countdown that afternoon. I had remembered that Randy had the wrong filter on her camera lens, and there was no way to tell her as she was a quarter of a mile away awaiting the flood. The crew had loudspeakers along the valley for giving instructions to everyone, and just before the countdown I went to the assistant director and told him about my daughter's camera.

Throughout this valley there was the echo of the booming voice of the British director, "Randy, your father says to change the filter on your camera!"

When it was all over and it was a "wrap" (movie slang for "finished"), the director kindly asked again on the booming P.A.

system, "Randy, did you have time to change your filter?" (Echo! Echo! Echo!)

There was a pause, and then from her end she got on the microphone and said, for everyone in the valley to hear, "Don't tell my father, but could you all do that again?" (Echo! Echo! Echo!)

It was the biggest laugh my daughter ever got!

Joy's husband, George Adamson, a former game warden, left their home and went to live in the bush alone in a *cage*. He lived in the cage to protect himself from the wild animals he was studying. He had a kerosene refrigerator which was generally full of meat for his lion friends. He deserves more credit than he received in the story of Elsa. He was well liked by the people of Kenya, both Africans and Europeans. When asked why he left the luxury of home with Joy, George said, "There are only three things I need in life: tobacco, gin, and Worcestershire sauce, and you see Joy is *none* of the three." When last I heard, he was still out there living alone.

The news that Joy Adamson was found dead in the bush was a shock. The first reports were that she had been attacked by an animal. I wondered at the time if it could have been murder either for money or for her imperial treatment of the Africans. Later reports said that she had been murdered.

Joy Adamson was a great, historic figure, talented beyond belief, sincerely and honestly dedicated to her animal preservation fund; she just was not a very pleasant or gracious person.

Randy and I did most of the filming on our trips to Africa. We had two cameras and a tape recorder interlocked, and I could start them by pressing a button that would send out a signal that would start both cameras and sound automatically. True, it was not motion-picture quality but was certainly adequate, considering that we were in remote areas. It is the only way I can work because I listen and look for many days to find a story. I could not have a crew of ten professionals following me around. The pressure is too great and too costly, as I do not shoot from a script but first find a story. After all, I reasoned, God made the world in only six days, but he had the advantage of working alone. He was a very wise man. Just think if our world had been created by a committee?

We once went up Mount Kilimanjaro in Tanzania by land rover to around six thousand feet and pitched camp. We built a fire because it was getting quite cold, set up my cameras and sound, placed some camp chairs around the burning logs, and after starting the cameras, rushed back to the center and began to talk to our friends who were with us: Jock and Betty Leslie-Melville and Miles Burton, a "white hunter." It was the first "talk show from Mount Kilimanjaro." That's a record that should stand. Now there are so many talk programs that children seeing the painting of the Last Supper must think it's a panel show.

I would chat away with my guests and pals and then have to stop, since my cameras were only able to take four-hundred-foot reels. I would then reload, start the cameras again, rush back, and act as host. I also had to use a clapboard as a sync mark for the sound, and once in my frantic hurrying around, I got my finger caught as I slammed the clapper down. They were wonderful days as I think back.

Around the campfire, I remember some of the men saying that at sixteen thousand feet both men and women lose all sexual desire. So don't say you haven't been warned. Remember what your mother taught you: "Do not go all the way."

Miles Burton was a wonderful young man. He had been a hunter but had given it up because all the blood and killing sickened him. Now he would only take out small busloads of visitors on camera safaris. He had recently had a group of German tourists for a few days, and he could imitate them perfectly. He said that he found the Germans behaved exactly as they did in the movies. "You give them an order, and they jumped to comply." After a week of lining up the visitors several times a day and saying, "Attention, you and you get in that bus, you and you get over there, and you go here and you over there in the last bus." They would obey exactly. After three days a little German lady came up to Miles and said, "Plis, Herr Tour Leader, tomorrow coot I sitten in zee boos noomer one. Zat's where my hoseband is, and I haven't zeen him in tree days."

Last year Miles was killed in a plane accident along with Gordon Parks, Jr., working for a film company in East Africa.

I heard a story about Bruce McKenzie, who was a most respected British colonial officer and was held over in the Kenyan government as the Commissioner of Agriculture. For some reason, he had some business with the mad Idi Amin and had an audience with him at the Ugandan capital in Kampala. We don't know what was discussed, but Amin was angry. However, as the plane was about to leave Uganda to return to Kenya, Amin had a present rushed to the aircraft at the last moment. I believe it was some kind of animal trophy. After the plane was in the air there was an explosion. A bomb had been placed in the trophy, and all were killed.

The plane went down in the N'gong Hills of Kenya, which may interest those of you who have read *Out of Africa*. This is the book by Karen Blixen (*née* Isak Dinesen) that I believe to be the finest book ever written on East Africa. In the true story, the N'gong Hills are where Miss Dinesen's lover went to his death in an airplane and where the modern legend still has it that animals come at night to guard his grave.

Another fantastic air story was in the Central African Republic. It's a landlocked country northwest of Uganda and very difficult to get to. A big status thing in Africa a few years ago was that each country wanted to have their own *jet* plane. The Central African Republic finally got a DC-8. There is only one airstrip in the whole country to land that size plane; it is located at the capital of Bangui. The plane was not licensed to fly internationally and did not have a crew with international credentials, training, or equipment, the only place it could take off from and return to was Bangui. So if you are ever going to Africa, would like tickets from Bangui to Bangui, and are having trouble, call me. I have connections.

19

Return To
The South Pacific

After I left the "Tonight" program, I had four months off before beginning a weekly, prime-time program on Friday nights, so I had time to think of something unusual with which to open the new series. A book had just been published, written by Robert Donovan, about President Kennedy's experiences in World War II in the South Pacific on a small attack boat, the PT 109. Nothing had been done on television or in motion pictures about the event. It was a thrilling story of heroism and had particular interest for me because I had served in that very same area. My idea was to make the long journey to the South Pacific and try to reunite the Australian coast watcher, Reg Evans, and a little Melanesian native, Ben Kevu, in the Solomon Islands where they had rescued Lieutenant Kennedy and the crew of the PT 109.

I was able to contact Reg Evans, who was now a quiet accountant in Sydney, Australia. I asked him by letter if he would like to accompany me and two members of my staff to return to the Solomon Islands in the South Pacific and film the area and mountains where the story took place. Reg agreed and said he would try to find Ben Kevu; he would rent a small boat and stock it with supplies for a ten-day journey. The Solomons are a British protectorate group of islands in the Southwest Pacific, where some of the most famous battles raged.

It was not only to be a story of Lieutenant John Kennedy but, more important, about the "coast watchers" who served so heroically in the war. The coast watchers were mostly Australian volunteers who had had experience in the area before the war, either as members of a trading company or plantation managers for Lever Brothers. Lever Brothers had used the palm trees on the island to make soap. These brave men infiltrated the many islands and went upon the mountain peaks and set up radio equipment in small camps. They lived alone for months, radioing messages about Japanese aircraft and shipping down the "Slot," a channel between the many islands of the Solomons. It was the route used by the Japanese for shipping and for planes going southward toward Guadalcanal. The coast watchers were alone, but at the base of their mountain hideaways there were Japanese troops on the shore, unaware that they were being spied upon.

All this area was in the hands of the Japanese at the time. The coast watchers needed the co-operation of the local Melanesian people, who were a dark, primitive race not at all like the Polynesians of the Central Pacific or the Hawaiians, the Tahitians, the Samoans, or even the stoic Fijians. (Incidentally, the Fijians are the only people I have ever seen who wear their hair like our Afro-Americans.)

The Melanesians are on the whole a short, African-looking people, very backward by the standards of the rest of the world. Some have been educated by Seventh Day Adventist missionaries. There are no pretty girls with flowers behind their ears. These local people were, however, very loyal to their former colonial masters and later to the Americans. I have never heard of a single instance of a Melanesian turning in any member of the Allied Forces to the Japanese. The natives knew the coast watchers were on the mountain and brought them food and scouted for them. It took exceptional and experienced men to hold the confidence of the local people, who had little idea of what the war was all about. Ben Kevu, the native boy, was certainly a hero by any standard, and I felt that to meet him and know him would be a great pleasure and might make one hell of a TV show.

I knew a great deal of the PT 109 story and was anxious to bring it to television with the film I hoped to get. Much has been written about the President's adventure when he was the skipper of the ill-fated little attack craft. The PT boats had powerful motors but were made of plywood and were only meant for a fast in-and-out attack on a destroyer. They had no armor and no sophisticated navigational equipment. However, on the dark night of August 1, 1943, PT 109 became lost and was accidentally rammed by a Japanese destroyer and cut in half. Two men were killed, and others were badly burned and wounded. Lieutenant Kennedy was responsible for saving the lives of all the remaining men eventually, but took a particular risk saving a seaman, Pat McMahon, who was badly burned. Kennedy took McMahon's life-saver straps in his mouth and swam a great distance, pulling him to a nearby island. The heroism was real. He saved all the sailors on the little boat. After putting all the living men ashore on an island, he swam out for two nights into the channel, hoping to find a PT boat or submarine that might be looking for them. His courage and fortitude and patience cannot be questioned. I later came to know every survivor of the incident personally and heard them tell the stories that were later on my television program. I also talked to the Commander of the Japanese destroyer, the *Amagiri*, which rammed PT 109, and had him on television from Japan. So I am quite certain that the legend of the PT 109 is true and that "Shafty," as Kennedy was nicknamed by his crew, was a genuine hero. My interest went further than the PT 109 accident; I wanted to know about these coast watchers. I spent nearly two years in that part of the Pacific during the war and never knew of these men.

John Reddy of the *Reader's Digest*, Tom Cochran of my staff, and I took off from Hong Kong, headed for the South Pacific. Despite the travel booklets—which usually say that "getting there is half the fun"—it is not so! New Guinea is one of the most remote places on the globe. We had been filming stories in Hong Kong and made arrangements to leave from there. Miriam had accompanied me as far as the Crown Colony, but she could not

go any farther, because once we arrived in the Solomons, it was to
be a really uncomfortable journey, in which we would have to
sleep on the deck of a sixty-foot boat at night for a week.

I left my wife at the Hong Kong airport with a tearful farewell,
because Miriam knew I would be gone three weeks or more, and
it was not all to be fun and games. But who do you think accompanied my wife to the airport and promised to look out for her
and get her back to the United States? The least likely person to
be in that exotic part of the world—Buddy Hackett! When the
chips are down, Buddy, whom you may know for his craziness, is
a very sound and intelligent friend.

Just for you trivia buffs: I'll bet there isn't one in a million who
would recognize our final destination by the printed name on our
return tickets. It was *Honiara*. You and I never heard of it as
such, but it was one of the most famous names of the war in the
Pacific—Guadalcanal. That's the only name now used by the little airline that flies in there every two weeks from Fiji.

By letter, weeks before, I had arranged for Reg Evans to rent a
boat to take us around the Solomon Islands. He finally contracted
for a sixty-foot boat to meet us at Munda with a native, barefoot
crew that spoke only pidgin English. The boat was called the
Kingfisher and was to be stocked with rations for ten days. The
rations turned out to be cases of canned peas, beer, and some
tinned crackers—that was it. The timing had to be perfectly
planned since airplanes only flew down there once a week.

After flying to Australia to pick up Reg Evans in Sydney, we
took off by Trans-Australia Airlines for the Solomons. We left
Sydney at nine o'clock at night in a DC-6 and flew most of the
night, passing over the Great Barrier Reef and the Coral Sea, and
landing at Port Moresby, New Guinea, at 6:10 the following
morning. There we changed to a plump-bodied, two-motored
Fokker Friendship for the remainder of the flight to Munda.

The weather in New Guinea was oppressively humid, with a
soft, warm rain falling, and the flight from there on was excep-
tionally turbulent. We passed through broken clouds and sudden
rain squalls, and our plane lurched and dipped as we flew across
the mist-shrouded Owen Stanley Mountains to Lae. At each stop
the airport facilities became more primitive. At Port Moresby, the

capital of the Territory of Papua and New Guinea, the airfield boasted a modern terminal building. At Lae, from which Amelia Earhart took off on her fatal flight, the terminal was a small, cottagelike building. At volcano-fringed Rabaul, on the island of New Britain, the terminal was a small shed with privies in back. At the island of Buka, across the narrow Buka Passage from jungle-choked Bougainville, the only facility was a shed with a corrugated metal roof. As we flew over the Solomon Islands, the clouds gradually dispersed and we could see patches of blue-green water and green islands clearly in the tropic sun. Evans, who knew the islands and surrounding waters intimately, identified the islands of musical names but bloody memory as we passed over them: Vella Lavella, Wana Wana, Kolombangara, Rendova.

The sun seemed to burn away the clouds as we neared the islands of New Georgia, and it was blazing hot when our plane set down on the deserted-looking airstrip at Munda, the scene of much fierce fighting during the war. In a small, shedlike building, which seemed to double as a post office and terminal, we waited in the stifling heat for what seemed like an eternity while native customs officials, in khaki uniforms with red piping, studied our passports as intently as if they were trying to decipher hieroglyphics. Flies buzzed around the uncomfortable little room, and about a dozen natives, men, women, and children watched the formalities solemnly and silently. Finished at last, Reg Evans led us through the little native village to where the *Kingfisher* was waiting.

Hot and tired from a night and most of a day flying, we were glad when Jack Nwame, the native bo'sun, put out from the dock and headed through Kula Gulf and Diamond Narrows for the Blackett Strait where PT 109 was sunk. It was then, while the sixty-foot *Kingfisher* threaded its way through the calm waters of Diamond Narrows, that I first got to know Ben Kevu. I was reading Robert Donovan's excellent book *PT 109* to familiarize myself with the details of the story we planned to film, and I decided to brief the native crew on our project. Several of them were sitting on the fo'c'sle, so I decided to try to get acquainted by talking with them and explaining our project.

I showed them the book, with its picture of the thin, boyish Lieutenant Kennedy on the dust jacket, and undertook to explain what we planned to do. Some of the crew nodded tentatively, but I had the feeling that I wasn't exactly getting through. I dropped into my best Hollywood Tarzan talk, pointed at the picture of Kennedy, and said, "Him President. You understand? Like chief." They smiled in a friendly way, but I suspected that I still wasn't making myself clear. Since the Solomons are a British protectorate, I decided to try a more British tack. "Him like Queen," I suggested, pointing again at the picture of the young naval officer. There were more rather mystified smiles.

Then a little man took the book from my hands and leafed through it. "Him, me," he said shyly, pointing at a photograph in the book. Sure enough, it was Ben, but looking not nearly so fierce in person as he did in the photograph in the book. From then on, he became a fast friend as well as an invaluable guide to the scenes we wished to film.

I had planned to go from island to island looking for Ben Kevu, filming my quest for dramatic effect, and there he was already on the boat! And he had to *tell me* who he was! I didn't even get to say, "Mr. Kevu, I presume." Damn! I always have good luck!

As the *Kingfisher* retraced the course of PT 109, through Blackett Strait and past Kolombangara, I heard firsthand the story of how Reg Evans, Ben, and some other natives had saved Lieutenant Kennedy and eleven of his men after their boat was sunk. Ben was a sort of silent partner to Reg's account of the incident. He sat by, showing his betel nut–stained teeth in a shy grin as Evans described the rescue. Occasionally Ben would add some comment, rolling his bloodshot eyes excitedly.

For several days we cruised the waters of the Western Solomons, rowing ashore and filming the three islands on which Kennedy and his crew had taken refuge. Since the waters of the "Slot" are filled with treacherous reefs, we would anchor at nightfall and sit on deck in the soft tropic night listening to the news in pidgin English from Guadalcanal. The islands were breathtakingly beautiful, the lush foliage a brilliant green, the sand white, and the water slate-blue in the open channels but greenish

over the submerged reefs. Sometimes there would be a sudden
rain squall, and the sun breaking through would paint shimmering rainbows in the sky. It seemed almost impossible to imagine
these hushed waters and vast skies, with no visible signs of life, as
the scene of the terrible air and naval battles that had raged
through them. Now their peace was broken only by a soft breeze
or a sudden tropical rainstorm.

As our boat, with its crew of natives, threaded its way among
the lush, green islands, amid treacherous coral reefs, Reg told me
one of the stories of the amazing coast watchers' operations.

"I landed on Kolombangara in February of 1943," he related.
"I traveled to the island by canoe from New Georgia with a native boy named James Malasa. We hid in the daytime and paddled at night. We passed so close to Munda that we could hear
the Japanese trucks working on the airstrip."

On Kolombangara, Evans said, friendly natives built him a
bamboo hut on a hill overlooking the jungles and ocean. He had
a radio, revolver, tommy gun, telescope, and binoculars. "These
are the same binoculars," he said, handing me the worn glasses.
"Take a look."

Peering through the binoculars, I could get a good view of
Kolombangara, a dark green, pyramid-shaped mountainous vol-
canic island.

"The Japanese were building an airstrip there on one of the
few level places on the island," Evans said, pointing to the near
tip of the island. "I was on the second knob there. It's called
Hipera. I had a wonderful view of the sea and the airfield."

I expressed amazement that his hiding place was so close to
where the Japanese were.

"It wasn't as dangerous as it looks," he smiled. "The jungles
there are so thick that even the natives build their villages on the
coast and rarely go inland. I would have natives perched in the
trees on sentry duty night and day. They would report anything
they saw, and I would radio Guadalcanal. Japanese barges moved
around those waters a lot under cover of darkness, and the American PT boats would hunt them down."

I asked Reg if he hadn't minded the loneliness.

"Not so much," he mused, rolling a cigarette. "You get used to it. Malasa was a mission boy and spoke English."

It wasn't the danger or loneliness he minded, Evans said, so much as the frustration. "Our island seemed to be jinxed," he said. "Inexperienced American fliers would bomb and strafe our friendly natives by mistake. Because Kolombangara was a Japanese-held island, the American fliers weren't too particular who they strafed and bombed there. It was probably a combination of green pilots and poor briefing. Our work was dependent on native help, and these air attacks were devastating to the morale of my scouts."

I asked Reg to tell me of the PT 109 crash, how he heard about it, and exactly what happened so that my planned program would be accurate and the definitive word on "Shafty's" experience.

This quiet, modest man played his part down and said that just before the incident he was discouraged and wanted to help the war effort more. As we were lying on the deck of the *Kingfisher*, Reg told us this story:

"Things got more and more discouraging, and I began to feel I was in a backwater of the fighting, which was moving farther west toward New Guinea. The coast watchers on neighboring islands did so much, but the main action seemed to pass us by. On Vella Lavella and New Georgia, on either side of us, they saved many American fliers and survivors of sunken U.S. ships. But on Kolombangara, I didn't save one. My native scouts rescued seven American fliers, but I wasn't personally involved in saving a single American. It was just the fortunes of war, I guess."

Finally, Evans told me, he decided to leave his Kolombangara hilltop and move to Gomu, a tiny island a few miles off the coast. On the new island he thought he would be closer to the action.

"Just before I left, we got a report that a PT boat had been sunk in Blackett Strait," Reg said. "I studied the strait through my big telescope. I could see some sort of floating object but couldn't tell what it was. There was no sign of any survivors. Later my scouts found three torpedoes on the beach that might have come from the sunken boat. I radioed this word along. When nothing more turned up, I decided to go through with my plan to move.

"I notified my scouts and radioed headquarters of my plan. Malasa and I slipped down to the coast at night and paddled across to Gomu. When we landed I heard a sudden sound. I raised my tommy gun, but it was one of my native scouts. He reported that natives had found eleven Americans on an island near Gizo. I radioed this good news to headquarters. Then several more natives arrived, all smiles over the news.

"The next morning I wrote a message to the senior officer of the stranded Americans and gave it to the natives to take to him. I advised him to return to Gomu with the natives, so we could work out means of rescuing his party. Then seven natives, led by Benjamin Kevu, paddled away toward the island where the Americans were. All day Malasa and I scanned the ocean impatiently waiting for sight of their return. Late in the afternoon we saw the canoe coming back. We could see only the natives who were paddling, but Ben Kevu was wreathed in smiles. As they glided up to the beach, an American navy lieutenant crawled out from under the palm fronds in the bottom of the canoe. He looked like a scarecrow. He was bearded and wearing nothing but skivvies. He was very young. His thin, half-naked body was sunburned and splotched with infected coral lacerations.

" 'Man, am I glad to see you,' he said.

" 'I'm bloody glad to see you, too,' I told him.

"I said that I had radioed headquarters where he and his men were. I suggested the natives paddle him back to his base while boats from the base picked up his men. He wanted to pick up the men himself. Finally it was arranged that our natives would paddle him to Patparan Island. There boats from his base would pick him up and he would lead them to the island where his men were. I gave him a pair of my coveralls and a Jap rifle and sent him off in the canoe with Ben and the natives. The next day I got word from headquarters that he met the boats according to plan. His men were taken off the island and returned safely to their base at Rendova."

Evans told me all this while our boat cruised the very waters where all this happened. With Ben Kevu we went ashore on Gomu Island, where the meeting with the young lieutenant had taken place. "The old shack where I lived used to stand right

here," Evans said. "There's nothing left." The clearing around the
house was now choked with palm and casuarina trees. The air
was filled with a sweet odor from dead leaves of the naqi naqi tree.

"It was strange," Evans said, standing on the beach where the
natives had brought the lieutenant. "That lieutenant was the only
man I saved in all that time as a coast watcher. He told me his
name at the time, but I forgot it. Not long ago I read a story in
the *Reader's Digest* about a naval incident in the war. Suddenly I
recognized the circumstances. It was the story of the rescue of the
young lieutenant. The man I had saved was your President Kennedy."

Benjamin Kevu, the scout who played the leading role in the
rescue of Lieutenant John F. Kennedy and his crew, is a frail,
dark native of Wana Wana Island in the New Georgia Group of
the Western Solomons. When I first encountered him, aboard
the *Kingfisher*, he was wearing a sport shirt and frayed shorts,
and was barefooted. His slight frame, bare legs, and silver-rimmed
spectacles gave him an appearance not unlike that of Mahatma
Gandhi. His thick, kinky black hair was streaked with a reddish
tinge from being dyed with lime juice, and his shy smile when we
were introduced revealed a few missing teeth. His large, expressive
eyes seemed to be permanently bloodshot. He scarcely looked the
part of a hero.

Besides the rescue of the crew of the PT 109, Kevu was the
leader in the rescue of seven more American pilots and seamen as
the war went on. As I type this, I wonder if anyone ever thought
to give him a medal. I gave him money, brought him to the
United States, and showed him a wonderful week in New York,
and he stayed for a few days at our home in Bronxville. When
President Kennedy saw the television program and learned that
Ben was in the United States, he called and insisted that he be
brought to the White House. The President sent up his friend
and a fellow survivor of the PT boat, Barney Ross, to take care of
Ben. Ben wrote me several letters and, strangely enough, never
asked for anything, although he was a smashing presence on my
program. He did want an American flag to fly on his canoe. A
year and a few months later, I received a note from him. It was
written from his native village in the Solomons on lined tablet

paper, and it said, "The message came through on the air local news that the great friend of J. F. Kennedy at the White House has get shot. It was a sad news . . . I feel deeply sorrow for his death."

The closest Ben came to any South Seas atmosphere amid the concrete canyons of New York was a party we had for the PT boat crew at Trader Vic's, a gilded Polynesian establishment with air-conditioned trade winds. The exotic rum drinks were flowing freely when we arrived, and there was much back-slapping and hugging when the crew met Reg and Benny again. They were embraced and pummeled by Pat McMahon, the badly burned crewman whom Lieutenant Kennedy had towed to safety; by George (Barney) Ross, the handsome, strapping lieutenant who had gone along for the ride on that fateful night; and by all the others.

The evening was a merry one, full of boozy reminiscences, raucous stories, and ribald speeches; and at times I got the feeling that some of the former fighting men might end up in a small war among themselves. They all spoke with obvious fondness of the President, whom they referred to as "Shafty." Benny sat quietly through all this cheerful confusion, saying little but grinning shyly at the speech and sallies. Because of this shyness, I had decided not to embarrass him by calling on him to speak, especially amid such rowdy surroundings. However, as the evening and the frozen daiquiris progressed, I felt Ben tug at my elbow.

"Aren't you going have me make speech?" he asked softly. Surprised but delighted, I introduced Ben. He made a brief but charming speech. His syntax was somewhat tangled, but his warmheartedness was so apparent that you could have heard a guest drop—and I think a couple did. He said he was glad to be in America and to see his old friends again. I'm not sure what else he said, but by that time it didn't matter much. He got a rousing round of applause from the surviving celebrants.

Ben's speech at dinner prompted me to suggest that he might like to say a few words on the television program, and he readily agreed. Although he had never seen television, much less appeared on it, Benny showed no concern about appearing before a national audience of an estimated 30,000,000 people, live and, as

NBC says, in living color. He apparently was resigned to the fact that America was full of mysterious and complicated inventions and faced going before the cameras and an audience with less trepidation than going up an escalator (the only thing that did throw him).

After we had shown films on the program of our trip through the Solomons, retracing the last mission of PT 109, I brought Reg and Benny on stage for a few words. My heart constricted as the crew, seated together in the audience, rose to give them a standing ovation. Reg chatted away with all the homey, hearty assurance you might expect of a man who hid out on a Japanese-held island, and Ben showed equal aplomb, although in a quieter vein.

He looked small and very frail as he stood center stage in the TV studio, with the powerful lights beating down hotter than any Solomon Island sun. He stood hesitantly a moment and then began to speak. He talked softly and shyly, in his curious but appealing way, his eyes darting about cagerly. His little speech was simple, and at times he groped for words I feared he might not find, but he found them and spoke with a gentle sincerity that made itself felt in the studio and, I'm sure, to viewers across the country.

It was a very dramatic and touching hour, and my first show in prime time went well. (I'm being modest, but what the hell good is it to be modest unless you point it out.) The august New York *Times* called it "an absorbing hour." Oh yes, a funny thing happened—several TV critics again, as always, said, "Another of Jack Paar's *home movies*."

Back to the South Pacific: When we took Reg Evans to the nearest island where he could meet the weekly plane back up to New Guinea and then down across Australia to Sydney, and Benny to an island where he had friends who would take him home, by canoe, we were on our own. This was a little frightening because I was now in charge, although I had little ability to communicate with the native crew. They were told that we were to be taken straight south to Honiara (Guadalcanal).

There must have been a ringing of ships' bells before that first night alone, but with Reg and Benny there to handle things like that, we had never noticed them. We had to sleep on the deck because although there was a small cabin on the sixty-foot boat, I had mistakenly used a bug bomb on the first night. (When we were in Sydney before the trip, an Australian friend of mine, Morris West, the author, took me to a naval store where I bought some provisions, including a bug bomb.) On the boat, when I sprayed the small cabin, literally hundreds of bugs crawled out from the mattresses and walls. We never went into the cabin again.

Since no one wanted to sleep in the bug-infested cabin, Reddy, Cochran, and I slept on the deck for a week. Cochran curled up in a pretzel position on the stern, and John and I were on a hatch cover. The ship was now pitching and rolling so badly in the heavy seas that we lay on our sides clinging to the hatch cover so as not to be dumped three feet below to the deck. All night long the *Kingfisher* labored through the swells, showering us with spray as she dipped her bow into the big waves. However, I learned to fall asleep still gripping the ropes.

The first night on our own, we were awakened by Tommy Cochran, who had crawled to our position and said frantically, "Put these on!" He had two life jackets: one for John and one for me. I said, "Okay, but why?"

Tommy said, "Didn't you hear the bells? We will have to abandon ship!"

I didn't know what to do, so I thought before jumping into the sea that I would check with our native crew. I did my best in pidgin English and learned that the bells were simply the ringing of the change of watch for the crew. They were only rung at night while the boat was under way. That is why we had never heard them before. If we had jumped into the Coral Sea, we would still be there or in a shark's belly.

The next day, with the mountains of Guadalcanal in sight thirty miles away, Tommy became very ill with a high fever. He had been ill before we left and should never have made the trip with us. We were in an area that I remembered from the war, the Russell Islands, where I had lived for many months. It was kind of a secret, hidden-away group of islands that was used by the First Marine Division for staging before fighting up north. I asked the native bo'sun if we couldn't put in there for the night and make the rest of the run to Guadalcanal the next morning.

Through binoculars I could see Banika, an island that I once knew very well. I could see some Lever Brothers' warehouses and activity and a dock. If we could pull in there, surely there would be a bathroom, showers, and something cold to drink and warm to eat. We went ashore and were immediately aware that a jeep was coming down the road toward us. Safe at last, a fellow European who would I was sure be glad to see us. He looked just like Ralph Richardson, the British actor, in khaki shorts, white knee hose, and all. He was *not* happy to see us because his opening line was, "What are you doing on this island?"

I was shocked. He was the first white man I had seen in ten days, and he wanted to play a smart-ass British quiz show emcee. I became angry and said that we were American, filming a television story about our President, and all we wanted was a shower, something cold, and some medical advice if there was a doctor available. He was not impressed. I then went on about "hospitality of the sea," and said that Lever Brothers could go to hell, that I had served in that area in the war, that the President of the United States was a personal friend of mine, and that he and the brothers Lever and the royal family could go pee up a palm tree. Trees, by the way, would not even have been there if it had not been for the Americans. I was livid and told Tommy and John that we should go back to that stinking little boat and make the run to Guadalcanal anyhow.

We turned and walked back to the dock to the friendly faces of our black brothers who were watching aboard the boat. He, Colonel Bogie, walked after us and said, "I *am* sorry. But you see, we must be very careful who comes ashore as the Communist labor unions are trying to organize the palm pickers. This island, my house, whatever we have is at your disposal. We have one air-conditioned bedroom up in that cottage on the hill, and we offer it to your sick companion." And then he used a rather *outré*, British phrase, considering that we were on a dinky island in the God-forsaken Southwest Pacific: "You gentlemen have the *courtesy of the port*." The British are just like their movies; and secretly I love them, but everything is drama to them.

Well, we went up to his house on the hill, where natives were pulling ropes that made ceiling fans work back and forth. He had a lovely wife who was delighted to see some new faces. Both she and her husband could not have been nicer. We shaved and showered with warm water; then we had scotch and sodas and a fine dinner.

Now before I give you one of my favorite stories, I must tell you that colonial people in Africa, India, or the Pacific read *Time* magazine, and you will almost always see the old copies piled up in the corner of their living rooms. The magazines arrive three or four weeks late, but they are saved.

Well, the wife was overjoyed to meet someone in the "telly" world, and to meet and have in her home a "personal friend" of President Kennedy was more than she could stand. She was thrilled! And when the British are thrilled, it's quite a sight to see. I think the English have a quota in their lifetime—two or three "thrills," and that's it!

I noticed the *Time* magazines piled in the living room, and remembering that the week I left "The Tonight Show" four months before, *Time* had done a brief story on my leaving the program, which included a picture of me in the television section. I went over in a grand gesture to prove my celebrity in America and found the old edition. Forgetting the caption that had been written under the picture, I said modestly, "Here, dear friends, read this." Unfortunately what was written, as our host read it aloud, was: *"Though at times he blew foul or fraudulent . . ."*

The next morning we made the trip to Guadalcanal. It was during the rainy season, which lasts for twelve months, and it poured most of the time we were there.

The village of Honiara on Guadalcanal was a shock when I saw it again. It was a sad little place with about five hundred white people, some Chinese, and a few thousand Melanesians. What was once a spic-and-span army and navy base with white coral roads and Quonset-hut hospitals for the wounded was now broken down and depressing. It was damp and humid; the only dangers now were boredom and the chance of mushrooms growing in your shoes. Once there were enough outdoor theaters where our show could play for three months and never repeat an audience; now there was one old building with benches for the natives where old Randolph Scott pictures were shown. Before the movie, there would be a five-minute showing of commercial slides advertising products with the background music of "Onward Christian Soldiers."

As was true on many of the islands in this area, the white people all seemed to be outcasts from Australia, New Zealand, or England. Among them were many alcoholics and quite a few homosexuals, noticeably among the clergy. (I don't use the word *gay* because these couldn't possibly be.) With the constant rain, I thought at the time it was the most melancholy place I had ever been. It made my memories of the war seem almost pleasant. I can remember the audiences, the bright lights, the music, and the GI's. Many a night I would do my routines to hundreds, sometimes thousands of soldiers and marines. And if I would sometimes look off to my right toward a fenced-in compound, there would also be Japanese prisoners enjoying the show.

Now the jungle had reclaimed all of those areas, and nothing remained. Even the tower at the famous Henderson Field was pulled down by the screwing upward of the jungle trees that were crushing everything. I didn't realize it at the time, but John, Tommy, and I were going to be there for longer than we planned. The report back in the States was that we were missing somewhere in the South Pacific. We were never "missing"; it was just that nobody knew where we were. Finally a radio report to Australia and then to the news service in the United States let Miriam and our friends know that we were safe, wet, and lonely. I would rather re-enlist in the Army than go through that experience again.

It was still raining buckets the day we were scheduled to leave for Fiji from where we would catch a jet for Hawaii and home. We were roused out of bed at 5 A.M. for an early takeoff on the long overwater flight. The reason for leaving at this ungodly hour, someone explained, was that the flight, with a stop at the New Hebrides island of Espiritu Santo, took twelve hours, and the Fiji airliner did not have proper equipment for night landings.

At Henderson Field, which was dotted with pools of water, we had our introduction to Fiji Airways, the last of the wood-burning airlines.

Our plane—a four-engine De Havilland Heron was sitting in the rain on the soggy runway while the flight engineer, clad only in trousers, warmed up the engines. We had met the crew the previous night when they flew in from Fiji. They were pilot George Washington, copilot Robin McGrath, and flight engineer Charles Ogilvie, all genial New Zealanders.

Finally everything was in readiness for our takeoff—Charlie had put on a shirt—and we boarded the plane. The Heron has a top speed of 120 miles an hour—slower than some sports cars. It seats twelve passengers in a seating arrangement that guarantees to-getherness. I took a seat directly behind pilot Washington, which meant I was almost riding piggyback. My knees were planted firmly in his back, so that if I'd crossed my legs we'd have done a nose dive. The rest of the accommodations were similarly infor-mal. The powder room was a bucket in the rear of the plane.

As Washington revved the motors, Charlie took his place in the forward part of the plane to demonstrate the lifesaving equip-ment as required in overwater flights. "Welcome to Fiji Airlines," he said. "Your pilot is George, Robin here is your copilot, and I'm Charlie, your stewardess." Taking a moth-eaten–looking life jacket, he grinned broadly and announced, "Now comes the ter-rifyin' part." He pulled on the life jacket over his head to demon-strate how to put it on in case we had to ditch at sea. "After put-ting on your life jacket, you pull this string to inflate it," he instructed. With that he pulled the string, and it came off in his hand. "Well, that happens," he said, "but don't worry. A light goes on if you're in the water for several hours. It doesn't work on this one." He then showed us a whistle dangling from the life jacket. "Ships will be coming for you, and you'll want to attract their attention," he added. With that he blew a feeble blast on the whistle.

While this reassuring demonstration was in progress, we had taxied to one end of the runway for takeoff. Then Washington gunned the motors, and the Heron began rolling down the run-way, throwing out sheets of water on either side. On and on we labored, without gaining sufficient momentum to be airborne. Finally we began picking up speed, and I felt Washington and McGrath tense in their seats. Suddenly George reversed the propellers and braked the aircraft to a skidding stop in a spray of mud and water. "There will be a twenty-four-hour delay," he announced with what proved to be undue optimism.

All that day and all night tropical rains continued to lash Guadalcanal. We sat moodily in the Hotel Mendana bar, actually an old Quonset hut, listening to the unremitting downpour and speculating gloomily on our prospects of getting away the next day. We commiserated with the pilots, who had some additional bad news. "Mud was thrown into two of the engines on our takeoff attempt," McGrath said. "We're trying to repair the engines."

The next morning it was still raining. Henderson Field looked like a swamp when we drove out to check on the prospects of our flight getting off. It was a dismal sight that greeted us as we pulled up at the field. Parts of the two engines were scattered around on the wet grass while the crew, clad only in swimming trunks, worked in the warm rain to repair them. "We need some new parts," Washington said, "but there's no way to get them while this rain continues. The field is too flooded for a plane from Fiji to land here." Every day we made our pilgrimage to the field to watch the crew struggling to get the engines fixed. And every night we sat around with the pilots, cursing the Guadalcanal rainy season—all twelve months of it.

As we waited each evening for the latest news from our friendly pilots, whom we would find drinking in the bar, I worried. Pilots are not supposed to drink twenty-four hours before a flight, nor to eat shellfish; nor are a pilot and copilot to eat in the same restaurant. (Guadalcanal only had two places to eat.) Also Henderson Field, though once famous in the war, is now just a coral airstrip with a thatched hut and one kerosene lantern. No ground crew, no parts; the "VIP Lounge" is a barrel under a tree.

After several days the rains stopped at last. Henderson Field still looked wet and muddy, but a relief plane flew in from Fiji with the necessary spare parts, and the crew finally got the Heron's damaged motors put together again. The following morning we were up again at 5 A.M. for another takeoff attempt. Due to the delay there were enough passengers to fill not only the originally scheduled flight, but the relief plane as well. Feeling that the first plane was jinxed, we tried to sneak aboard the relief plane that was scheduled to leave a few minutes later. However, we were herded aboard our original plane along with a motley group of passengers. The runway was still soggy, but this time our Heron managed to get up just enough speed to be airborne, barely clearing the palm trees at the end of the field.

As we headed out over Ironbottom Sound, where so many Japanese and American ships were sunk—hardly a comforting locale for a group of nervous passengers—the two damaged engines began acting erratically again. The pilots feathered one propeller, and the other engine continued going but with the spasmodic rhythm of a 1923 washing machine. "The trouble is we put metal shields over the air intakes to keep them from getting clogged with mud again," George explained. "Now the carburetors aren't getting enough air."

As we limped toward Espiritu Santo, Charlie decided to relieve any anxiety among the passengers by announcing that he would serve a box lunch. Judging by the way things had been going, I fully expected these to be CARE packages. A few moments later he was back with a correction. "There's been a little error," he announced cheerfully. "The box lunches were put on the relief plane by mistake. However, we have some soft drinks for you." He went to the rear of the plane again, and we heard the rattle of bottles. Then he was back for still another correction. "I guess we won't have the soft drinks after all, folks," he chuckled. "Someone forgot the bottle opener."

So for hours we droned over empty seas while the only passengers who enjoyed any liquid refreshments were the native babies who were being nursed by their mothers. The rest of us looked at the feathered propeller on one engine, listened to the cha-cha rhythm of the other balky engine and recited the Twenty-third Psalm. You are always over open sea; there are no radar or beacons in that part of the world.

There was a wholesale sigh of relief when we landed safely at Espiritu Santo about midday. While the crew climbed resignedly

out of the plane to resume their uphill battle with the two problem engines, an airline station wagon took us into the little village of Luganville for lunch. Luganville is the most curious town
in the Pacific; it is one street wide and six miles long. "There is a
French restaurant there," the pilot said, "so they might have very
good food." On the way into town, we amused ourselves by total-
ing up the mishaps of the jinxed flight: the delayed takeoff, the
motors acting up, and forgetting the lunches and the bottle
opener. "Has it occurred to anyone," I suddenly remembered,
"that today is Friday the thirteenth?"

At a little tropical restaurant called the Corsican, we ordered
lunch and decided to celebrate our safe halfway arrival with a
bottle of good French wine. Cochran, a wine connoisseur, had a
long conversation in French with the proprietor, earnestly discussing brands and vintages. The proprietor produced a dusty bottle
that he proclaimed was his very finest vintage. Tommy sniffed the
bouquet knowingly and then sipped the wine with the skeptical
expression of the true connoisseur. "An engaging little wine," he
pronounced it. "Full-bodied but not too pretentious."

The wine did lend a festive air to our lunch, and we ate it with
the gusto of condemned men eating their last meal—which is
what we felt like. "You have the last," I said, pouring the end of
the wine into Cochran's glass. "Oh dear God," he exclaimed,
looking at his glass. Along with the last of the wine, three very
dead and soggy flies had plopped into his glass. Vintage flies, no
doubt.

Back at the old drawing board, we found our crew putting the
finishing touches on another repair job of the temperamental De
Havilland engines. Climbing aboard with all the enthusiasm of
Kamikaze pilots, we took off on the last leg of our trip—six more
hours overwater to Nandi, Fiji. The last lap of the flight was perfectly normal—the two engines began acting up again! George
again feathered the propeller of one while the other resumed its
bongo-drum rhythm. I looked at Cochran and thought I saw his
lips moving in prayer. "If you're saying a prayer," I suggested, "be
sure to include me in."

"It's not you I'm worrying about," Tommy said. "I'm praying
for the pilot."

Hour after hour passed, with nothing below us but endless
stretches of ocean. It began growing dark, and I remembered the
reports we had heard that our plane was not equipped for night
landings. I sat peering into the darkness and silently composing
slogans for Fiji Airlines—"Pray now, fly later . . ." As darkness
fell, George began to take star shots to calculate our position. It
did nothing for our morale to see him take a shot with his sextant
and then sit down to plot our position, furrowing his brow and
shaking his head in apparent bafflement. We knew we were
scheduled to land in daylight, and our apprehension increased as
we droned through the darkness with nothing beneath us but the
dark sea. George continued to stand up and take sightings with
his sextant, until I began to wonder whether he was taking star
shots or imploring divine intercession. It may have been my imagination, but it seemed to me that George's brow had been fur-
rowed so long over his calculations that it was more wrinkled
than Lillian Hellman's. I'm ordinarily not the nervous type about
flying, but a feeling kept growing that an airline which could put
the lunches on the wrong plane, and even forget the bottle
opener, might be capable of missing a tiny group of islands in the
midst of thousands of miles of empty ocean in pitch blackness. I
wondered if the obituaries would remember that Paar is spelled
with two a's. Finally George stood up and smiled. On the far horizon was a faint flare of light. It was the airport lights at Nandi,
and to us they looked more beautiful than the Northern Lights. A
few minutes more and our poor, weary Heron limped in for a
landing like an exhausted gooney bird. *Terra firma* never felt better.

An airline bus whisked us to a smart, modern hotel with the
improbable name of the Mocambo. After the deluge on Guadalcanal and the terrors of the flight, we were suddenly transported to
the lap of luxury: air conditioning, a native orchestra playing, a
swimming pool shimmering under a tropic moon. It was almost
too good to be true. All the earmarks of civilization, including
American tourists complete with sport shirts and cameras. "Hey,
Jack," one of them yelled. "You keep me awake every night."

I knew we were getting near home.

20

Shoveling Smoke

At least once or twice a year, either NBC, CBS, ABC, or PBS
makes the request that I co-operate with them in doing an hour
or two documentary on my career in television. All I will have to
do, it's explained, is show up at the studio where their staffs have
been busy thinking up fascinating questions about my life. It will
be a great tribute to me, I am told, and it will finally honor my
contribution to television. There is just one small problem:
Where are the Jack Paar archives, scrapbooks, awards, and thousands of hours of film and tape? When I tell them that there are
none—that NBC saved *nothing*, not even the ten selected hours
that were picked for their own historical files—I am never
believed, not even by the new young executives at NBC who
should know better than I what NBC has in its inventory. Nearly
all my work in television was unscripted, as unrehearsed as a hic-
cup, and was either good or not; it has all been lost. My career
was like *shoveling smoke*—it's up there somewhere but useless.
My cupboard is like Mother Hubbard's, even more bare I fear
than Jimmy Carter's Presidential Memorial Library will be.

It has been said by many people that I have a most unusual
memory, especially regarding incidents that I find interesting or
amusing. It's become rather selective, I confess, and my attention
span is about thirty seconds. I don't really have time or patience
with the luxury of *déjà vu*. Some years ago a play called *I Am a*

Camera was written based on the Christopher Isherwood stories of his days in Berlin. It later became a musical play and motion picture called *Cabaret*. My point is that my memory works that way, and perhaps I should call this chapter, "I Am A Polaroid."

The other night my daughter suggested that I write about "fame" and what a disaster it is or can be. Any success or celebrity I may have had is not nearly as interesting to me now as the fickle finger of fame. These stories quickly flash before me as fast as I can type.

A few years ago, after more than six months of my turning down a most lucrative offer to take over their late-night show against Johnny Carson, ABC had the idea that I would only have to do *one week* a month. Their theory was that I would get so caught up with the business that I would want to come back into television regularly. Since they were going to drop Dick Cavett in any event, if I would come back, they would keep Dick on for another year at *one week* a month. They would then fill in the other two weeks with other programming. I had an interest in Cavett and had started him on a career in television working on my staff. I also genuinely liked him. I made it quite clear in my agreement with the network that I would try it for a year as long as they *kept Cavett!* I am afraid that Dick never believed this and was terribly hurt, but there are many lawyers and agents and network executives at the highest level who know that what I write is true. If Cavett still doesn't believe it, I am sorry, but that's the way it was. A year later, when I knew the idea wouldn't work, my only choice was to take over the whole show every night or quit altogether. You understand that on ABC, five nights a week part of the season because of the football games on Monday nights meant *four* nights, and in much of the Middle West, ABC affiliates would pre-empt Friday night for basketball games so we were down some weeks to three nights a month. It was hopeless, and I told ABC officials that I just didn't want or need the burden of a nightly show. To this day I have the finest relations with all of the ABC management; they were disappointed, but they understood.

The theater that ABC used for their late-night program was on Fifty-eighth Street, and there was no continuity for an audience to get used to. It was pretaped at seven o'clock to show at eleven-thirty. My own mother never knew when I was on, and my wife figured if I wasn't in bed, I must be on ABC. Actually, Jack Douglas, my old pal and writer, worked for me as always from his home in Connecticut. He would mail the stuff in, or if he had something topical, he would phone me before the program. One night he called at home and said, "Forgive me. I didn't send any material last week. I didn't *know you were on.*"

When I was at NBC in Radio City, the line would form for a block inside the heated or air-cooled lobby. They were a classy audience, people who had written in sometimes six months in advance to reserve tickets, as they do now for Johnny Carson. At the ABC theater they had to drag people off the streets, and it was an embarrassment after what I had known. At ABC we had to hold the crowds back with dental floss.

With few exceptions, my old staff of the "Tonight" program was scattered over all the rest of the "talk-show circuit": Carson, Griffin, Frost, and Cavett. My director, Hal Gurnee, had quit television and moved with his family to a beautiful estate in Ireland, but he offered to fly back from his home there one week a month. There was a fine young writer whom I had discovered by simply trimming some bushes between my property and his parent's home in Bronxville. When I could see over the bushes, I saw this big guy sprawled out on a chair sunning himself. I said, "You must be David. I have heard so much about you from your parents. They tell me you want to be a writer and that you are very clever." He was Yale graduate and a classmate of Dick Cavett's and had just returned from the Navy as a lieutenant. I hired him, and he worked with me for many years. Since he was then working for Cavett on the ABC late show, I offered him the week with me also. Incidentally, this David is David Lloyd, who turned out to be one of the most respected comedy writers in television. He has won several awards, especially for "The Mary Tyler Moore Show."

I got my darling Mitzi to return from motherhood to television as my assistant. I asked Bob Carman to be the producer. Dick Nelowet, the man who had always handled our financial affairs and who had a very important position with Arthur Andersen and Company, joined me to oversee the entire operation. We rented offices in the Plaza Hotel and held most of our meetings in Trader Vic's.

They were all old friends and believed in me, but I am afraid I let them all down. The truth was that I had lost interest in television. I couldn't seem to adjust to the new music, which I found embarrassing and to a studio audience made up of mostly street people in T-shirts. The big laugh subjects were mostly pot, dope, and deviant sex. I was underwhelmed!

NBC had a tremendous advantage in a station lineup nationally of more than two hundred outlets, most of which I had built up from my original inherited fifty stations. ABC had fewer than 160 stations with the Cavett program and was missing some important cities.

This explanation of my lack of success is not really meant as an apologia but is for those of you who are interested in what happened.

But don't let me interrupt myself again . . . back to the opening night of this new attempt to make a triumphant comeback on ABC. It had been heralded as a minor "second coming" for at least two months before the event. It was certainly the main topic of conversation of professional show people. I really had no opinion as to what would happen because it had never been attempted before: A man, once the most successful in television and who quit at the top, was attempting to return against a successor who was already established as a smash. I never really thought of it in those terms, but that's the way it was.

I began to think only of the opening night and what I would say. Over the weeks I had written many good, literate lines that I was confident were fresh and funny. It was a very exciting evening. The theater was packed with many professional people. There was no warmup . . . just the band tuning up, then the sound in the theater and backstage on the P.A. system: "Two minutes."

I had wanted to try something as different as possible from my old format, which Johnny Carson had naturally copied (what little there was to copy). I hired the first woman announcer, Peggy Cass. She and I were very comfortable with each other. She is a fabulously witty and natural person. Peg has a voice that always sounds like she is trying to overcome a bad connection, and I adore her.

Opening Night

P.A. SYSTEM VOICE (Hal Gurnee, my long-time director): "*Thirty seconds, everybody. Good luck, Jack . . . Twenty seconds . . . Ten seconds . . . Five seconds . . . On air . . . Take camera one. Theme! . . . Cue, Peggy.*"

PEGGY CASS: "From New York City . . . *Jack is back!*"

Applause . . .

I entered from the wings to thundering applause, very nervous because for the first time it really dawned on me the enormous task that I had committed myself to. I was, however, very touched at the reception because the audience stood and applauded—an honest-to-God standing ovation! It went on and on. I must confess that a tear came to my eye, and then I spoke softly and in character repeated the funny thoughts I had in my head, and they all worked. Every line got a laugh, and I was "rolling," but big, into three minutes of the monologue. And then, and then—

P.A. Voice from Booth: "Jack . . . Jack . . ."

I knew instantly what the problem was. It had never happened to me before or since, not in Africa, not in Russia; it just couldn't be happening to me now! I refused to stop and kept talking. It was either that or open my poison ring and take the powder and kill myself right on the stage.

P.A. Voice from Booth: "Jesus, Jack, I'm sorry. We have a picture, but they forgot to open the audio lines to the tape machines . . . We'll have to do it over!"

Now if thousands and thousands of people read this book, only a few hundred, maybe only a handful, will realize the problem. There wasn't time for a discussion; there wasn't time to rewrite what took weeks to write; there wasn't time to stage or reinvent a sincere standing ovation, or to think of new lines. There wasn't even time for a tantrum! For a few seconds, I thought perhaps I could turn this into a disaster event and tell the audience in the theater my problem. Perhaps, I could ad-lib around it with some sarcastic, putdown lines of the ABC technical staff, but surely not on an opening program, a *premiere!* Then, too, while it might have been a hilarious "inside" routine in the theater, it wouldn't mean a thing to the millions who would be watching later at home. Besides, I am a *pro*, or would like to think I am. I looked toward the control booth and said, "Whatever you say. Do you think Peggy Cass can *remember her* line again?" That received a laugh in the theater, and the studio audience knew that there on that stage they were involved in an event and wanted to help. We did it all over, and honest to God without any mention or suggestion, that same wonderful group of many professional people stood and applauded and laughed at mostly the same material again. But honestly, since it had never happened to me before or since or ever will again, I have never, ever recovered. It is another of my constantly recurring nightmares. My wife, being quite a special person, realizes that if that's the bad dream, she only has to say, "Just do it over, like Hal says, and the studio audience will understand."

En passant: It might be of interest that while I did only thirteen of these programs four times a week, in that brief time two very important talents were discovered and presented by our program. They were Jimmy Walker, the young black comedian who could have had a promising career but blew it, and Freddie Prinz who became a star overnight, only to get caught up in drugs and to shoot himself. What a pity! But although they were talented, neither of them were ready for success because they had not paid their dues anywhere. They both wanted to be on our program very badly, but it took weeks to find just five minutes of their material that was presentable on television.

Among the stories collected of my career, the following one seems to be the favorite. It happened one afternoon when they were rehearsing singers and the commercials. I never had to attend these mostly technical meetings, but Mitzi, my assistant, had decided that I was not doing enough public service or disease announcements. I have a low tolerance for the sincere actor types who will make any announcement for the publicity or who sometimes appear at telethons as hosts or emcees when in many cases a certain amount of money has been paid for their appearance. I am not making any great judgment—it just isn't my style! Well, dear Mitzi had arranged to have a plea for a certain cause to be put on the TelePrompTer, and if there was time at the show's technical rehearsal in the afternoon, I would put on a tie, jacket, and a little makeup, and she could get me to run a minute announcement off on video tape. Then it could be sent out to the stations showing America Jack Paar's great interest in this disease.

The point of this story is that I can read as well as anyone the copy on a TelePrompTer *cold*, without ever having read it beforehand. This comes with years of doing it on many television shows. A TelePrompTer is a roll of yellow paper that rolls automatically just above the camera lens with written copy on it one line at a time. The audience is not aware that when the actor is looking straight at you, he is actually reading with great, natural sincerity. Well, to please Mitzi, I went down on the studio floor and said I am prepared whenever they are ready and let's make it in one take. I began, with no idea of what I was saying but pouring on the sincere, professional charm.

PAAR READING FROM TELEPROMPTER: "Friends, are you frequently awakened in the middle of the night with anxious pains in the chest? Do your hands perspire? Are you tired and listless? Are you sometimes irritable and unreasonable with those you love? Do you have fears of fainting after bending over?" (At this point I am told that I froze and just stared into the camera, saying nothing.)

P.A. VOICE FROM THE BOOTH: "Jack, this is Hal, what's wrong?"

PAAR: "What do you mean, what's wrong?"

HAL ON P.A. SYSTEM: "Well, you've just stopped reading, and you are staring into the camera."

PAAR: "Well! I just realized that I have all these symptoms! Roll to the end so I can see what the hell I've got! What is this announcement for? Whatever it is, I've got it!"

Well, we rolled to the end. The announcement was for a form of diabetes, and I saw a doctor the next day.

A good, fickle fame story is about when Richard Burton opened on Broadway in *Hamlet*. I was then doing my Friday night NBC weekly program, and since my daughter had a crush on Burton from seeing him five times in *Camelot*, I decided to take her to the premiere. This meant formal clothes, renting a limousine for the evening, and filming the whole scene for my weekly program. NBC was to have a camera crew ready at the theater entrance to film all the stars' arrivals but mainly Randy and me.

Her mother got Randy a new formal dress, and she looked lovely. Since I was seldom seen in a tuxedo or in formal society, the audience would get a small chuckle later when it was shown on television. The big, black limousine pulled off the West Side Highway and started down toward the theater district on Forty-fourth Street. The police had wooden barriers to hold the street crowds back on the curb. Randy asked what we should do if the crowds applauded, and I said, "Like Prince Philip, I'll just give a little raised hand, and you should give them a short wave."

Well, my dears, there wasn't a lot of applause; a few stared, and then some crazy bag woman broke out from the police lines and followed our car all the way down Forty-fourth Street, thumbing her nose at us. It really caused a great laugh because there was this one poor soul chasing a big Cadillac and thumbing her nose. Thank God she didn't try to bite the tires!

Now, for my style on television, that would have been a howl, but it was bad luck that the cameraman missed it. Most so-called stars would have been grateful not to have it on film, but I had a different personality, and things like that are naturally funny to me and my type of audience.

Our car pulled up in front of the theater, and I looked again for the NBC cameraman who was filming a *different* Cadillac. Since I was halfway out of the limousine, I could hardly get back in and go around the block again, but I knew NBC had missed the shot of Randy and me getting out of the car into the spotlights.

We entered the theater with all the celebrities and took our seats. Having decided to eat after the theater at a fine restaurant, we had not eaten since lunch. We are Midwesterners, who usually dine *en famille* at six o'clock, so my empty stomach began to rumble. As you know, there are many soft soliloquies in *Hamlet*, and my stomach rumble in the background was giving Burton a certain rumba beat.

Then *zing!* My formal shirt front was not starched properly; my studs were coming loose, and my shirt was flying up. Randy was becoming very embarrassed and began leaning toward her left to make believe that she was with someone else. Then one of the studs fell into my pants, and as I reached in to get it from the top of my trousers, it fell right to my crotch. They were very expensive sapphire studs. It was really a disaster at this point, and at intermission I told Randy we simply had to leave rather quickly and she could come back another night. I got up and felt the sapphire about to fall farther down my leg as I walked up the aisle. I was bending over, grabbing my crotch with both hands, and when I got to the lobby, there was an ABC cameraman yelling, "Great! Here comes Jack Paar!"

Everything went wrong. The whole idea of a father and his daughter out on the town for a TV vignette was lost, but the next week I told that story with embellishments. It was among the funniest monologues I had ever done. So I must have been doing something *wrong!*

Allen Funt, who had a similar idea in radio, later turned it into *Candid Camera*, and it was a most unique idea. The trouble was it looked cruel in some instances until he came on "The Tonight Show" and showed the same film to a studio audience, and that made the difference. He had been doing it without an audience, but with people laughing along with the action, it became a durable hit and lasted for many years. He asked me on his program several times, but I didn't have the time or the desire to do guest shots. Finally I consented. Here's what happened:

I was dressed as a parking lot attendant, was in the cashier's booth, and was supposed to give people a hard time about their cars. The cameras were rolling in a hidden location, and I was stamping tickets. The first person to approach the booth was a beautiful mother. She was a real knockout, and the poor darling had a little baby draped over her arms whose nose was running and who was crying. The mother looked so sweet that I hated to do this routine, but this is how it went:

PAAR: "Is this your ticket madam?"

LADY: "Yes . . . it's a blue Plymouth station wagon."

PAAR: "We have a problem here . . . When you left the car this morning, a wheel fell off and rolled down the street. Also, the upholstery was on fire, and I would like to know why you would want to bring a car in that condition into this parking lot?"

LADY: "Wheel fell off—on fire? I can't believe this. I have had such a bad day."

PAAR: "I'm sure you have, but our day has not been a great success either. I would like an explanation."

The lady looked at me with her lovely face, and with tears coming down her cheeks, she tried to tell me that only that morning she had told her husband to check the wheels; she also said she didn't smoke and—now she was sobbing.

I had tears in my eyes, and I rushed out of the booth to put my arms around her and help her with the child. I said, "I am so sorry. Forgive me! . . . Look at me! Don't you see . . . I'm Jack Paar!"

LADY: (Sobbing) "I don't care who you are . . . where can I buy a new wheel?"

That bit, of course, was never used on TV, mainly to avoid a lynching. Another time, I was to be a uniformed policeman in a little New Jersey town which put up special, crazy signs that would confuse everyone, like: "Left turns only permitted on Thursdays and odd number days," "Right turns permitted only at certain times," "Stop, then go, then stop again" . . .

I was stationed across a street from Allen Funt's film crew so they would have a good shot of whichever car I blew the whistle on. Then I was supposed to get the person to leave the car and walk across the street to me so I could do my bit as a new policeman. Well, a car came down the road, and no matter what the driver did by the signs, he would be wrong. He was a big, tough-looking guy, the perfect type for my bit. I blew the whistle. He stopped his car, rolled the window down, and said, "What did I do wrong?" Well, I had to get him over to me where the camera could pick us both up. I said, "You come over here, and I'll tell you what you did wrong." The camera was back on his car, and the big guy opened his automobile door. First out came a crutch, then a leg in a cast, and then the man began to hobble over toward me. I knew I was in trouble. I looked over at Allen Funt hiding behind a tree. He was giving me the "hands across the throat" signal, meaning to cut. Sure "cut," but then what? The big guy came toward me and asked, "What the hell is going on?" I said, "I'm terribly sorry—there has been some mistake, and that man over there hiding behind the tree will explain it."

That was another bit that never made the air or my diary. You see, I've saved all the best material for you, my dear reader.

One of my favorite restaurants in America is Joe's Stone Crab in Miami Beach, Florida. The owners, Jessie and Grace Wise, are dear old friends of mine, and my fame among our chums in Florida is that I am one of a few people who can go in the back way with the fish. Otherwise, it's an hour's wait for a table. A few years ago Miriam and I were enjoying a wonderful meal, and I noticed someone who seemed to recognize me. He looked familiar, but I wasn't sure exactly who he was. I noticed that he and his friend were finishing their meal and were about to light two dinky, cellophane-wrapped, awful-looking cigars. I had three cigars made of the finest Cuban tobacco with me that I had brought back from a recent trip to Europe where they are legal. I asked the waiter to please give these two cigars to the gentlemen with my compliments. As the waiter left the table, I suddenly realized that I was sending two illegal eight-dollar Havana cigars to J. Edgar Hoover and his friend. And that's all I know about the FBI. Don't ask me for more details!

Since this portion is getting rather confessional, I will now admit that on a network-show guest shot I once had a little bit I did with three basset hounds. It was very funny because the trio of dogs were supposed to register affection for me, which they did in abundance, even licking my face. It was very touching and funny, and the audience couldn't believe that one man was so beloved. The trick was that just before entering the stage I had smeared liverwurst behind my ears.

Another trick I used to do on the "Tonight" program was my own invention. I would go among the studio audience with the latest magazines and pass them out to anyone. I would then return to the stage and ask each person who had a magazine to pick a page, a line, and then a paragraph and tell me the page, line, and paragraph number. I would immediately repeat exactly the line. Here is how it was done . . . In all studios the stage manager is wearing a headset with a radio communication link to the control room. I also wore a headset hidden by a turban. After the person in the audience had picked the page, line, and paragraph, I would ask the cameraman to take a picture of the exact page and show it to the audience at home and to the studio audience monitors. I would then blindfold myself with a long scarf. When the control room got the picture, the assistant director would count the line and paragraph and tell me on the radio link exactly the line. I would repeat it to an amazed audience. The first time I did it was one of real wonder, but it really wasn't any fun until I, by various giveaways, let the audience in on it but pretending all the time that it was a great gift. It only became entertaining after everyone *knew* how I did it and then went on in mock anger about my unappreciated psychic gift. It was a strange thing about that bit . . . it was amazing but not entertaining. When most people *knew* and I pretended that they *didn't*, it became a sure-fire bit that I would do often on a slow night.

In my early years on "The Tonight Show" before the video tape was perfected, everything of course was live. There was a very popular program that Edward R. Murrow did on CBS called "Person to Person." At that time it was just about the most technologically involved program possible because they had to get a video link between the subject's house and the top of the Empire State Building, which was usually miles away. When Murrow interviewed me, it meant at least three weeks of preparation because the technicians had to put telephone poles in our garden to get the wire to the highest peak in Bronxville, thirty-five miles from midtown Manhattan. They went through all this each week to interview a famous person who could have been interviewed in a studio with no trouble at all. This idea, "Person to Person," was unique in that it came "live" from some famous guest's home, and the celebrity could walk around the living room or bedroom with the fireplace roaring; it was very popular.

I was working that night at NBC on my own program, and the idea CBS had was to see me at the end of "Person to Person" get into a big Cadillac and drive off toward New York City and my theater on West Forty-fourth Street. It was the first time they had a camera in a car, and Ed conducted the last portion of the interview talking to me in the car from New York.

Well, Murrow was a fine gentlemen but not particularly a good interviewer. He was frightened of actors, so everything was pretty well prearranged. On the morning of the show, I was amazed when a large moving van with about fifteen people arrived. I never knew we were in for such an invasion and told Miriam to immediately start making sandwiches and coffee, because we were going to be hosts for about ten hours.

It was a cold autumn day, and I asked the men in the studio truck to come inside. The house was soon full of cameramen, electricians, directors, and producers. I looked outside and saw a very attractive girl in a leather jacket, jeans, and boots; she was obviously the script girl that you find on all TV and motion-picture locations. I asked her in, and we had coffee. I showed her the whole house—the basement film studio I had, my paintings, Miriam's clothes, everything. She was a very nice, quiet girl, and finally she said, "You've been so nice to me, Mr. Paar. Could I go out to my car and get my girlfriends to come in and see your home and have some coffee with you?"

I was dumbfounded. "Aren't you with CBS? Don't you work with this crew?"

"Oh no," she said, "we were driving by and wondered what all the activity was, and you practically dragged me into your house!"

For Miriam and Randy it was an experience that they won't soon forget because CBS had placed in their brassieres small transmitters with microphones that sent their every word to the truck in the driveway. And after an hour or so, say in their own bathrooms, they would forget that they were broadcasting to fifteen men in the control booth.

Everyone has experienced living near a nutty neighbor, and we certainly did. "Person to Person" had as guests the most distinguished artists, educators, entertainers, and politicians in the world, including a President and several former Vice-Presidents. One would assume that your neighbors would be proud to live near you if you were the guest on this famous show. Well, just before the program, the police arrived and with great embarrassment said that a neighbor wanted the program canceled right then because the neighborhood was only zoned for residential homes, and they didn't want any commercials originating from our street. I told the police to tell the nut either to get a lawyer or take boxing lessons. Of course, the program went on, and the incident made a funny routine for me later on the "Tonight" program.

Live television was so much more exciting and better in many ways. Now two men and a tape machine can do it over and over till they get it just right, and then some half-assed star wants it all done over again because there was a shadow on her forehead. My advice to anyone with anything important to say is to insist that their portion be live or guaranteed in writing to be unedited. And if you are in business and Mike Wallace calls, for God's sake, hang up!

The "Tonight" program originated many ideas that later had a life of their own. "Real People" is in part my Friday night program. For instance, we used to do a weekly series of very short non-sequitur blackouts, not more than fifteen or thirty seconds long. It became one of television's greatest success stories, "Laugh-In." The "bloopers" idea of "out-takes" from motion pictures was my idea and has become a popular series with Dick Clark. My favorite comedy invention was the "translation bit," which was very difficult to do, but when it worked well, or rather when it didn't work at all, it was a great hit.

I would hire a group of skilled linguists from the Berlitz School who spoke at least three languages. They were not within hearing distance of the others, who were kept in a sound booth. I would tell a simple story to the audience and a guest in English; they would then repeat it in French to the next person, who would then tell it in German to another person, and so on. The idea was that it would always end up being told in Spanish to our musical conductor, José Melis, who would listen to his native tongue and then immediately tell it back to the audience in English, *exactly* as *he* understood it.

Sometimes we would use Zsa Zsa Gabor, who speaks five languages, but she is so hard to control and would get off the subject. (I always said that if one could put a gag on Zsa Zsa's mouth, she could talk *intravenously*.) It's great fun because as the studio audience hears the story in different languages, there are similar sounds that get screwed up. Also many people in the audience would understand one of the languages and would know when the story was going astray. And, of course, the language speakers would naturally embellish in their quick translation.

One night, for instance, the joke was this:

"Two birds built a nest with a hole in the bottom. Another bird came along and asked them why. They said they built the nest that way because they were crazy about marriage but didn't like children."

I told this in English to our first Berlitz teacher, and she repeated it in German to Zsa Zsa, who repeated it in French to another, who told it in Italian to Eva Gabor, who repeated it in Spanish to José. Then he quickly told me in English. Here is how it came out:

"Two birds were building a home without a roof. A neighbor came by and said why do you have a roof and also a hole in the basement? They said that they didn't like the neighbors' children but were crazy about sex."

So you can imagine the problems at the United Nations . . .

More than any of the present talk-type programs, my show traveled to many cities in the United States, but I would also do a show anywhere there was enough electricity—Cuba, Hawaii, London, Berlin, and by film from Africa, the Soviet Union, Brazil, Rome, Dublin, Madrid, Amsterdam, and this, if I may indulge in a small amount of vanity, is where you have to separate the men from the King.

When the "Tonight" program would travel with about twenty-five people, naturally NBC would arrange or barter for hotel rooms by having me mention the hotel we were staying in. So everyone knew, if they cared, exactly where I was. You would be surprised at the phone calls I would get from lonely women, crazy women, and quite a few drunks late at night. So I always registered under the name of Primrose McGoo; this code name was known to my staff, NBC, and my family. It also cleared the hotel of any responsibility for saying that no one by the name of Jack Paar was registered. This happened at the Beverly Hilton.

I walked into my hotel room one afternoon, and the light on the phone was flashing, indicating that someone had called while I was out.

I called the operator. "This is Jack Paar. My light was blinking."

There was a long pause. Then the operator said, hesitantly, "This is rather embarrassing, Mr. Paar. Are you staying with Miss McGoo?"

Miriam had flown home to Bronxville to be with Randy for Thanksgiving, so I decided to call and wish them a happy holiday. However, I had just changed my unlisted number and couldn't remember it. I got the Bronxville operator and said, "Honey, this is Jack Paar. I know this sounds crazy, but I can't remember my phone number. Would you ring my house for me?"

"Yeah," the operator said cynically, "that's what they all say."

"I kid you not," I said. "Really, this *is* Jack Paar. Don't you ever watch the show? Don't you recognize my voice? Listen, I'll hum our theme."

When she hung up midway in the first chorus of "Everything's Comin' Up Roses," I could see it was a losing battle. I got the hotel operator back and asked her to ring my assistant, Mitzi Moulds, figuring that she might have my new number.

"I'm sorry," the hotel operator reported presently, "but Miss Moulds has a 'Don't Disturb' on her phone."

"But this is Jack Paar," I protested, getting madder by the minute. "I'm her boss. I've got to talk to her. It's important."

"I'm sorry," persisted the operator. "We have no Jack Paar registered."

"But I *am* Jack Paar," I insisted. "I'm staying right here in Room 1120."

"I'm sorry," the operator said sweetly. "Miss Primrose McGoo is registered in Room 1120."

We spent a week in Hawaii doing five "Tonight" programs, and while I am very fond of the outer islands and the mountains, I can get my quota of their music rather quickly. I also am not crazy about being served a drink that has flowers or a little bamboo umbrella floating on it. When I have my nightly martini, I want a cool drink and not presents. Who needs a little canoe in his drink?

Hawaii is famous for its informality of dress, and we spent some of the time dressed like beachcombers, but one of my sponsors decided, one night, that I should wear a dinner jacket on the show. I didn't mind the dinner jacket as much as the accompanying black bow tie. Trying to tie one of those frustrating strips of black obstinacy is like trying to wrap a package with a live serpent.

That night I popped out of the shower and, before getting dressed, began to practice. For some minutes I sat on the bed, barefoot up to my Adam's apple, tying and untying the tie to make sure I could get the bow to look right.

As I wrestled with it, I began to feel a chill from the air conditioner over the bed. Since I couldn't figure out how to turn it off, I decided to put a towel over it to cut down the cold air. It was quite high up, so I put a footstool on the bed, climbed up, and was stuffing a towel against the unit when a little Hawaiian maid popped in to turn down the bed.

There I was, with nothing on but a black bow tie, teetering on a footstool on top of the bed and waving a towel! Although I've spent most of my adult life ad-libbing, all I could think of to say in my embarrassing predicament was "Aloha."

One experience I had in Tahiti still makes me smile. Some of the women are quite lovely, and they were unspoiled fifteen years ago before all the jets landed there. As you know, frequently experienced photographers ask their subject to say "cheese" since it forms the mouth into a natural and smiling expression. It works nearly everywhere but in Tahiti, where the second language is French. I had these three lovely girls in a closeup shot and said, "Say cheese." All three said, *"fromage"*—French for cheese— which has just the opposite effect.

In Hong Kong, NBC had arranged for me to meet some of the social leaders and Chinese businessmen who live in the Crown

Colony. It was a formal dinner, and at the cocktails beforehand, I was introduced to one of the most important and wealthiest Chinese men on the island. He was dressed in beautifully tailored English clothes, and I had some difficulty finding a conversation starter. I said to him, "Have you ever been to America?" in a slow, overpronounced, Tarzanlike speech.

He said, "Yes, I go many times. Have penthouse on Park Avenue."

Well, obviously I was not speaking with a former waiter and switched to a more normal delivery . . . a long pause; then I said, "Do you like Americans?"

The Chinese gentleman replied, "Frankly, I am not fond of you people in America."

"But why?" I asked.

He said, "I do not like Americans because they all call me *Charley*."

So watch it, you boobs! There are now over a billion of them, and one lives on Park Avenue.

There is a very famous international playboy by the name of Jorge Guinle, who lives in an unbelievable two-story penthouse atop the Copacabana Hotel, which his family owns, in Rio De Janeiro. He is a marvelous little guy and is just crazy about actors; I really mean actresses. He has a spy system and knows exactly which famous star is heading for Brazil, and he just takes over, which is his great pleasure. He knew everyone and had romances for a few hours with Veronica Lake, Lana Turner, Rita Hayworth, Jayne Mansfield, Kim Novak, Susan Hayward, and Marilyn Monroe. But on a slow week, the Jack Paars were the best catch. He turned on the charm and champagne, and we spent a few days with him. I read a story about him in the New York *Times* recently; he's getting on in years and is very short—five feet two. He's the only man I ever knew that wore built-up shower clogs around the pool. I felt sorry as I read about him getting older and shorter. And there really aren't many glamorous movie stars anymore. Diane Keaton dresses like Charlie Chaplin, and the new so-called sex thrill is Pia Zadora, who looks like a young Mickey Rooney. I think we are all becoming impotent or senile at just about the right time.

I recall one evening in this super living room, like nothing we had ever seen, with a view of Sugar Loaf and the beach at Ipanema, when we got talking about the recent revolution. Brigitte Bardot, the French actress, was there at the time and said, "What a lovely revolution. How very chic."

Drinking champagne in this beautiful setting, I wondered what a revolution was like for the very wealthy living atop a penthouse. Jorge Guinle told me he watched the whole revolution from his bed. "It was an interesting revolt," he said, "but the sound was bad."

"What in the world do you mean by that?" I asked.

"Well, the long-range cameras could get good shots of the fighting and military maneuvering," he explained, "but it was impossible to get microphones in close. Consequently you could see the action very well on TV, but the sound was terrible."

He continued, "It was most amusing to see the tanks coming down the street going toward the Palace and then suddenly stop at the corner because the light had turned *red!*"

The Brazilians are a delightful people and very aristocratic, dignified, and independent. I heard a story illustrating this trait on Rio's ancient *bondes* or open trolley cars. A crowded *bonde* was rolling along with passengers clinging to it. A tall Brazilian man tried to get off the rolling trolley, tripped, and fell flat. His fellow passengers roared with laughter. The man got up, brushed himself off with dignity, replaced his hat jauntily back on his head, and said, "Everyone descends from the *bonde* in the way he wants to."

For all their tolerance of government vagaries, the independent Brazilians don't like to be pushed around by officials. One lady got a tax form which said in one place, "*Do not write in this space. For official use only.*" She wrote in the space, "*I am a Brazilian, I am vaccinated, and I write where I please.*"

In my many trips to South America, I found that the middle class and the wealthy had no interest at all in the United States. If and when they left South America, they would go to either London or Paris. Fifth Avenue, Broadway, American food, and restaurants did not interest them at all. However, on my last trip there had been a big change. Everyone—rich, poor, middle class, children, and old people—wanted to come at least as far as Orlando, Florida. Disney World became the greatest asset the United States had for the South Americans.

On one of our trips to Brazil, we decided to go one thousand miles up the Amazon River to see something which I had read about and had always fascinated me. Little was known about it in 1965, but Manaus at the turn of the century was one of the richest cities *per capita* in the world and the most remote. If you took a string from the center of the city, made it twenty-five thousand miles long, and circled the globe, you would not find a place more remote on earth. Nothing but the most primitive Indians lived there; the waters were full of caymans (the Amazonian version of the crocodile), and the deadly piranha fish were supposed to be able to devour a man in two minutes. We were told that skeletons were found of fully clothed men who were devoured by a school of piranha that ate everything but bones and clothes. The fish are usually only a foot long or less and swim in groups of hundreds.

Because of the rubber trees which were discovered there, at the turn of the century plantation barons, mostly British, built incredible Victorian mansions in this absolute jungle. The streets were paved with terrazzo. Seldom had history recorded such wealth. The European people who lived there in the early nineteen hundreds sent their laundry to London or Paris. There were no roads or bridges and no way out but by boat. They had built a docking system that cost forty million dollars eighty years ago. It was the quickest get-rich community that the world had ever known. What intrigued me, and I just had to see it, was that they had built an opera house which was one of the small glories of the world. It was still standing, and while the city is now only a shell or remnant of a culture that lasted fifty years or less, there was this crazy opera house where the stars of Europe were brought by boat at fabulous salaries to play and dance. Legend has it that the great Pavlova danced there and that one ballet company lost twenty of its members because of malaria.

At night we had to walk around the streets with flashlights, since there was no lighting and the city had open manholes; garbage was collected by the vultures which flew about. There was one traffic light run by a car battery. It was the craziest place we had ever been. When I complained of the heat in the rooms, the management of the hotel told me that the air conditioning was jammed with frogs. Also, would I wish to buy the hotel for fifteen thousand dollars?

The famed opera house is something to see. We had heard stories that it was falling apart, and I had visions of the jungle creeping in to reclaim it, but this, like so many Amazon stories, proved to be spectacularly incorrect. In fact, it had recently been refurbished and was gleaming in fresh gilt and red velvet. Although the architecture is early Charles Addams, the opera house is overpoweringly sumptuous. It is set in a huge square of serpentine mosaic and is decorated inside with lavish murals and frescoes featuring armies of plump cherubs. The scenery is still hanging in the flies, as though awaiting the ballerinas who died of yellow fever while dancing there. I asked if they ever have performances there now. "Only a local string quartet a few weeks ago," I was told.

For all its plush and new paint, there is a sadness about the old opera house standing in the tropic sun, literally a thousand miles from nowhere. For the dense jungles of interior Brazil around Manaus are among the least-populated areas in the world. Only Antarctica has a larger area with less population.

This weird place of beauty fell apart in a few years. As suddenly as it had skyrocketed, Manaus plummeted. An Englishman smuggled some of the rubber seeds out. They were planted in the Far East, where they grew even better than in Brazil. Soon Brazil could no longer compete in the world market. In 1912 the crash came, and Manaus became a ghost town. The few characters we met all looked like Humphrey Bogart and had a scheme that for a few thousand dollars they would let me in on a diamond mine that had gems the size of bagels. But I found that in bad taste and explained that the people I knew simply wouldn't wear a diamond as big as a bagel. I just mention it in case . . .

On two of our trips to Brazil, we spent a week with our dear friend Mary Martin, one of the most glorious stars of the theater. She and her husband lived in a remote but heavenly place. It's a ten-hour flight to Rio, then a two-hour flight to Anápolis, where we would be met by Mary and her husband Richard Halliday, and then a one-hour trip on a red dirt road to their ranch, Nossa Fazenda (Our Ranch).

Mary's house was beautiful but had no electricity and no telephone, and refrigeration was by kerosene. It is 1,200 acres of fertile farmland, with hundreds of heads of cattle, many horses, and chickens.

The guesthouse is a hundred yards away from the big main house, and you really live there in great luxury. It is all gaily decorated by Mary in bright Brazilian colors, with gaucho blankets and even a piano covered in white wicker.

We quickly fell into a comfortable routine. When we woke up in the morning, Randy would give a blast on a horn, hung in our bedroom, to notify the Hallidays that we were awake. From the main house would come the answering sound of Mary tooting a bugle to let us know they had heard our signal and that breakfast was on its way. Moments later the Hallidays' American butler, Ernest, would be rapping on our door with breakfast, and what a breakfast! Juicy melons, just off the vine, flavored with freshly picked limes. Scrambled eggs gathered that morning. Strong Brazilian coffee, freshly roasted, smoking in the cups. With a breakfast like that, who needs civilization!

Mary and Richard loved their *fazenda*, and their warm pride in it was plainly evident as they showed us around. They had six thousand chickens in a series of long chicken houses with nine hundred cages. They also raised Brahman cattle, pigs, and turkeys, and had twenty thousand coffee trees, avocados, limes, lemons, and corn, rice, and other vegetables.

Audiences who saw Mary as Nellie Forbush in *South Pacific* or as Peter Pan on television would scarcely recognize Doña Maria, as the Brazilians call her, in blue jeans, herding her Brahman cattle, feeding the chickens, whizzing over dusty roads in her jeep, or supervising the damming of a spring to create a little pool. I have always considered Mary Martin one of America's natural wonders, since first hearing her sing "My Heart Belongs to Daddy," but this was a new and startlingly different Mary from the one I knew in *Annie Get Your Gun* or *The Sound of Music*, or from visiting her in her luxurious New York penthouse overlooking the East

River. Yet she's as much a revelation in one world as she is a star in the other. She's a marvel.

It's sad to write about all this as it came to an end when Richard died a few years ago. Mary will have to sell the ranch because it's now a big responsibility. The reason that Mary and Richard decided to live there part-time at first was that their friends Janet Gaynor and her late husband Adrian had found the property and built their home there. When Adrian died, Janet never returned; once Mary and I rode over on horses to see the home that Janet had left. It was a rather modern, Moroccan-designed home with a *Beau Geste* fortress look, as I recall. It was very new and very white and handsome, but in just a few years the jungle had reclaimed it. Trees went in one window, twisted out another, and crushed nearly the entire house. As I write this, Mary and Janet were just in a terrible auto accident in San Francisco, in which one of our best friends was killed. If you live long enough, they say, life will eventually break your heart. I just don't know how you can beat that. Perhaps, try and have a good evening.

If there was any secret to doing the "Tonight" program, it possibly was this: Let the guest get his laugh; let him or her have the last word. The audience loves to see the host in trouble. I would purposely go way out on a limb, hoping they would saw it off. After all, I was on every night, and this was the guest's one shot. No matter how funny the guest's remark was . . . if you waited, you could top it by simply looking into the camera in "close-up" and doing a take. I had a switch at my foot that we called the "take-me switch." It was a signal for the director to cut to me. On a scripted show, the director would know when to cut to close-up, but on a free-wheeling, ad lib show, you couldn't count on anyone anticipating a reaction shot. Johnny Carson does this superbly.

There were times when nothing would save me, and I just had to go along with the flow and look like a fool. I'll give you an example: Fred Astaire had to be on the program because there had been a book cowritten by him, and he had to plug it. He had never been on a live talk show before and was frightened to the point of being ill. I assured him before the program that it would be easy, and if he wished, whenever I felt he was uneasy, I would

say to the audience, "Fred, I know you have a late supper engagement, and thank you so much for honoring us, and you go now
and have a good evening."

Fred said, "Oh, thank you, but please make my appearance
short, and you will get me off the hook. You will say that, promise?"

I agreed. Well, he came out the first time ever, hearing himself
talk without a script, and he realized how easy and enjoyable it
was. The greatest stars are thrilled to hear their own words get
laughter without a script. You can be a star and never in twenty-
five years get a laugh on your own in front of an audience. Then
suddenly you hear laughter and feel a warmth from an audience
that you had never experienced before.

Well, dear Fred was a big hit . . . He relaxed and talked of his
life and career, and it was magic. No one enjoyed it more than
Fred.

I kept my word later and said, "Fred, I know you have another
engagement tonight, and thank you so much for being here."

Fred looked hurt, the audience groaned and glowered at me,
and Fred didn't help matters any by saying, "You want me to
leave . . . haven't I done well?"

There was nothing for me to say, and if I had pressed the
switch in a close-up, it would have been worse. There are times
when you must play the fool. That was one of the worst experiences I can recall, but that's show biz. Fred Astaire is one of the
truly great gentlemen of the theater, but never again did I try and
help him. He can take care of himself.

In this book of memories, I haven't written at length about my
disagreements with the press, and it would be difficult to do so
since all my adversaries are dead. I can honestly say that I never
objected to a bad review but became quite angry with an out-and-
out falsehood or a personal attack. Since no one else had ever answered the columnists back with a nightly program, with an audience in the millions, it became an exciting event for the viewers.

Walter Winchell, the most famous gossip columnist ever and
the most successful of his type, wrote a really silly column, but it
was fun to read, and he had tremendous power. He could and did
ruin many a career. No one would ever think of challenging him

or needling him as I did night after night for two years. And to have him practically screaming into his typewriter was great fun. He finally not only left me alone but had intermediaries try and stop me and arrange some *détente* between us. I kept after him until the public saw what a vulnerable old fraud he was. He finally brought a million-dollar suit against me, but it was never brought to court or settled. In fairness I should say that he invented a type of journalism and style that, for a man who was unschooled and unread, was remarkable. Most of his wit came from press agents, but he really was a power for more than twenty-five years. He was a big hit on radio, but finally when television came along and the public could *see* through his act, he ended up a sad old man and became a joke. If I played any part in his fall from power, it gives me no great pleasure now. Jack O'Brian, then a television columnist, was often critical but always fair to me, although he was a close friend of Winchell's. I have heard that O'Brian was going to write a book called *The Man Who Killed Walter Winchell*. I hope he doesn't.

For character assassination and fear, there was nothing ever like Walter Winchell, a yipping, pistol-packing—they actually gave this nut a gun permit—fire-chasing, posturing, pontificating ex-hoofer. He was a bully and had just about everyone frightened to death of him. My program became a place for people to come if they had the courage to answer any of Winchell's charges.

Once a press agent got an item in Winchell's column for his own client by planting the phony story that a well-known actress had cancer. The actress, who had never felt better, was naturally indignant. She submitted X rays, doctors' reports, and other evidence of her good health, together with a demand from her lawyer that Winchell retract the story.

Winchell immediately began his own research to find out if the actress was really ill and to wreak vengeance on her or the press agent who had given him the phony story. This struck terror in the hearts of Broadway press agents. For days they waited in trepidation to see on whose head Winchell's wrath would fall.

One night a few of the nervous press agents were speculating over the ominous situation. "All I can say," one of them mut-

tered gloomily, "is that if that lady hasn't really got cancer, she
sure is in a lot of trouble with Winchell."

The actress appeared on my program, and she was the wrong
one for old Walter to take on. You know her still as a great lady
of courage and one of the movies' most important stars. It was
Bette Davis. We still embrace when we meet, for we both survived Winchell.

A few years ago Nunnally Johnson, a screenwriter and producer
and a great wit, told me this funny story about Walter Winchell.
Winchell made the claim that he knew everything that was going
on, that he was in touch with the Presidents, an intimate of
J. Edgar Hoover, a friend of Senator Joe McCarthy, and that he
knew all the secrets of the Communist conspiracy in this country;
he was a nonstop talker. Later in his life he became a little wacky
and was always alluding to things he claimed to know that "if I
told you, you would be frightened to death." He said to Nunnally, "You have no idea what a responsibility it is for me to have
all this information, to know what is going on in the military,
who is sleeping with whom—sometimes the pressure of all I know
frightens me. I have too much in my head and am afraid of being
kidnapped."

Nunnally said, "Walter, that must be a great responsibility.
But tell me just one thing that you know that is a secret. I would
like to know a real important secret!"

Winchell looked around the table and said, "Later . . . later."
When the others left the table, Winchell leaned over and said to
Nunnally, "You know that professional wrestling on television
. . . *IT'S FIXED!*"

I cannot leave the name of Nunnally Johnson without telling
you my favorite story about him. He married very young and had
children and then grandchildren. He then remarried and started
the cycle of children again, ending up with quite a few. He once
said, "I have spent the last forty years reading *Little Black
Sambo!*"

NBC had great faith in my ability to know the laws of libel
and how far I could go, and they never tried to stop me (other
than with that silly water closet story). However, one issue of *TV
Guide* contained not an item but a story that ran for a page and a

half and contained a supposed phone conversation that I had had with an agent. It was quoted verbatim as if it had taken place, and it showed me in a very bad light. Fact one: I never made the phone call. Fact two: I never knew the person to whom I was supposed to have spoken. Fact three: The other person admitted that I never made the call and that I had never spoken to him.

I asked for a retraction of the entire story. I never received a reply. Then I decided to get their attention! Each night I would tell what I knew about the publishing family that owned *TV Guide* and the *Philadelphia Inquirer*, the Annenbergs of Philadelphia. I told stories about the seedy beginnings of the Annenbergs, stories that the family had striven mightily to suppress. Walter's father, Moe, had criminal connections and had served time in prison for income tax evasion. I kept this up for several nights and then was called to a meeting with Robert Sarnoff, the President of NBC.

Mr. Sarnoff, as I always called him, had always been extremely fair in all his relations with me. He said, "How much longer are you going to keep up this attack on Walter Annenberg? You realize he's a friend of mine."

I said, "I assume that two such powerful men would be friends, but I plan to keep up the attack, tonight for instance, unless *TV Guide*, which he controls, prints a complete retraction. The other alternative is for you to dismiss me. I should think that you would be concerned about a story that is harmful to your most successful program. I want a retraction or I will tell the rest of the Annenberg story, and the audience is dying to hear it."

And then Sarnoff said a strange thing, "Do you realize that Walter Annenberg has a deformed ear and is really a very nice person. And I think you are being thin-skinned!"

"Well, Mr. Sarnoff," I said, "we all have our problems. He has a deformed ear; I am thin-skinned. The fact remains that a magazine that he controls has printed vicious untruths about me and NBC's "Tonight" program. You might tell him in either ear to print a retraction."

It was late in the afternoon, and my mind was on that evening's program and not on long discussions in the executive suite.

I agreed that I would not mention the Annenbergs that night, and Sarnoff could have a chat with his friend Walter and let me know. It was a few days later actually that I received word from the NBC press department that there would be a *complete retraction* in a forthcoming *TV Guide*.

TV Guide is printed in perhaps fifty different editions. The front and back color editorial part is the same in all issues, but the center part that contains the local listings changes in each city or state and is inserted locally. At about this time, our show moved to California for a few weeks, and I got a call one morning from the NBC press department in New York saying, "You won. There is a retraction. You won!" I grabbed the latest *TV Guide* and looked on the page they mentioned, and there was nothing. What had happened was that the *TV Guide* editors thought I would be in New York City and only printed the retraction in one city after libeling me across the country. Now that's tacky!

But it made a great story on television that night. I told the story as it happened, and then I remembered a story about a young English writer, John Osborne. There was an important critic who for years had been knocking everything Osborne had been writing in the most vicious attacks. Then John Osborne wrote a play, *Look Back in Anger*, that was the biggest hit of the London season. It brought raves from all the critics. In the men's room of the theater on opening night, the most unlikely thing happened. There standing at the urinals was the critic, and there next to him was Osborne.

The critic was embarrassed but said, "You have written a great hit. I apologize for whatever I have written in the past. I am sorry."

And Osborne, peeing slightly on the critic's shoes, said, "That's all right, but next time insult me in the *men's room* and *apologize in public*."

Sometimes the TV critics would amuse me with their vitriol. It's difficult to knock a successful program night after night, and then have the man you dislike quit the show and leave a hit, and then return later in prime time and stay three more years, and begin another successful series, and *then* continue to do specials that were mostly well received and highly rated. What can you write about a man who wants to leave a career at forty-five? I was the best target they ever had.

A year or so after I retired from television, there was a late-night phone call at about two in the morning. Since few people had my private number, I immediately thought it must be some emergency. My first thought was that something had happened to some member of my family.

"Is this Jack Paar?" a voice asked.

"Yes," I said, beginning to do a slow burn. "Who is this? How did you get my number? I have an unlisted bed."

I could hear two voices on the call. "We're from *Time* magazine," one voice said. "We'd like to ask you a few questions."

Suddenly, I heard a telltale beep. I knew that the conversation was being recorded as there's a law that there must be a beep every ten seconds if a phone call is being recorded. I realized that the call must be some kind of a joke and was even madder at being awakened at two o'clock in the morning.

Then I recognized the voices. They were Johnny Carson and Steve Allen calling from Steve's TV show in Hollywood. Johnny was guesting on the program, and they got to talking about the fact that all three of us had done the NBC "Tonight" program. At two o'clock in the morning, it seemed like a hilarious idea to call me.

"Did we awaken your wife?" Johnny asked apologetically.

"Yes, my wife's awake, our dachshund's awake, and the German shepherd puppy's awake," I grumbled.

"I hope we didn't wake Randy," Steve said.

"Well, she doesn't sleep with us anymore. She sleeps with the lion cub." I said, "There's just my wife, me, and Noël Coward."

Since I was awakened to find myself talking to a national television audience, I tried to toss off a few merry quips, and I could hear the studio audience laughing in the background. They seemed to be enjoying it, even if I wasn't. Then Carson and Allen hung up, and I spent most of the rest of the night trying to get back to sleep.

A couple of days later, I read a review of that Allen show in a TV column. It said that Allen's program was sparkling and that Carson was a delightful guest. Johnny and Steve were great together, the review added. *"Jack Paar's phone call,"* it concluded, *"was nothing."*

The truth is I was thin-skinned, and a greater truth is that we are all thin-skinned! I don't want to leave the impression that all of the press was unfair or unkind to me. I realize now that I was good copy. I never avoided a question, and I believe that I am the only person who would ask as many of the press as wished to come on my show in a group and spend an hour asking me anything about my life or show. To this day I have many friends in the newspaper business and like some of them very much. Many were very helpful to me in the beginning and later.

Television has its faults, heaven knows, of which I was probably one, but it still manages to do an occasional good turn for the country. I was a party to one such good turn as the party of the second part, so to speak, when I unwittingly assisted in bringing about a suspension of the Federal Communications Commission law granting equal time to Presidential candidates during the 1960 campaign.

Actually, the equal-time law was a good one in intent, aimed at not letting any legitimate candidate for major political office get more free air time than his opponents. However, it reached a point of absurdity when applied to campaigns for every office down to coroner, and also when a whole gaggle of splinter parties began to get into the act with raucous cries to be heard on the public airways.

In no time, the FCC was being bombarded by requests for time from such obscure groups as the New Party, the Mississippi Black and Tan Grand Old Party, the Christian National Party, and the Vegetarian Party, whose slogan is "Our steak is in the future."

Typically, I got mixed up in the equal-time question more or less by accident. One of the more hardy perennial splinter candidates in the country was an eccentric Chicagoan named Lar Daly.

Daly, who campaigned in an Uncle Sam costume, complete with whiskers, had been stumping for years as the America First Party's candidate for President.

During the 1960 Presidential campaign, Senator John Kennedy and Vice-President Richard Nixon both appeared as guests on my

show. Senator Kennedy appeared first, and when Lar Daly heard
of his appearance, he promptly demanded equal time.

However, Daly wasn't kidding. Moreover, the FCC decreed
that under the law the lanky Chicagoan in the Yankee Doodle
getup was entitled to his equal time.

Well, Mr. Daly showed up to claim his rights, and it was quite
a night. He wore his Uncle Sam suit and had a scraggly white
beard that might have adorned a goat. He also wore a grim expression which left no doubt that he was not happy with the state
of the world.

I explained to the audience that giving Mr. Daly equal time
was the FCC's idea—not mine. This introduction did not faze
the "tireless candidate." Although I tried, in fairness, to interview
him on his views as I had Senator Kennedy, he insisted on turning the interview into a harangue.

"Your only choice is America First—or death," he intoned. "I
say shoot first if necessary."

The audience, which originally seemed to think that the candidate in the Uncle Sam suit was part of a comedy sketch, began to
catch on that he was in dead earnest. They began to boo and hiss
his wild proposals for dealing with other countries.

Daly blasted Red China for holding some American captives
and suggested that in dealing with them we drop an atom bomb
first and argue afterward.

"But if we did that," Alex King broke in, "wouldn't our American captives be killed along with the Chinese?"

"They'd be better off dead," said Daly, "than living the way
they are."

"I'd like to get their opinion on that," Alex snapped.

I have never heard such wild proposals as Daly put forth. If
nothing else, he achieved one historical TV first—he left me
speechless. On and on he droned, hammering home what he
called his "three-point program."

Finally someone in the audience yelled, *"If he'd take off his
hat, we could see his fourth point!"*

Daly's appearance on the program, ridiculous as it was, served a
good purpose. For millions of Americans it dramatized vividly the
flaw in the FCC law granting equal time to all candidates. A bliz-

zard of mail hit the FCC and Capitol Hill. Congress wasted no time in passing a resolution suspending the equal-time provision for the 1960 campaign, and President Eisenhower hastily signed it.

For me the hardest thing to handle was a sincere zealot in front of a studio audience that is conditioned to laugh at anything outrageous. (During my time on "The Tonight Show," one of the most *outré* personalities was Christine Jorgenson: the man who had the sex-change operation. I never wanted her or him or them on the program because I saw no way to handle the subject.)

Sometimes I would get mixed up with a person who made predictions—they were hilarious but dangerous. Astrology leaves much to be desired in my opinion, but once I had a real nut case on, and she said, "Since you, Jack, are Taurus and I am Venus, next month my Venus will touch your Taurus."

The interview was over when Hans Conried said, "Congratulations!"

The Lar Daly episode above explains the telegram appearing in this book that Jack Kennedy sent me before he became President. And the letter from his father, the Ambassador, is a little confusing because I never said *I was for Richard Nixon*. I had made a secret bet with Hugh Downs that I *thought* Richard Nixon would win, and he naturally with glee read my bet on the air. What the letter does provide is evidence that everyone on "The Tonight Show" was treated fairly.

Many of television's finest writers once worked with me in my early days: Hal Goodman (now with Carson), Pat McCormick (also now with Carson), and Gary Marshall, the most successful writer-producer in Hollywood today. I can still remember one of his earliest lines. We were doing a bit about kids writing letters home from summer camp. It went: "Dear Mom—Why don't you sew my name on my underwear like the other boys. I am tired of being called *Fruit of the Loom*."

Jack Douglas is a legend as a writer and eccentric. We have been friends for thirty years, and my biggest, wildest written jokes were usually his. When comedy writers gather, and the subject gets to original jokes, Douglas is always the favorite topic. When

I first met him and asked him about his background, he volunteered the information that he had been a part-time smoking instructor in a boys' camp. He had formerly worked for Bob Hope, and there is the famous story of him accompanying Bob to the Rose Bowl game, where the comedian was to make an appearance between the halves. Gazing over the gathering of a hundred thousand people, Jack was gripped by an uncontrollable urge. Grabbing the microphone from Hope, he growled at the huge throng: "This is a stick-up. Don't anyone move."

He later wrote some funny books with titles like *My Brother Was an Only Child* and *Never Trust a Naked Bus Driver.*

Lines of his that I remember I did include some about taking a girl to the Radio City Music Hall and going to the ladies' room. She made a wrong turn and was *kicked to death* by the *Rockettes.*

He wrote on such bizarre subjects as a funeral parlor that had a funeral for only twelve dollars, but the corpse had to sit up front with the driver.

He wrote of a Hollywood starlet who wanted to commit suicide in a glamorous manner, so she jumped into twenty gallons of lanolin and *softened* to death.

When we wrote together in radio, everything then had to be scripted and go through a board of censorship. Doug would find ways of outwitting them, and one example, quite harmless by the standards of today, went like this:

I introduced the then buxom queen of all time, Jane Russell. Doug just wrote in the script, SOUND EFFECT: TYMPANI. It got by the censor, but on the air I said, "And now, here is Jane Russell." SOUND: Boom! Boom!

Doug met and married a charming little Japanese girl, Reiko, who spoke very little English and then mostly phonetically. They would both come on the "Tonight" program, and I would ask him what I should talk to her about. Doug said, "Oh, just ask her what she is doing in America."

I had no idea what would happen, but I asked her what she had been doing in America, and she repeated without understanding a word of what she was saying, "I am here to photograph American Military Installations."

As you know, the Japanese have trouble with the letter "L,"

and Doug had taught her to sing "Rove Me or Reve Me or Ret Mc Bc Roncry." Nothing was funnier on the "Tonight" program than Reiko, the French girl Genevieve, and Dody Goodman just talking without forethought or script. No one could write or stage the laughs—those three would get talking seriously about anything.

One night on our show, I was holding forth at some length, and it came time for me to do a Norelco shaver commercial. I held up the shaver, which looks remarkably like an ocarina, to go into the commercial, but Douglas kept on talking. Finally, looking at me holding up the shaver, he said, "Well, either sell it or play it."

I sit here typing and laughing at a few of the lines that Doug wrote over the years. He is a very quiet man and not at all an extroverted comedy writer. He mumbles lines like these:

"Speaking of yoga . . . anyone can be a yogi—all you need are a dirty sheet and two broken legs."

"I lost my second wife in a wishing well—those things really work."

"An electric blanket without a cord . . . for Christian Scientists."

"New York has everything . . . There's a pet shop on Second Avenue with children in the window."

"I remember the advice my father gave me. He said, 'Son, save yourself for your wedding night, and then be gentle . . . the second night.' "

"English muffins are just virgin bagels."

"He wrote an announcement for flat-chested women: 'Send for our *two* free booklets.' "

"Doug, who doesn't drink, discovered a new cure for alcoholism—where the doctors drink right along with the patients. It hasn't cured anyone of alcoholism, but the days seem to *fly by!*"

"A captain on an airliner . . . 'This is your captain speaking . . . the next voice you hear may surprise you.' "

"Herman Raucher said a funny thing here the other night. We had finished dinner, and Miriam walked around the room, passing out chocolate mints. Herman said, 'Oh, I didn't know we were *landing.'*"

Doug lives here in Connecticut, and I remember his first home in Northridge in the San Fernando Valley. Doug, like me, has a passion for privacy. He jealously guarded the boundaries of his rural domain, which was enclosed by a steel fence and three separate gates on his endless driveway. As you entered this long private road, he would open the gates electronically. You would pass signs like DANGER, MAD DOGS. A short distance beyond was another sign which said, BRIDGE OUT—SLOW TO 60. Yet another sign said, HAVE YOU TELEPHONED THESE PEOPLE?, HOW DO YOU KNOW YOU'LL BE WELCOME? And finally there was NORTHRIDGE LION FARM.

When he moved farther north from us in Connecticut, he asked Miriam and me up and just gave me the name of a mountain road he lived on. There were no numbers on the rural mailboxes, and the road was two miles long. I was sure I would spot his place, but I drove back and forth for an hour, swearing and saying I don't even have his phone number. I was ready to return home when I spotted a mailbox that said, LUCKY LUCIANO. Sure enough, there was Doug waiting with his wolf (honest to God) and a shotgun. I knew we would have an interesting afternoon.

Doug loves animals as Miriam and I do, and prefers them to some people. On one visit he invited me to swim in his pool, which was filled with floating lumber and orange crates. He methodically threw the debris out of the swimming pool to enable us to swim. When we finished, he carefully threw it all back in. I said, "Why did you do that?"

Doug said, "If a squirrel or a rabbit should fall in, they deserve a fighting chance, don't they?"

I confess that this chapter of "Shoveling Smoke" is in free form and quite rambling, but I have written it in a hospital room. I have had my first operation that was mildly serious. I was frightened to death of hospitals, and now here I am with tubes going in me and some I assume coming out. Doug just phoned me and said, "I didn't send you flowers. Do you want a bullet to bite on?"

My operation was abdominal surgery, and I have been kept

quite sedated, but still I would try and write when I could to meet the deadline with the publisher. One rather intimate but clinically true note is that to avoid spasms or trauma I have been given opium suppositories. The first night waking up from the anesthetic, sedation, and opium in a darkened room, I thought I was dying. My whole life passed before me, and I wondered what I could have done better, what I had done wrong. I thought of everything, forgave everybody, was sorry if I had ever harmed anyone, and then came to the euphoric conclusion that I was a real swell person. In this semiconscious state, the only thing I had ever done wrong, the only mistake I ever made, was that I SHOULD NEVER HAVE SOLD MY ROLLS-ROYCE!

An isolated hospital room is not the best place to write a book. I missed my reference library and dictionary. I had wonderful nurses who would come running whenever I pressed the button, only to discover that I was fine but did they know how to spell "anaesthesia" and "proctology"? They would go and look it up and help me. Later I pressed the button and said to the nurse, "Bedpan."

She said, "Do you want one or shall I spell it for you?"

21

A La Carte

If you don't wish to read from the main menu, here are some little stories, bits of information, and miscellany—what W. C. Fields would call a *mélange*. I would make notes like this before a "Tonight" program and wait for an opening to introduce a subject that might prove provocative, interesting, or amusing as a conversation starter. Here, then, is a "Paar-pourri" of observations and stories.

You can always start a nice argument by saying that the term *anti-Semitic* is imprecise and has nothing to do with race or religion, lexicographically speaking. The Semites are only a language grouping that includes Hebrew, Aramaic, Arabic, and Amharic. I learned that from Abba Eban, the former Israeli Ambassador to the United Nations. I have won a few bets on that one.

I am addicted to radio call-in shows because you can hear such wonderfully dumb things. The other day, I heard a guy call in to defend somebody, and this is what he said, "Well, nobody is perfect. There was only one perfect man in the world, and that was Jesus Christ. And you know what happened to Him? They shot Him!"

We had a wonderful housekeeper for more than twenty years. Often we would discuss religion, and she was willing to accept

the fact that "Jesus was Jewish, but surely his mother was Irish."
I tried to explain that both Mary and Joseph were Hebrew and
were happily united, and that mixed marriages do not always
work out.

We had quite a problem when the Jehovah's Witnesses would
ring our bell in the country. They made our maid very angry. I
would try and head them off by explaining that I did not wish to
discuss *religion* in the *driveway!* The irony I rather enjoyed, because they were nearly always black members of their faith and I
found the reversal of the missionary role interesting. However
devoted and sincere they were in the propagation of their beliefs,
they were at times quite pushy. I always wondered how one
would say *chutzpah* in Swahili.

To the eternal question, "Is there life after death?" the most
certain answer is: "Perhaps, now that we have *tape* or *kinescope!*"

I was raised by a religious mother, and we always attended Sunday school as children. It didn't matter what denomination—we
were always sent off to the nearest church.

I believe that I live by the Ten Commandments but would like
to think that as a civilized man I would live my life much the
same without them. I certainly do not *covet* my neighbor's wife. I
play tennis with many of them, and the only thing I covet is one
or two of their backhands.

Incidentally, a moment ago I wanted to check the Ten Commandments, and I admit that I had trouble finding them. I knew
they were in the Old Testament, but I am used to looking for an
index. There was none. I had hoped to find a listing under
"Moses: mountain climbing."

I much prefer to read the Bible in the modern English version
than in the King James text. I find that all those *saiths, cometh,*
and *goeths* make it sound like everybody in the Bible had a lisp.

When I was once asked whether I thought I could walk on the
water, I had to answer honestly: "I really don't know, since I
have never *tried*. I did walk down to the Hudson River and did
think about trying it but figured that even if I could cross, I
would only end up in Newark, and there was no point in getting
the bottoms of my socks wet for that."

The concept of Heaven has never really interested me. I figure it's much like San Francisco—a nice place to visit, but I wouldn't want to die there.

To win by a landslide vote in our country, you need only fifty-four percent of the vote. Quite naturally, one cannot be liked or admired by everyone. So on my tombstone I would like "You had your chance, now he's gone" or simply "Keep the line moving."

I have always been moved by any action of unsolicited kindness for another human being. I heard John Ehrlichman say that before he entered prison to serve his sentence for his participation in the crimes of Watergate, he received a letter from a prisoner who offered this advice: "Be prepared for the slam of the gate as you enter the prison. It is inevitable and a shocker. But be prepared. The clothes they give you will not fit, but make the best of it. The food is wholesome but fattening, so be careful with your diet. Your bed will be lumpy, but if you stack newspapers under the mattress, it can be quite comfortable. Make the best of your time by reading and seek out others with common interests—they are not all congenital criminals. Make use of the library. Try to get involved with others who may seek or need your advice. It will be most rewarding."

The letter went on and in detail told him what he would find and how to adjust to prison life. Ehrlichman said how very helpful the letter was and how grateful he would always be to the prisoner who took the time to prepare him for his ordeal.

And then every single day in prison he received a letter from a Mr. Levine, a complete stranger. The letter each day would contain bits of philosophy, humor, and things to think about. There would be clippings from magazines, things Mr. Levine had heard on the radio or television, anything and everything to keep Ehrlichman's mind occupied. There would be letters of humor, religion, or argument. Every single day for two years there was a letter from Levine. And when Ehrlichman was released, he sought out Mr. Levine in Baltimore and took him to dinner to thank him. Mr. Levine was an artist but made his living by being a masseur in an athletic club.

When John Ehrlichman asked how he could repay Levine for his kindness and his two years of faithful letters, the mysterious man replied, "There is nothing I want. And you will not be hearing from me again. There are others who need me!"

One of the most touching love stories I have ever heard I read in the letters of Harold Nicolson. He was telling his wife a little-known story about Queen Victoria and her devotion to her husband Prince Albert. When the Prince died, the Queen went into a mourning that lasted more than twenty-five years. When they were young, they had visited Florence, Italy, several times and were quite taken by the beauty of the city but particularly the Brunelleschi Dome. Many years after his death, the Queen returned to Florence, got into a carriage, and was driven to the plaza outside the Dome. There had been wonderful repairs to the great buildings. And she rolled down the window of her carriage, looked at the restoration of the Dome, and then, reaching into her bodice, pulled out a locket, a miniature of Prince Albert; she slowly panned it up, down, and across so that he could see the wondrous repairs. Then she slowly drove away.

Here is a story of marriage on a different level but nevertheless involving great love. Each year Miriam and I attend an awards dinner gathering of the *crème de la crème* of Hollywood personalities, many of whom are old friends. Since we live in the woods of Connecticut, this is our opportunity to see everyone we ever knew at one gathering.

The producer of the show is one of my oldest friends, and Miriam and I are always seated next to the producer's wife at the table. The women wear their latest gowns and look smashing; the men wear the same evening black tie, which doesn't change from year to year. Now during the awards the camera pans and picks up in close-up two or three people at a time. These shots are later incorporated into the program that you see at home a week later.

Two years ago, sitting as usual next to the producer's wife, I was seen with her. I remember it well because she was wearing a stunning green dress. The second year, the same lady was wearing a red dress. But when the program was shown on TV a week later, there was a picture of me and the lady, but she was wearing a green dress. I looked the same.

What happened? I called my friend and asked him to explain the mystery. He said, "What could I do? She was there at the editing of the tape and decided that she liked last year's *green* dress better, so I reran the shot."

A few years ago I was talking with Joan Fontaine, the actress, about religion. She told me that whenever she heard the Lord's Prayer, she cried. Something in her past, some inexplicable nostalgia moved her deeply. Well, one day she was making a movie with Ray Milland, a perfectly proper and nice person but a cool personality. Now let me explain how pictures are shot. First there is the long shot; this would take in profile the two characters in the story. Then comes the over-the-shoulder shot, which in this case was a close-up of Milland in the same scene with the same dialogue. Next would be a reversal over his shoulder and a close-up of Miss Fontaine. In this case the close-up shot of her had her breaking into tears, a very hard thing to do which is usually saved for the last setup of the day. What will surprise you is that very often, most often, the other actor has gone home by this time, so here pretty Joan was left alone to cry staring into a camera lens. Not an easy thing to do. And Milland, being a very businesslike and tired actor, headed for his dressing room.

Joan tried to get into the mood, but it was difficult looking at that lens and trying to cry. Take after take, and it wasn't working. Then, on the final signal from the director, "Action." Joan tried again.

From the darkness of the empty sound stage came Ray Milland's voice, "Our father, who art in heaven"—tears filled her eyes, and it became the best scene in the picture.

We had a very worrisome experience here the other day. Our housekeeper seemed very distressed and told me that her young nephew had been missing for two days. He was ten years old and could not be found or traced anywhere. On the third day, his bicycle was found in the woods, but there was no trace of the youngster. By the fifth day I had little hope for him because the weather was very cold. And the signs were not very hopeful.

On the fifth day he was found alive, sleeping under the Connecticut throughway. How did he survive?

Well, his mother worked, and during the day the kid would come home and take just enough food from the refrigerator and take a few clothes from the closet, but not enough to be noticeable.

You see, the boy's mother and father had separated, and the kid thought that the tragedy of his being missing would bring his parents back together.

I know we all like happy endings, but in the real world it doesn't always work out. He's well, but the parents are divorcing.

One of my former associates is a diabetic. He has to give himself several daily injections of insulin. The poor guy has used up every reachable part of his body. His physician told him to teach his wife to inject the areas in the rear where he could not reach. The doctor explained that to teach his wife the action of the hypodermic needle it was advisable to have her practice on an orange. Last week he gave her the orange and the needle and taught her the wrist action. She held the fruit in one hand. She thrust the needle into the orange and fell to the floor. She had fainted!

My Tonto on the "Tonight" program, Hugh Downs, had to have a tooth extraction, which required a nerve block given by needle from inside the mouth into the cheek. The dentist held Hugh's jaw firmly with one hand and with the other injected the novocaine from the inside but went through the cheek and anesthetized his own *thumb!*

Hugh also had a frightening experience in a hospital recovery room. It was a minor operation on his throat and required a slight anesthetic. When he awakened, he found a Catholic priest over him, mistakenly giving him the Last Rites. Hugh, a Protestant, could hardly speak, but he managed to say, "Father, there must be some mistake. I'm only here for a little while."

The priest pushed Hugh's head down and said, "My son, we are all only here for a little while," and went on with the prayer.

Our good friends, Betty and Jock Leslie-Melville, who live in Nairobi, Kenya, come to the United States several times a year. If they are coming for more than a month, they try to bring their dog, a black Labrador, with them. East African Airways allows only seeing-eye dogs to enter the cabin of a plane. However, they bend the rules a bit for the Leslie-Melvilles if the plane is a late-night flight and is not full. Betty and Jock, waiting in the lounge at the airport, gave the Labrador a few sleeping tablets to make the flight easier. The dog fell soundly asleep, and when the flight was called, Betty and Jock carried the big Labrador to the gate and said, "This is our seeing-eye dog!"

I thought that this was a very witty and perhaps true remark made by Senator Dan Moynihan of New York: "The only social action that is one hundred percent effective is *castration!*"

Senator Eugene McCarthy, the former senator from Minnesota, is a very engaging personality and a first-class conversationalist. Senator John Pastore of Rhode Island, a very short bantam-rooster–type person, was given to extravagant phrases. He said to Senator McCarthy, "I must vote against you on this issue. I know that I am right. I can look God right in the eye and say no." Eugene said, "If you can look God right in the eye, he must have been *bending* over."

One of my favorite political personalities is the former governor of New York, Hugh Carey. I enjoy his company very much. He is well read and a highly intelligent, very engaging man. We met a few years ago on the island of St. Martin in the Caribbean. Miriam and I had the cottage next to his, and we would spend time on the beach each afternoon. He was with his then lady friend, Ann Ford, and with two other people whose names I did not quite catch at the time. The woman, I later learned, was an absolutely stunning lady by the name of Katherine Du Ross. She was great fun, and we played tennis with her because her older companion didn't play. He was a rather grumpy type, and I would occasionally go swimming with him. We talked mostly about how expensive breakfast was at the hotel. He said, "Do you know that the food this morning cost twenty-four dollars?" Our breakfast cost eighteen, which to me was quite a bit. One day, after a swim and a rather dull conversation, I joined the Governor, Ann and the super, ginger, peachy cream lady, Katherine. I don't know how I tactfully said to her, "What in hell are you doing with that guy?"

She replied, "I thought that you never knew who he was, but I am going to marry him."

She did, and his name was Henry Ford!

Speaking of attractive women, I saw one the other morning on one of the early news shows, and she was a beauty. Seldom have I been so taken by a woman that I never knew but saw only on television. She was so chic, poised, and attractive. She was the wife of the great symphony conductor, Zubin Mehta.

My wife became quite annoyed and said, "So that's your type?"

"No, my dear, you are my type, but if ever I am found dead stabbed by a *baton*, you'll know who did it!"

I am not good at all in remembering names of people I have just met because I am so busy trying to charm them that I forget who the hell everybody is. Miriam is very good about this social grace. Some years ago we walked into a living room, and Miriam was introduced to the late Orvil Dryfoos, the publisher of the New York *Times* who was married to Marion Sulzberger, daughter of the owner of the prestigious publishing empire. As Miriam met him, she repeated, "Orvil? Orvil! Like the Wright Brothers!"

I realized and knew that she was using the mnemonic method of remembering by word association. But a few hours later, as we left, My Darling went up to Mr. Dryfoos and said, "Good night, Wilbur."

I am a great gadget person, and anything electronic gives me enormous pleasure. A few years ago, when CB radios were the fashion, I bought the kits, installed them in my cars, and set up a home base in the kitchen. The fun was putting them all together,

but when the time came to use them, I, supposedly one of the
great talkers in the country, found myself very shy and could say
nothing. Here I had earned a living all my life by talking, but as
soon as I had the three radios and transmitters installed, I was
too shy to start a conversation. I think this was mainly because
the jargon is so silly and special. My first try was when I pulled
into a gas station because I was too nervous to talk, work the
damn CB radio, and drive. I said, embarrassed as hell, "Breaker
Fifteen, can you read me?"

"I read you perfectly," said an unknown voice. "You have a
great signal."

I said proudly, "What is your twenty?" (meaning "What is
your location?").

And the phantom voice came in with, "I'm at the next pump!"

The only sport that I am really addicted to is tennis. I really
enjoy playing and watching the game. Here are some stories
about my experiences on the court.

In Key Biscayne, Florida, Miriam and I used to play with a
couple from Argentina. The señora was a good player, but her
husband, a very Latin, *macho* type, was new at the sport. We were
told by her that we were not to hit to his backhand because it
upset him. I was already a bit angry because of this and had lost
my concentration. It was his time to serve. He threw the ball up,
smashed it across the court, and *hit a bird!* Can you imagine the
odds on that—hitting a bird in flight on a serve? With the poor
little bird flopping about the court, we got a Dixie cup of water,
put it to his lips, and placed our feathered friend in the bushes
until he recovered from the experience. I was so upset that we
lost the match!

Miriam and I always enjoy having weekend guests to play tennis. But I dread the Monday mornings at the Post Office sending
back all the clothes, rackets, and paraphernalia that the guests
leave. Phyllis Diller, a fine player when she was here last time,
left her brown, silk tennis underwear pants. I never knew where
to mail them back, so the next day, when a church bazaar for the
missionaries was collecting things to auction off for the needy, I

offered "Phyllis Diller's silk underwear." I would like to think
that her contribution helped a deserving Ubangi in Africa.

On our tennis court, I have installed two TV cameras and have
been photographing on tape the two-hour matches. Afterward we
come inside to the den and watch the whole two hours. But what
is interesting is that experienced sports announcers like Joe
Garagiola, Frank Gifford, and executives like Gene Jankowski,
president of CBS, Pete Rozelle, president of the NFL, and many
others are difficult to get to come to dinner. They want to watch
every play and always seem to know, during the entire two hours
of replay, when their next good shot is coming.

The wittiest remark on tennis is Alan King's. He said that because he was Jewish, he naturally had an aggressive and hard-hit-
ting forehand, but because of two thousand years of persecution,
he had a weak backhand!

Miriam, Randy, and I love going to La Costa and hitting balls
with the great Pancho Segura, who is the pro there. Last year,
Pancho wanted us to watch a young twelve-year-old player whom
he thought had great potential. The kid had been barred from
the courts for a month because of his use of profanity. This
would be his first time on the court since his disgrace. Well, the
kid was really remarkable but so intense that when he missed a
shot he would either cry or swear like a sailor. Pancho stopped
the match and said, "How dare you use such language again in
the presence of Mrs. Paar. You should be ashamed. You *little
asshole!*"

We enjoy the company of tennis pros more than any other
group of people. I have played with Roy Emerson and Fred
Stolle, the Australian greats and with Tom Okker of the Nether-
lands. I most enjoy having lunch or dinner with them and listening to their stories.

The subject of Billie Jean King usually comes up, and I have
heard the legend of this truly great woman tennis player. She was
a real champion and is responsible for the stature of ladies' tennis
today. She is well liked and respected by all the players and has
been the social and professional leader of tennis.

Then came the unfortunate publicity about her gay affair with

Marilyn Barnett. All the players spoke well of Marilyn and said the relationship went on for five years before it was broken off.

I also learned that this is not uncommon in women's tennis, that a high percentage of the women play doubles in more ways than one. The male pros had an explanation for this by saying that it was not that common when the tournaments featured men and women, but that now there are only about three important contests that feature both sexes—the U.S. Open, the French Open, and the Wimbledon.

The life on tour is a tough one. The men practice each morning for two hours, have lunch, rest, and then have two more hours of afternoon practice followed by dinner; and the match is that evening. After the contest the male players go to the nearest bar and drink five or six bottles of beer. And then off to bed.

Women players just cannot enter bars as a group without being accosted and harassed by the local boors. So they began to gather in their hotel rooms and stay among themselves. As this went on year after year, relationships were formed that led to the present problem.

In other words, I gathered that Lesbianism is caused by *room service*.

I have mentioned Peggy Cass often in this book. She is a favorite of Miriam, Randy, and me. When I first met her, in the early days of the "Tonight" program, she was appearing on Broadway in the part of Miss Gooch in *Auntie Mame*. Later, when it was made into a movie, she was nominated for an Oscar.

Whenever the program traveled, we always took Peggy with us, for she is the most wonderful company. Peggy is the most naturally funny woman I know, although she has a voice like a passionate Brillo Pad. Her best friend is Jean Kerr, and the play that Jean wrote for Broadway, *Mary, Mary*, is based partially on Peg's life. When they finally cast the play, Peggy applied for the part and was told, "she just wasn't the type."

On our first trip to Ireland, we were invited to stay at the American Embassy for five days. The residence of the Ambassador is in Phoenix Park outside Dublin; it is a beautiful Georgian

home. This is the same house that Winston Churchill lived in as
a young boy, when his father Randolph served the British government there. There were only two guestrooms left over. Miriam
and I had one, and Peggy and Randy had to sleep in the other.
Each morning at eight the servants would come into the room
and light the peatfire; then they would serve breakfast in bed
with wonderful Irish bacon, a rose, and the *Irish Times*. It was as
elegant as any of us had ever lived.

I remember walking down the hallway in my bare feet late one
night, the same hallway in which young Winston had walked,
and telling Peggy and Randy to "shut up and go to sleep." Peg
was teaching Randy what was then a new game called Password.

After we had returned to the United States, I hadn't heard
from Peggy for a few months; then I finally got a phone call, and
she told me this horrendous story. She had an operation on her
knee in a hospital that specialized in injuries to athletes. Well,
when she awakened from the anesthetic, she reached down to feel
the bandage on her bad knee, only to discover that they had operated on the *wrong* knee!

Peggy is a screamer, and who is to blame her? The doctor said,
"I operated on the knee with the Magic Marker on it—no prob-
lem, we'll just put you to sleep again and do the other knee."
And they did!

Now that's really "grace under pressure." It's a good thing they
didn't use any old Joe Namath parts. She was frightened that if
they had any ether left, they might do a hysterectomy. The poor
darling still has trouble walking, but she did the right thing. As
soon as she came out of the anesthetic, she phoned her lawyer. I
think now she will be able to afford that new home in the Hamp-
tons.

During my days visiting Washington, I was often in the company of lobbyists. I cannot at the moment think of one commercial, industrial, religious, or ethnic group that does not have a
paid public relations advocate to influence legislation in the
Congress or to influence action elsewhere in our vast bureaucracy.
These advocates are highly skilled and personable people with

vast expense accounts; they wine and dine our representatives of government.

This story is, obviously, apocryphal, but is not too far from the truth as I saw and experienced it. The cheese industry agent of the dairy lobby was given a high-priority assignment: Get "The Lord's Prayer" amended to read "our daily bread and cheese." He went straight to the Vatican, pleaded the humanitarian case for his depressed clients before the papal nuncio, and offered a $25,000 contribution to the Cardinals' Fund. Outraged by the lobbyist's presumption, the papal nuncio refused.

The lobbyist redoubled his arguments for equity and justice and increased his proposed contribution to $50,000. Even more resolutely, the papal nuncio refused to consider the amendment. Driven to desperation, the lobbyist made his final offer: "Look, we'll match whatever the *bread* people have been giving you."

There are times, I must confess, when I wish I were back on television for just a few moments to pass on something interesting or amusing that I heard that day. Recently, I had dinner with Nancy Reynolds in Washington. She is the least publicized but most intimate confidante of President and Nancy Reagan. She told me: "When the President returned from the hospital after the attempt on his life, he stayed in the living quarters upstairs in the White House. At that time there was a renovation going on, involving many workmen, carpet layers, carpenters, painters, etc. It was very noisy, and Reagan wanted to get to the far end of the long hallway to the Lincoln bedroom and get some rest. He was wearing a bathrobe and slippers, and was walking slowly because of his injury when he came across a card table with about six workmen crowded around it having lunch. The President walked slowly over to them and said, "You wouldn't think that such a far out of the way eating place would be such a big success."

If John DeLorean is such a great automobile designer, how come his car has windows that do not roll up or down? The door does go up—the whole damn door goes up! You could be going fifty-five miles an hour down the highway, and if you want to throw out your gum or a cigarette and have to open the door, you could lose your hairpiece that way . . . even your underwear. The DeLorean car could bring back the spittoon.

I read something in a British paper this morning that surprised me. The highest paid athlete in the world is not an American baseball player, a football star, a tennis champion, or a world soccer player. His name is Eddy Merckx. He made over two million dollars last year in winnings and endorsements. He is a Belgian bicycle racer.

At the moment the big sports news is the NFL football strike and how will ABC fill the Monday night TV time. I have an idea. I would call it a "Gang Bang, Tag, Talk Team" and have Howard Cosell interview Mike Wallace, Barbara Walters interview Rona Barrett, and Sarah McClendon interview Sam Donaldson. At the half, they all switch. (Does Sam Donaldson remind you of someone from "Star Trek"?)

Years ago, when I was riding the late-night train from Grand Central to White Plains, a very prim and proper lady got on the midnight train in New York. As she sat down, she was joined by a fellow who was really quite drunk. He was harmless enough and fell asleep. She leaned over toward the window as far as she could to avoid the fumes and took off her gloves. As she slipped one off, the glove fell right in the drunk's lap. The problem was how to retrieve it without an incident because it was right on his fly. She tried reaching for it on the trip but didn't have the courage. The stop before White Plains is Scarsdale, and as the conductor announced "Scarsdale," the drunk awakened, saw the glove, thought it was his shirt, stuffed it into his trousers, and got off the train. So there's a lady in White Plains with only one glove and a drunken husband in Scarsdale without an explanation.

Last summer we had a youngster visiting us, and I swam in our pool with him. He was eight years old and very bright. I was interested in this observation: He said to me, "I would say that you were on the *rich* side."

Rich side? "Why do you say that?" I asked.

The youngster said: "Well, I've noticed that poor people have swimming pools, but they are always *above* ground, and rich people have pools *below* ground."

This experience I had last spring was the strangest I have had in awhile. I hired an Italian carpenter to do some building on our house. He was a handsome, virile guy, strong and muscular and a first-rate carpenter recently arrived from Naples. We became friends over the weeks he worked for me, and I was very surprised by his gentleness with children and our dogs—so very Italian. Well, I was putting up screens on our second floor windows and was on a high ladder. I asked him if he would go inside and fasten the screens as I hooked them over the outside. He raised the window as I tried to hook the screens on the fittings. Then he slammed the window down, not realizing that both my hands were on the ledge. He could easily have broken all my fingers, and I was in such pain that I screamed, still trying to hang on to the ladder. He opened the window and didn't know what to do to help, so he grabbed both my hands and kissed each finger. It was one of the craziest, most painful, and touching moments of the year.

If you have a friend you are not too crazy about, I have a suggestion for you. (Please don't do this to me as someone already has.) Go to a second-hand book store and buy any thick, dull, preferably technical book. Wrap it nicely and enclose this card: "You may be amused, and possibly angered, by the mentions of you in this book. A friend."

My Jewish friends are always talking of their mothers and how funny they are or were. Listen, we Presbyterians have a few funny mothers. My mother was a very attractive woman; she looked like a socialite, although actually her education came mostly from magazines, television, and movies. She could put on great airs and pretend to be very *au courant*. When she visited us in New York, I would take her to the best restaurants, but she preferred to go to the places that she would hear me mention on the "Tonight" program. The Stage Delicatessen was owned by a lovely man, Max Asnes, and he really liked me. So I took Mother there. Max had his best table ready and said to my mother in that gravel-throated Brooklyn accent, "What is your pleasure?"

My mother said, "Let the innkeeper decide." (Where she got that line, I'll never know.)

Max said, "I recommend da Kosher Corn Beef."

Mother said, "Ah, yes, Kosher Corn Beef. Tell me, is it in *season?*"

My mother was always concerned about my notoriety in the newspapers but secretly loved all the publicity. She cautioned me with, "Do what you think is right. You can't win them all. After all, if everybody obeyed the Ten Commandments, there wouldn't be any eleven o'clock news!"

I mentioned earlier in the book that once Robert Kennedy and I were sued by James Hoffa for two million dollars for a remark Bobby made about Hoffa on the "Tonight" program. In this case, since I had not said the words, NBC would have its law firm defend me; Kennedy would have to get his own lawyers. It turned out that because Hoffa had filed his suit in Michigan, I could not be served in New York. So NBC warned me not to go to Michigan until this all blew over.

My grandmother, then in her eighties, lived in Saginaw, Michigan, and she had always been my favorite relative. I adored her. She became very ill, so one weekend I decided to visit her, since I felt it could well be my last time to see her. The hell with Hoffa! I flew to Detroit, wearing dark glasses and a mustache, rented a car, and drove to Saginaw and my Uncle Harry's home late that night.

Grandmother was pretty far gone yet beautiful and cheerful, but she didn't seem to know me. I said, "Come on, you are only pretending. I am a big TV star. Harry says you used to watch me every night on television."

Grandmother said, *"Television*—what is that?" I realized she was slipping away from us, but on I went with the big-star routine.

Now in our family an evening always ended with a glass of beer and a pretzel. To this day we still do. I was trying so hard to reach the old dear and wondered if I was getting through. I knew I was always her fair-haired boy. She was in bed, of course, and she asked me what time it was. I told her. She took her cane and rapped on the bedroom floor. My uncle came upstairs and said, "Yes, Mother."

Grandmother said, "It's time for my beer and a pretzel . . . and get one for . . . what's-his-name!"

22

And Now . . . Goodbye

When you reach your sixtieth birthday, there is not a lot to look forward to except falling down in the bathtub and breaking your hip. This always seems to happen to all my older friends exactly as they reach sixty-five. At sixty-four, I plan to outwit fate and begin to basin and sponge regularly.

While I have had many offers to return to television, I cannot imagine myself doing it. Since I retired, I have only appeared on TV when friends have asked me—Joe Garagiola, Arlene Francis, Mary Martin, and Merv Griffin. When last I was on Merv's show from California, he wanted to know my future plans, and I said, rather dramatically, "I guess the next event in my life will be my death."

This shocked dear Merv, and he repeats the story quite often when my name comes up on his show. He seemed very disturbed by my frankness. Well, last week I had a physical, and they found in blood tests that I had several factors which indicated longevity. So, Merv, I am now worried about you and what I will say when you are no longer with us. For there is nothing more certain in life than death, taxes, and another Bob Hope special.

I have never been a hypochondriac and have spent little time with doctors. I have always been concerned by the Hippocratic oath that all physicians take: *Premium non nocere*—which means, "First do no harm!" That makes you think before you rush off to your next appointment.

I am also weary of dentists and their constant X rays. I told my dentist recently that couldn't we skip the X rays this time. He said that they were not harmful, and then he put on lead shorts and left the room. BUZZZ!

I once spoke at a dermatologists' convention and was surprised that they had seminars all day long, mainly on how to make their waiting rooms larger. There was a serious moment when someone announced a breakthrough, a new wonder drug . . . Calamine lotion.

Doctors now believe in a *second opinion*; they have their own and then call your bank!

I have remained very healthy most of my life by a diet, tennis, and at least ten hours in bed every night, many hours just reading.

My only wish, and not a small one, is that this book be entertaining. For years I have been giving all this material away, and my friends encouraged me to put it down on paper. It is even possible that this effort was written under the influence of money. It is not a *mea culpa* (or a "you-a-culpa") but the best I can do. No one was to blame; things happened to me the way they are presented here. You may have noticed that there are no explicit sex scenes in the book, and the few words of gutter speech I used I felt were necessary.

If this book is *entertainment*, I did it without a single "car-chase scene," and aren't you tired of those cornball movies with the endless screeching of automobile tires? I prefer the old-fashioned Western movies where a horse can go around a corner without all that noise.

And aren't you getting a little turned off by these endless Broadway plays with a five-minute idea stretched to two hours?

This is not yet another cookbook, nor have I mentioned *nouvelle cuisine*. This would be pretty pretentious, considering that my favorite food is chili.

I haven't given the advice so many of those endless "self-help" books of psychology offer: "You're OK, I'm OK." The truth is that I *am* OK, but I am not really sure about you!

There have been so many books written in the past year by former stars who now rush to tell us that they lost their fame because they became addicted to drugs. Some of this sounds as if they are building up their past just to put a little drama into their lives for the sake of the book. If all this sniffing of cocaine were going on, destroying their nasal membranes, you'd think some of them would have had their noses "Tefloned."

Another bit of drama is the "I-wasn't-ready-for-fame—it-came-too-soon" type of biography. Not for me, it didn't. I was ready for fame when I was six years old, and I spent my youth in a crouching position.

As I look at the best-seller list each week, I find that pornography is most popular. I thought I would try and write a sexy-pornographic travelogue—it would be about the Eskimos. But I only got as far as the part where the boy Eskimo and the girl Eskimo were sitting around in their igloo, rubbing noses. Finally, the girl Eskimo said to the boy Eskimo, "That's enough foreplay . . . let's *kiss!*"

The antihero is now the important character in literature and films. I liked it better when justice triumphed, when decency prevailed, when at the end the main character was heroic, as he might be and often is in real life. I knew that this was over when it was announced that they were going to make a picture called *Lassie Kills Chickens.*

Another sure best seller is "How to Live a Longer Life." I have no suggestions to offer, so you will just have to take your chances along with the rest of us.

What I would hope that this book will accomplish is to answer the tiresome question, "What was Jack Paar *really* like?" And more seriously to answer the often asked, "How was the Paar show different from all the others?"

Television was so very exciting when it was live and spontaneous. I worked with wonderful people who were loyal and devoted, and if I were to come back to TV tomorrow, I would rehire every single one of them. They all loved the old "Tonight" program: the tension, the crazy hours, the pressure. One evening before the program, Hugh Downs took a friend to our offices in Radio City. By the way, in the years I worked there, I was in these officcs only twice. The friend remarked to Hugh, seeing the frenetic activity before the show, "These people seem crazy. If they act this way, what is Paar like?"

Hugh said, "The surprising thing about Jack is that he is quite sane, but he is a *carrier* of mental disease!"

I believe that the only unreal thing about my work was the "king" bit. It was to me what Jack Benny's alleged stinginess was to him. Also, it allowed me the semantic advantage of not having to say "I" all the time and allowed me to speak in the third person when I was referring to myself. It also gave me a funny, false character. I broke up when last I saw Robert Morley in London. He said, "Dear boy, the world was so much better when you were running it!"

Jack Douglas just telephoned me and said that since I had been in the hospital, could he help me in any way to finish the book. I was very touched by such an offer. He then said he was worried about the title, *P.S. Jack Paar*—that for a book to be a best seller, you had to have sex in the title. I explained that in my condition sex was the farthest thing from my mind at the moment. He wanted me to change the title to *It's Ten O'Clock—Do You Know Where Your G-Spot Is?*

I am recovering very well from my operation, which turned out to be a serious prostate condition. The only reason I mention this now is to give confidence to men in their fifties and sixties who have a similar problem, which is quite common at that age. Seriously, I recommend that you rush off to your friendly, neighborhood prostate dealer and get it over with. I wish I had done this years ago. I feel so much better and will be playing tennis in a few weeks. I now get a full night's sleep and can pee like the Jolly Green Giant. I don't want to brag, but actually my only fear is that now I might *crack* the *porcelain!*

I don't mind really growing old, as long as I have interests and can travel. The saddest story I know is about the father of Al Hirschfeld, the artist, who when he reached the age of seventy-five used to spend his days, all day, filling in with pencil the O's in the New York *Times*. The father of another friend used to spend most of the summer sitting on a stepladder with a hose, watering the lawn. He insisted that that is the way nature intended it to be: water falling from the sky. Still the sad but funny story of the man who read the obituary page every day in the newspaper and came to the conclusion that people died alphabetically.

I sometimes believe that there are too many "how-to" books, too much amateur medical advice available on television, too many "instant experts." I heard this the other day, as a true story from my writer friend, Herman Raucher, but I would not wish to defend with my honor its truth.

In a restaurant, a woman got up to leave her table to go to the rest room; she stood and momentarily put her hand to her throat, simply to scratch an itch.

She was immediately pounced upon from behind by a waiter in what is called the Heimlich maneuver. This is where you are approached from the rear and the person trying to save your life with clasped hands pulls his thumb's knuckles into your abdomen to force out something that is stuck in your throat.

The poor lady was so stunned that she fainted when another person said, "Don't you see, she's hyperventilating; get a brown bag and put it over her head." (This is another emergency first-aid treatment.)

Then a third person threw a glass of water in her face.

The poor darling came to, wet, frightened, and said, "Please don't help me anymore. I was just trying to scratch an itch!"

We used to play a mental game on television. The premise is that if you were ill and in the hospital, three to a room, who would you wish for company on either side of your bed. I would usually say Peter Ustinov and Robert Morley. Lately, I have thought about it and realize that I have left out Jonathan Miller, the most amusing and urbane, interesting, and witty man around today.

You'll notice that all of the aforementioned are British, but when I think about all the friends I have made, the most stimulating and articulate American was easily Alexander King, and he really was Austrian. I miss him very much since his death ten years ago.

Now, right this minute, if I could pick any two people to share a hospital room with, I would have to pick Alex King, and the other would be *you*, the reader. You see, we would have to have someone to *listen!*

I have much enjoyed writing this book. I started after Christmas, and it's now late fall. You were splendid. You didn't interrupt, there were no commercials. Now it's time to leave you.

I have told you everything, some of it not very flattering to me, because that's the way it happened. I wish I could have done things better, but this book was pretty much, "warts and all," to use a rather unappealing cosmetic cliché.

Before he died, Alex King wrote something and gave it to me as a gift. I used it once in a preface to a book many years ago. I would like to repeat it now in a much-edited version, since nothing was ever written about me as touching as this. Of course, it's kind and complimentary, but then surely you have read in the past, if you remember at all, mostly unkind things, many of them untrue.

So I give you Alex King:

A WORD TO THE WISE GUYS

So what does Jack Paar actually do on that show of his?

I'll tell you what he does. He somehow manages to distill the most worthwhile aspects of the TV medium into the most flexible form of unrehearsed, adult entertainment. He does a nightly verbal striptease in the company of some of the most articulate and amusing people in the country, and the public, almost completely stultified by the hodgepodge that is usually slopped onto its home screens, is only too eager to stay up until all hours of the morning to participate joyfully in this unpredictable charade.

The show has other virtues, too, of course. It has cleared the paths for a lot of talent and made the way easy for people with remarkable gifts to place their accomplishments before the public.

But I think its truly unique contribution to TV, and one that can only be identified with Jack's own peculiar aptitudes, lies in the fact that people with rich lives and lively imaginations have

suddenly found themselves able to display their unique attributes
in an atmosphere of almost unlimited freedom.

You see, the actors and various professional entertainers who
appear as his guests have, mostly, only two or three stories to
offer on the altar of split-second improvisation. Anyone who
knows actors at all will tell you that most of them aren't really
much good without a memorized script. Only the highly exceptional ones among them can draw on a wide enough variety of
experience to be granted a free passage to those dangerous pre-
cincts where swift verbalization is expected as a matter of course.
Well then, let me tell you that Jack has an absolutely uncanny
faculty for guessing the approach of the exhaustion point on the
part of his guests, and by an adroitness that has become second
nature to him, he manages, almost miraculously, to steer them
into the less turbulent areas of more generalized conversation (or
steer them offstage altogether). To do this without embarrassment to your visitor—to do it so that it sometimes seems that
it is the host who is fumbling around in waters too shallow for
his navigation—therein, I say, lies some of the great, undercover
skill of a truly great professional interlocutor.

Jack is a quick-witted *hombre* with an absolutely fabulous
memory. He has, of course, the instant appeal of his considerable
good looks, as well as his carefully fostered Midwestern awk-
wardness, which make him so irresistible a fetish for middle-aged
ladies of all sorts. I say carefully fostered because I think it is an
attitude he feels is highly consistent with the public image that is
best suited to his personality. He is certainly quite genuinely
square about some things, but he is fully aware of it and sees no
reason to ameliorate it as long as it is good for the show.

Actually, he has proven, over the years, to be one of the least
hypocritical of men, and I can vouch that he is quite free from
any sort of misleading or evasive pretenses. Why should he
bother? After all, he has made it absolutely on his own terms,
hasn't he?

For Jack's many envious detractors who believe, or pretend to
believe, that he is just a very lucky guy, without a shred of talent,
I offer the following little parable.

Once upon a time, in the ancient kingdom of Persia, the Shah
established a rest home for some of his superannuated camp fol-
lowers. In one room of this quiet retreat there were six beds
placed along the wall, and since there was only a single window

at the end of this chamber, it naturally came about that the prisoner placed nearest to the window was the only one who had a view of the colorful world which still went on about its business on the outside.

And so it happened that this man, whose name was Dschafar, would for many hours each day keep the rest of the inmates informed about the lively things that took place beneath that window. He never seemed to weary in describing the various people who passed on their way to the market place: the soldiers, the merchants, and the many seductive women who jiggled their undulant curves while pursuing their multitudinous errands in the street below. Lacking such subjects, Dschafar would, from time to time, expatiate at length on the many changes that he observed in the aspects of nature as they occurred in the gardens across the way, and by suchlike discourses he made the other members of the dormitory forget, for a time at least, that their own active days on this earth were almost over.

"The fledgling swallows in that almond tree," he said, "have taken their first flight this morning. Their parents are flitting with pride and anxiety all around them."

At another time he said, "That milkmaid in the pale blue scarf has had a letter of good news today, and all day long she walked about her duties like a queen."

Now then, the man who lay prone on his back in the bed next to Dschafar's was a man called Mirza, and, after a while, this man became extremely envious of Dschafar. He couldn't bear the thought that all the riches and splendors of the world should be spread out so freely right outside their chamber, and that no one really had access to them, excepting his fortunate neighbor. This envy eventually turned Mirza's heart to bitter hatred against Dschafar, and finally the wretched man even decided to kill the chronic blabberer, and perhaps obtain the use of the one bed that allowed a view of the city beyond the rest home walls.

And this he did.

Through a visiting friend he managed to obtain a quantity of some particularly virulent poison, and while the unsuspecting Dschafar was soundly asleep, Mirza poured this evil thing into his neighbor's tea.

The following day Dschafar was dead, and the secretly rejoicing Mirza was promptly moved into his place.

And then, when at last Mirza raised himself on one elbow and looked eagerly out of the window, he beheld only a barren field that seemed to reach as far off as the horizon. Mirza blinked his eyes like a man bereft of his senses and frantically clutched at his bedposts.

There was nothing to see—nothing but a desolation of bare ground and grayish rubble and a bit of dirty paper blown fitfully about by the evening wind.

With a great cry Mirza fell back upon his pillow, for he suddenly realized that all those visions beyond that window had only existed in Dschafar's mind.

—ALEXANDER KING

And now . . . goodbye. *Ciao*—Jack Paar.

P.S.: If you rented this book, thank you; if you bought this book, thank you *and have a nice day!*